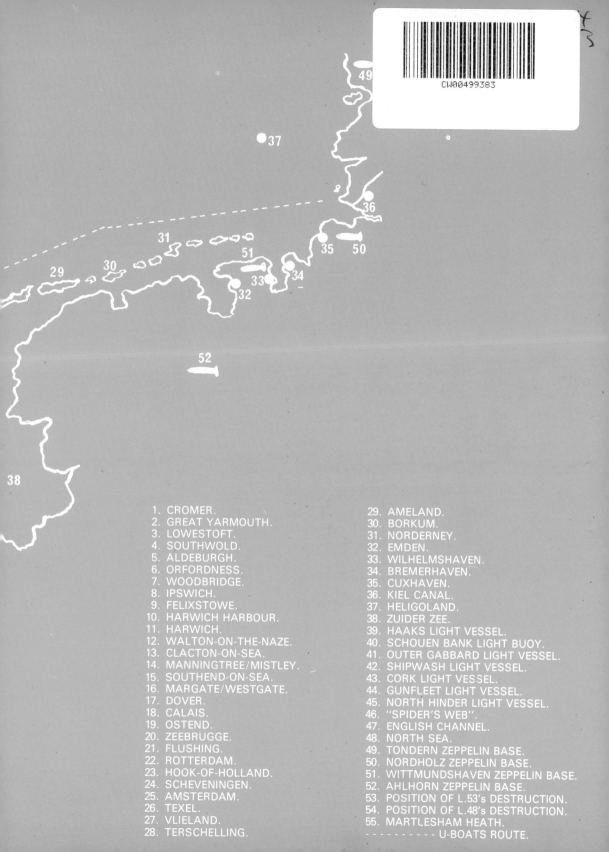

1. CROMER.
2. GREAT YARMOUTH.
3. LOWESTOFT.
4. SOUTHWOLD.
5. ALDEBURGH.
6. ORFORDNESS.
7. WOODBRIDGE.
8. IPSWICH.
9. FELIXSTOWE.
10. HARWICH HARBOUR.
11. HARWICH.
12. WALTON-ON-THE-NAZE.
13. CLACTON-ON-SEA.
14. MANNINGTREE/MISTLEY.
15. SOUTHEND-ON-SEA.
16. MARGATE/WESTGATE.
17. DOVER.
18. CALAIS.
19. OSTEND.
20. ZEEBRUGGE.
21. FLUSHING.
22. ROTTERDAM.
23. HOOK-OF-HOLLAND.
24. SCHEVENINGEN.
25. AMSTERDAM.
26. TEXEL.
27. VLIELAND.
28. TERSCHELLING.

29. AMELAND.
30. BORKUM.
31. NORDERNEY.
32. EMDEN.
33. WILHELMSHAVEN.
34. BREMERHAVEN.
35. CUXHAVEN.
36. KIEL CANAL.
37. HELIGOLAND.
38. ZUIDER ZEE.
39. HAAKS LIGHT VESSEL.
40. SCHOUEN BANK LIGHT BUOY.
41. OUTER GABBARD LIGHT VESSEL.
42. SHIPWASH LIGHT VESSEL.
43. CORK LIGHT VESSEL.
44. GUNFLEET LIGHT VESSEL.
45. NORTH HINDER LIGHT VESSEL.
46. "SPIDER'S WEB".
47. ENGLISH CHANNEL.
48. NORTH SEA.
49. TONDERN ZEPPELIN BASE.
50. NORDHOLZ ZEPPELIN BASE.
51. WITTMUNDSHAVEN ZEPPELIN BASE.
52. AHLHORN ZEPPELIN BASE.
53. POSITION OF L.53's DESTRUCTION.
54. POSITION OF L.48's DESTRUCTION.
55. MARTLESHAM HEATH.
- - - - - - - - - - U-BOATS ROUTE.

SEAPLANES—FELIXSTOWE

Also by Gordon Kinsey

MARTLESHAM HEATH
A History of the Royal Air Force Station
1917-1973

AVIATION
Flight over the Eastern Counties
since 1937

SEAPLANES—FELIXSTOWE

The Story of the Air Station 1913-1963

by

GORDON KINSEY

Foreword by
Harald J. Penrose, O.B.E., C.Eng., F.R.Ae.S., M.R.I.N.A.

TERENCE DALTON LIMITED
LAVENHAM   .   SUFFOLK
1978

Published by
TERENCE DALTON LIMITED

ISBN 0 86138 039 8

First published 1978
Revised edition 1985

Text photoset in 11/12pt. Baskerville

Printed in Great Britain at
The Lavenham Press Limited, Lavenham, Suffolk

Contents

Index of Illustrations

Acknowledgements

IN HELPING me to compile this history very many people and organisations have gone back in time and searched their memories in order to furnish me with valuable and interesting information and facts. All are worthy of individual thanks and notes, would only space permit, but within these limits, I would like to record alphabetically the main sources, first individuals and then organisations. My sincere thanks to everyone concerned.

First the Men of Felixstowe over the decades: Mr R. W. Angell, Seer Green—Mr L. F. Asbury, Colchester—Squadron Leader L. P. Coombes, South Yarra, Australia—Group Captain Stuart Culley, D.S.O., Italy—Captain G. Fane, Feering—Squadron Leader F. J. French, Felixstowe—Mr W. T. Good, Dovercourt—Mr G. Hill, Ipswich—Mr J. T. "Tolly" Hill, Witnesham—Mr C. F. Hippersley, Chelmondiston—Mr George Hodgson, S.S.G.M:, Montreal, Canada—Mr E. T. Jones, Twickenham—Mr H. F. King, O.B.E., London—Mr P. S. Leaman, Farnborough—Group Captain G. E. Livock, Blandford—Mr Earl MacLeod, Vancouver, Canada—Mr E. C. Middleton, Oxford—Mr B. H. Millichamp, Ludlow—Mr Milward, Heacham—Mr Parke, Felixstowe—Mr C. V. Pettitt, Cowlinge—Mrs L. Pyke, Fawley—Mr R. C. Rowbotham, Ipswich—Mr S. D. Snell, Ipswich—Mr E. Symonds, Felixstowe—Mrs M. Tillyer, Fawley—Mr Frank Woolley, Nova Scotia, Canada—and Mr G. L. Wright, Birchington on Sea.

Enthusiastic individuals who assisted in many ways; Mr C. H. Barnes, North Wales—Warrant Officer Peter Barker, R.A.F.V.R. (T), Ipswich—Mr David Barton, Ipswich—Mr E. Bell, Felixstowe—Mr T. Bloomfield, Ipswich—Mr H. E. Booth, Bramfield—Mr Keith Bowman, Felixstowe—Mrs Burch, Needham Market—Mr R. S. Butcher, Felixstowe—Mrs Campbell, Ipswich—Mr C. Chandler, Ipswich—Mr Peter Claydon, Felixstowe—Group Captain J. L. Crosbie, O.B.E.—Flight Lieutenant A. Cowan, R.A.F.V.R. (T), Felixstowe—Mr Richard Crier, Woodbridge—Mr Peter Crowhurst, Ruislip—Mr Alan Farrow, Orford—Mr S. J. Fetherston, Kirby le Soken—Mr L. C. Firman, Ipswich—Mrs I. Freeman, Little Bealings—Mr Roger Freeman, Dedham—Flying Officer J. Fuller, R.A.F.V.R. (T), Felixstowe—Mr Alan Gotelee, B.A., D.S.C., R.N.V.R., Ipswich—Mr and Mrs Grace, Ipswich—Mrs Grant-Jones, Needham Market—Dr Helena Hamilton, Chesterfield—Mr A. J. Jackson, Leigh on Sea—Flight Lieutenant J. Jay, R.A.F.V.R. (T), Ipswich—Mr John Langford, Ipswich—Mr and Mrs K. Leighton, Ipswich—Mr Robert Malster, Ipswich—Mr Minns, Felixstowe—Mr J. W. Mitchley, Lowestoft—Mr L. W. Moore, Diss—Mr W. C. Newman, Felixstowe—Mr R. L. Olley, Ipswich—Mr Palmer, Felixstowe—Mr F. V. "Sandy" Powell, Felixstowe—Mr and Mrs R. J.

Pratt, Devon — Inspector Claude Rush, Felixstowe — Lieutenant Commander Sir Peter Scott, M.B.E., D.S.C., R.N.V.R., Gloucester — Mr Donald Smith, Ipswich — Lieutenant Commander I. C. Trelawney, O.B.E., D.S.C., R.N.V.R., Cornwall — Major John Venmore-Rowland, Lavenham — Mr A. C. A. Wansford, I.S.O., Harwich — Mr Keith Wickenden, Felixstowe — and Mr G. Williams, Margate.

Organisations and their representatives who all co-operated with such splendid vigour: Air Historical Branch — Anglia Cameras, Mr Jim Empson — Messrs William Beardmore, Glasgow — British Aircraft Corporation — British Airways — British Hovercraft Corporation, East Cowes — Brooke Marine, Lowestoft — Mrs V. Rayner — *East Anglian Daily Times* and their associated newspapers — *Eastern Daily Press* — Elfan ap Rees, Yeovil — European Ferries, Felixstowe — Felixstowe Dock and Railway Company — Hawker, Siddeley Aviation, Brough, Mr E. Barker — Hatfield, Mr Philip Birtles — Kingston on Thames, Mr J. I. Triddell and Manchester, Mr G. Allen — Ipswich and District Historical Transport Society and its members — Ipswich Borough Library, Miss King and Miss Wood — Ministry of Defence (Air) — Rolls Royce (1971) Limited, Derby — Shorts Limited, Belfast, Mr White — Vickers Limited, London — Vosper Thornycroft (U.K.) Limited, Diana O. Floyd — and Westland Helicopters Limited, Yeovil.

My special thanks to Harald Penrose, O.B.E., C.Eng., F.R.Ae.S., M.R.I.N.A., for honouring me by contributing the foreword, Mr A. R. J. Frost, A.I.I.O., A.R.P.S., M.I.R.T. for his photographic skill with the older prints, prolonging and enhancing their informative life, and Mr C. E. "Holly" Hall for once again producing the colourful dust jacket.

Finally, once again my deep gratitude and thanks to my wife, Margaret, whose ready assistance and advice in so many ways is beyond measure. Many thanks also to my publishers and their able staff for full co-operation, quiet guidance and excellent workmanship.

Gordon Kinsey,
Roundwood Road,
Ipswich.
August, 1978.

Foreword

by

HARALD J. PENROSE, O.B.E., C.Eng., F.R.Ae.S., M.R.I.N.A.

THE brown-green North Sea and long low coastline of East Anglia, with its shingle-banks, havens and open landscape, linger in memory as if still seen from the skies of my early years. Down there, at the centre, is the glittering fissure of the Stour and Orwell estuaries; and opposite Harwich, within the curved arm of Landguard Point are the docks of Felixstowe, adjacent to which was the Marine Aircraft Experimental Establishment of old, a mile from the centre of that seaside town.

On the other side of Felixstowe, imagination sees the quiet River Deben, flowing almost parallel with the distant, bigger Orwell, and at its head, just short of Woodbridge, is Martlesham Heath, the landplane counterpart of the Felixstowe establishment. Both were the Mecca of my student days, for my home was half-way between the two, and aeroplanes were then, as now, my hobby. Many an hour was spent on the fringe of the Heath, or the muddy shore by Landguard Martello Tower, watching the flying, though often it was a cycle ride in vain.

Later, as a test-pilot aeronautical engineer, I knew both intimately and found that despite their stern military purpose, they remained places of romance, each with individual emphasis—the great heathery spaciousness of Martlesham; the sea tang and mud of Orwell Haven as I stood on the slipway apron outside the big R.A.F. hangars. As with Martlesham, what an amazing variety of aircraft I saw at Felixstowe; the last of the F.5 flying boats, the little Peto for stowage in a submarine, the advanced Rohrbach monoplane, Iris and Southampton flying boats, the six-engined Sarafand, Fairey seaplanes and the beautiful Schneider Trophy machines.

Though my experience with flying boats and seaplanes in those days between the wars was all too limited, there is no doubt that it was the art of piloting marine craft which enthralled me most, combining as it did, high-speed motor boating with transition into buoyant flight. Who better than Saint-Exupery could describe that pleasure?

"The motors are running free and the plane is already ploughing the surface of the sea. The pilot feels the ship charging itself with power as from second to second it picks up speed. The metal organs of the controls become the messengers of the power in his hands. And when his power is ripe, in a gesture gentler than the culling of a flower, the pilot severs the ship from the water, and establishes it in the air."

That is the essence as felt by a pilot: but Gordon Kinsey has much more to tell, devotedly tracing the story of flying in relation to Felixstowe from pre-Great War days, reincarnating not only the many aircraft of outstanding historical interest but also portraying the men who designed, maintained, and flew them — for without men there could be no such epic.

Harald Penrose,
July 1978.

Felixstowe's longest living resident is moved from the mudflats at Felixstowe Ferry where it had lived for a number of years as a houseboat. This Supermarine Southampton all-wooden hull has been preserved for display at the R.A.F. Hendon Museum and is believed to be the only wooden flying boat hull still in existence. *Courtesy of The East Anglian Daily Times*

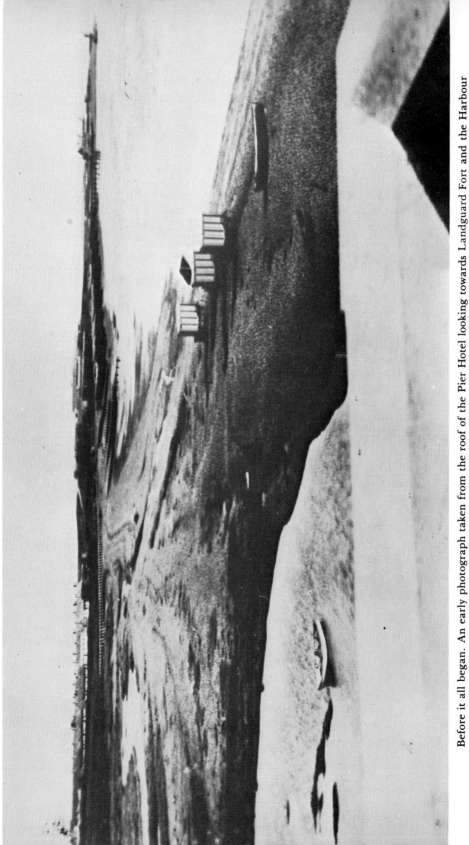

Before it all began. An early photograph taken from the roof of the Pier Hotel looking towards Landguard Fort and the Harbour mouth. The Air Station was constructed in the middle foreground with the slipways positioned just the other side of the bathing machines.

C. F. Cordy

CHAPTER ONE

Times and Tides

THE Admiralty did not take kindly to the idea of aircraft of any description, and basically up to the end of 1911 kept an eye on their development, and nothing more. Kipling had written that the Navy is very old and very wise, and in that thinking, old traditions died very hard.

At first the Admiralty favoured the lighter than air craft, but after Bleriot had conquered the English Channel on 25th July, 1909, their thinking was more in the direction of the aeroplane.

During February, 1911, the Royal Aero Club told the Admiralty that one of its members, Mr Francis MacClean, would loan two of his aircraft, at his own expense, to train four naval officers to fly. Another Royal Aero Club member, Mr C. B. Cockburn, offered his services as an instructor, and it was through these two public spirited gentlemen that naval aviation was born.

Two of the four original naval officers taught to fly became household names, Lieutenant Colonel Charles Romney Samson of the Royal Flying Corps and Air Chief Marshal Sir Arthur Longmore of the Royal Air Force, these two also being the first serving officers to qualify with Aviators Certificates numbered 71 and 72, dated 25th April, 1911.

The lighter than air machine lost most of its favour with the Admiralty after the loss of the *Mayfly* which broke its back on 24th September, 1911, without even flying, but up to this time the machines used by the Navy were those which had been loaned by private individuals. The first British naval officer to take off from water in a hydro-aeroplane was Commander Schwann, flying an Avro biplane fitted with floats of his own design.

The Royal Flying Corps was formed on the 13th May, 1912, with the subtitle "Naval Wing" but the latter part was soon dropped, and the force comprised 22 officers, 8 of them aviators. Previously on the 25th April, the Air Committee of the Committee of Imperial Defence recommended that landing rights should be obtained at or near Harwich Harbour, among other sites. As a result of this decision, Lieutenant L'Estrange Malone visited the area, accompanied by a Works Department official, Mr Pearson, and together they surveyed the possible sites. Ideally they were looking for a place with launching facilities for marine aircraft and anchorage for attendant motor boats, railway access for goods and housing for personnel.

This was followed up on 3rd June, 1912, when Samson flew to the Orwell Estuary from Burntwick Island, near Sheerness, Kent. His passenger in the

Samson's hydro-aeroplane on the slipway outside its shed at Shotley during 1912. The shed was a temporary structure to house the aircraft whilst it carried out the Harwich Harbour survey.

Richard Crier

Short hydro-aeroplane, S.41, No. 10, was Charles E. Risk, and the object of the visit was to carry out a survey for the possible site of a hydro-aeroplane base at Shotley or up the River Stour at Mistley. Samson appeared to be more attracted to the eastern banks of the River Orwell, as on 14th July, he made another visit with E.R.A. O'Conner as passenger, again flying in the Short S.41 from Portsmouth and along the South Coast.

Another early aviator, M. Henri Selmet, who was named as one of the *Daily Mail* Flying Men,* visited the area on 10th August, 1912, as part of his tour of the Eastern Counties. Later in the day he flew on to Ipswich, his 50 h.p. Gnome-engined Bleriot monoplane covering the 12 miles in about 10 minutes.

Samson came again on 26th August, 1912 in the S.41 and again in October, and he paid particular attention to the Felixstowe site, circling Landguard Common and surveying the river banks. Some of the flights also included an attempt to see if it was possible to detect submerged submarines from the air, but owing to the muddy nature of the shallow waters in the area, the exercise was not very successful. Another experiment was the carrying of early wireless equipment, and with this Samson was able to pick up messages at ranges varying from three to ten miles.

Daily Mail Flying Men were young potential aviators sponsored by that paper.

An announcement in *The Times* of 14th April, 1913, stated that the Admiralty had given instructions for a naval air station to be constructed in Harwich Harbour. The following day, the *Eastern Daily Press* carried the following announcement: "The Admiralty has given instructions for Naval Air Stations to be constructed at Great Yarmouth and Harwich on similar lines to that of the naval hydro-aeroplane station commissioned on the Isle of Grain last December. The Yarmouth station will form the centre of a group of stations on the East Coast and will be placed under the command of Lieutenant Reginald Gregory who holds the rank of Commander in the Naval Wing of the Royal Flying Corps." An announcement from the Admiralty stated that the term "hydro-aeroplane" would be replaced by that of "seaplane" as from 17th July, 1913.

Felixstowe Air Station was commissioned on 5th August, 1913, and became known as "Seaplanes—Felixstowe", and was commanded by Squadron Commander Charles E. Risk, who established his Headquarters at the Melrose Hotel, now the North Sea Hotel, on Felixstowe sea front.

The first aircraft was a Borel monoplane floatplane of French design and manufacture, powered by a 80 h.p. Gnome rotary motor and this was later joined by Maurice Farman Longhorns, also of French design. Of the popularly

The Bleriot monoplane of M. Henri Selmet flies over the district during his visit to Felixstowe and Ipswich during August, 1912. *via Robert Malster*

Farman built hydro-aeroplanes Nos. 115 and 139 are prepared for flight from the Felixstowe shore during 1913. Note the crew being carried out to the aircraft with H.M.S. *Ganges* and a sailing barge in the background.   *Richard Crier*

dubbed "box-kite" type, these latter machines were powered by a variety of motors, but all were capable of about 60 m.p.h.

Felixstowe saw a few more aircraft on 16th August, 1913, when machines taking part in the *Daily Mail* Seaplane Competition, whilst on the Ramsgate to Great Yarmouth leg of the event, passed over or called at the Station. One of the contestants was Mr. Harry Hawker, flying a Green-engined Sopwith seaplane with Mr H. Kauper as his passenger.

Construction of the new seaplane base went on apace and three large hangars, or sheds as they were known, were erected by Boulton and Paul Limited of Norwich, and slipways and jetties were built out into the River Orwell.

In a letter dated 7th November, 1913, Mr Winston Churchill, as First Lord of the Admiralty, asked the Director of Works to ascertain certain alterations be put in hand in order to make the Coastguard Station at Felixstowe suitable for housing officers and men of the Naval Air Station. The nearest aerodrome to Felixstowe was Aldeburgh, Suffolk, with the large station at Great Yarmouth rapidly taking shape.

Mr Winston Churchill visited the Station to see for himself how the works were progressing, and was then tempted to take a flight in the Borel monoplane. This flight, however, was short lived, as the seaplane side-slipped into the Harbour from about 150 feet, and the shaken First Lord was taken to the Melrose Hotel for a change of clothes and a hot meal.

A few landplanes also operated from the site using Landguard Common as their airfield, and Mrs M. I. Freeman of Little Bealings recalls a Lieutenant Nansen flying from Felixstowe to Kesgrave Heath to visit her parents who lived at Bracken Hall, Kesgrave. As photographic proof shows she was allowed to sit in the aircraft, but not allowed to fly in it.

Events at the Air Station now began to appear in the local press as on 12th March, 1914: "Captain H. R. Fawcett, R.M.L.I. who yesterday flew in a Farman seaplane from Yarmouth to Felixstowe met with an alarming accident on descending onto the sea at Felixstowe. For some reasons at present unexplained, the seaplane capsized on the water and became a complete wreck. Captain Fawcett and his passenger were rescued fortunately uninjured. Captain Fawcett was in an accident not long since off the East Coast when he landed on the Maplin Sands when returning from the South Coast and the aircraft was a total loss."

On the 24th April of that year Mr Winston Churchill was on his way to Felixstowe from the Isle of Grain, with Lieutenant Wilfred J. Seddon, R.N., in a Short Type 74, No. 79, when it was forced down off Clacton, Essex, with an engine malfunction. The seaplane was taken in tow and brought into Harwich Harbour, after Short type S38, No. 19, had been sent from Felixstowe to pick up the First Lord. Just previously, on the 1st April, another seaplane on

Mrs Freeman of Bealings sits in the cockpit of an aircraft which Lieutenant Nansen landed near Bracken Hall, Kesgrave, having flown from Landguard Common, Felixstowe.

Mrs Freeman

Sopwith Bat Boat No. 1, Serial No. 38, manhandled on the shore. 1913.   *Richard Crier*

passage flying from Isle of Grain to Felixstowe was forced down off St Osyth, Essex, the pilot and passenger being rescued by a passing barge, whilst Clacton lifeboat salvaged the wreckage of the aircraft.

During May, 1914, a Yarmouth aircraft, Henri Farman No. 142, was flown non-stop from its home station to Felixstowe by Lieutenant Bone, accompanied by Wireless Operator Hendry, and returned to base the same day.

An official announcement read: "The Royal Navy Air Service forming the Naval Wing of the Royal Flying Corps will comprise all naval aircraft and personnel, either for action or reserve service, and will be administered by the Admiralty. It will consist of: The Air Department, Admiralty, The Central Air Office, The Royal Naval Flying School, the Royal Naval Air Stations. All seaplanes, aeroplanes, airships, seaplane ships, balloons, kites and other types that may from time to time be employed for naval purposes. All ranks and ratings of the Royal Naval Air Service will be borne on the books of one of His Majesty's ships, and will serve under the provisions of the Naval Discipline Act accordingly."

The Royal Naval Air Service (R.N.A.S.) came into being on 1st July, 1914, and aircraft from the new air arm took part in the Spithead Review during July. Seaplanes from Felixstowe participated and were known as "C" Flight for the purposes of administration. Squadron Commander Risk led the local contingent which consisted of three Maurice Farman floatplanes fitted with 100 h.p. 12-cylinder Renault motors and one powered by a 130 h.p. Salmson motor.

About this time a Short Tractor seaplane was detached from Felixstowe to Clacton in order to carry out coastal patrols, whilst on 27th July, 1914, several additional seaplanes arrived at the Station to carry out extended coastal patrols. Two aeroplanes also arrived for the same reason and these operated from Landguard Common.

The European political situation rapidly deteriorated and at 11.00 a.m. on 4th August, 1914, the chimes of Big Ben in London told the world that Great Britain and Germany were at war with each other. It is recorded that the British Foreign Secretary had remarked the previous evening, "The lamps are going out all over Europe. We shall not see them lit again in our lifetime."

As soon as hostilities commenced the patrols from Felixstowe intensified, linking up with those from Great Yarmouth and Clacton. Squadron Commander Risk was in charge of these operations and his responsibilities lay from Southwold to Clacton. Additional seaplanes were also drafted in from Eastchurch to carry out this work. It was also decided that as the R.N.A.S. had superior numbers of aircraft to the Royal Flying Corps, it would be responsible for the air defence of the British Isles.

The Dock Basin adjacent to the Air Station became a base for destroyers, minesweepers, coastal motor boats and boom defence vessels. This unit remained at the Dock, alongside the Air Station, until 1925.

Felixstowe did not have its own wireless equipment at this time but had to use that of the Royal Navy base at Harwich.

Lieutentant C. E. H. Rathbone left the Air Station for France, but later returned to be Commanding Officer. Whilst operating from France he was shot down and taken prisoner of war, but not being satisfied with his surroundings, he, together with 28 fellow inmates, dug a tunnel and escaped from the prison camp at Holzminden. Another serving officer at Felixstowe was Lieutenant C. H. Finch-Noyes, playwright and author and also the inventor of an incendiary bomb.

Short seaplane S.41, No. 76 with Commander Samson as pilot and Mr Winston Churchill as passenger, prepares to take off during 1913.   *Short Brothers*

On 26th July, 1914, the Union Jack emblem carried on the mainplanes and fuselages of all R.N.A.S. machines was replaced by the blue, white and red concentric rings, sometimes with a thin white line on the outside of the outer blue ring. The three colours were also carried on the vertical tail surfaces as upright stripes with red the furtherest aft. Christmas Eve, 1914, saw the three ex-South Eastern and Chatham Railway Company's Channel packets, *Engadine*, *Empress* and *Riveria* now converted into seaplane carriers, escorted by the light cruisers *Arethusa* and *Undaunted* and eight destroyers, slip out of Harwich Harbour for the Heligoland Bight. Carrying nine seaplanes, they were to attack the Zeppelin sheds at Cuxhaven, but fog obscured the target, and they bombed alternative targets on the Kiel Canal, only three of their number making the return flight to their parent ships. One of the seaplanes carried as her observer Lieutenant Erskine Childers, R.N.V.R., the author of the pre-war thriller *Riddle of the Sands*, the story of which covered the area over which he now flew.

The newly commissioned seaplane carrier *Ark Royal* sailed from the Harbour on the 1st February, 1915, bound for the Dardanelles, and was followed later in the year by the *Ben-My-Chree*, another ex-packet vessel.

War came a little closer during the last week of February, when two German airmen were picked up in the North Sea about 40 miles off the coast. Landed at Lowestoft, they appeared very apprehensive, fearing that they would be lynched as soon as they reached the shore.

Clacton's lifeboat was busy again when it went to the rescue of the one and only Admiralty 1000, No. 1358, three-engined, twin-fuselaged seaplane which had suffered continual mechanical trouble since leaving Cowes, Isle of Wight. Loaded to almost ten tons, the AD.1000 had taken almost 15 miles to take-off and had alighted at Newhaven to repair an oil pipe and drop one of its passengers. Another oil pipe fractured off Clacton, and it was then towed along the coast to Felixstowe, where it remained, unused and unwanted, its R.N.A.S. heavy bombing duties being taken over by the Handley-Page 0/100 landplane.

Mr Winston Churchill visited the Station again but luck ran out once more on him. Staying at the Pier Hotel, he inspected the Station, watched a flypast of marine aircraft, and when about to take a flight himself, the seaplane being brought alongside the landing stage, capsized and sank, so he abandoned the idea.

It was ironical that at this time the German base at Zeebrugge used the captured ex-Great Eastern Railway Company's packet s.s. *Brussels*, whose home was just across the water from Felixstowe at Parkeston Quay, as quarters for their base personnel.

Around midnight on 29th/30th April, 1915, a German Army airship made its first appearance off Felixstowe on a brilliant moonlit night, and crossing the coast, made her way inland, dropping bombs on Ipswich and Bury St Edmunds before re-crossing the coast at Aldeburgh on her way home. The L.11 also crept into the area near Orfordness, but suffering engine trouble, turned and made for her base.

Mr R. D. Milward of Heacham was at the Air Station at this time and remembered the incident: "One evening after dark when the Station was flooded with light whilst we were manhandling all the aircraft back into the sheds, bombs started falling and we saw the Zeppelin which had dropped them as it passed from cloud to cloud, heading out to sea. The bombs mostly dropped where they did not matter in a line between the area of the Station and Landguard Fort."

A small seaplane carrier, H.M.S. *Vindex*, operated from Harwich and carried two Bristol Scouts which took off from an improvised platform on the forward deck. Planned for operations against the Zeppelins, they carried out one sortie on 2nd August, 1916, but the pilot, Flight Lieutenant Freeman, was forced to come down in the sea and was interned in Holland. If beyond reach of land, they would have to alight in the sea and be picked up by the parent vessel.

Captain G. Fane, an ex-R.N.A.S. pilot attached to H.M.S. *Vindex* recalled to the author the hazardous nature of flying off the Bristol Scouts, and

Short 184 seaplane attempts a "carrier landing" on Felixstowe New Pier, 22nd May, 1920, whilst an assorted group of servicemen study the salvage situation. The track for the electric pier railway is clearly visible on the right. *Richard Crier*

other aircraft from the extremely short runway, made more dangerous by the sharp rise and fall of the vessel, which had to steam at full speed into the eye of the wind in order to create the necessary windspeed for take-off. When fitted with floats, these small aircraft were very vulnerable to damage whilst being hoisted inboard by the ship's crane after alighting on the sea alongside the parent vessel.

Later in the year on 13th/14th August, the Zeppelin LZ.10 passed over the Estuary and dropped bombs on Ipswich, Woodbridge and Harwich. Commanded by Oberleutnant Friedrich Werke, the bombs dropped by the LZ.10 at Woodbridge killed seven inhabitants when they fell on St John's Hill, whilst others crashed down on Castle Street and the yard of the Wagon and Horses Inn at the corner of Bredfield Street. It is reported that Werke claimed to have bombed the railway and seriously damaged the electrical plant of the Harwich Naval Base.

A curious incident occurred on the night of 31st March, 1916, when, during the hours of darkness five Zeppelins passed over the district, and,

Aerial view of the Air Station taken during 1924 showing the three hangars with their attendant slipways and jetties, the sheds of the Old Station in the top distance and living quarters to the left.   *Mr Good*

during this time it was discovered that all the telephone lines to the Station had been cut, but by whom it was never ascertained.

On 14th April, 1916, the enemy sallied forth when five torpedo carrying seaplanes attacked the Greek steamer *Antonios* five miles from the Sunk light vessel, but without success. They then attacked another small steamer, still without damaging it, but finally sunk the *Kankakee* about one mile from the Sunk.

A unique experiment was jointly carried out by the R.N. and the R.N.A.S. during April and May, 1916 when the Harwich Force submarine, E.22, carried two Sopwith Schneider* seaplanes to sea aboard her decking. After launching the seaplanes at sea, the E.22 submerged and the seaplanes returned to Felixstowe.

Aircraft used by the Royal Navy seaplane carriers, *Vindex, Engadine,* and *Campania*, were serviced at the Air Station and consisted of Sopwith Babys, Bristol Scouts, Sopwith 1½ strutters, and Short 184s. One of the hazards of these operations was launching the frail craft onto the surface in choppy conditions, which caused many aircraft losses.

An unusual defensive measure taken in the district was the R.N.A.S. mobile anti-aircraft gun batteries, and one of these, named *Rattler*, armed with naval pom-pom guns, operated in the Rushmere district near Ipswich.

The German High Seas Fleet appeared off the Suffolk coast on 25th April, 1916, when they shelled Great Yarmouth, Lowestoft and Southwold. Making out to sea they were pursued by R.N.A.S. aircraft, but without effect. The same night a Zeppelin dropped bombs across the harbour at Harwich and Parkeston Quay, where at the latter place a very large bomb fell on soft ground and was never recovered. Naval guns in the area fired at the raider which dropped her water ballast and gaining height made off out to sea, where she dropped the remainder of her bombs in the region of the Sunk light vessel.

Zeppelins were overhead again during the night of 30th July, 1916, and aircraft took off to engage them but without success, whilst on the night of 2nd August, the L.11 flew over the Harbour at great altitude, ringed by the flashes of anti-aircraft shell bursts, and she was believed to have been damaged by the defences.

An act of heroism out in the North Sea was enacted by Flight Lieutenant George Reid who was flying a seaplane in a heavy snowstorm, off the enemy coast, searching for a fellow airman who had been forced down. Flight Sub-Lieutenant John Hay had been flying along the Dutch coast when engine failure compelled him to alight, and whilst so doing his single seat seaplane capsized, and he clung to one of the floats which had broken away. Flight Lieutenant Reid put his seaplane down on the rough surface and his observer, Chief Petty Officer Richard Mullins, reached down to managed to grab Hay and drag him aboard. After several attempts to take-off again, but

*This Sopwith type was so named because it raced in the pre-First World War Schneider Trophy events.

11

The large angular all-metal Rohrbach designed Beardmore Inverness N.183 taxies along the "Sea-Front" with Harwich in the background. This was the first one of the two aircraft ordered, the second following two years later.   *S. D. Snell*

without success, Flight Lieutenant Reid was forced to surrender to a German patrol boat which had loomed up alongside. The occasion of this incident was the raid on the German bases at Schleswig-Holstein in which five Felixstowe men were posted missing.

Felixstowe was at this time responsible for the extra training of flying boat pilots and regular courses were held in order that First Pilots could qualify as Senior Captains.

The famous "Spider's Web" Patrol System was inaugurated on 13th April, 1917, and the exploits of this operation are described in the chapter "War Flight".

Norman Wilkinson, the now famous marine artist, arrived at the Station to examine the effects of "dazzle painting" as a means of camouflage for flying boats. This was the only use made of this scheme for aircraft, although some of the earlier machines had been vividly painted in order that they could be seen if forced down on the surface. This scheme was to be revived again at a later date.

The Zeppelin L.48 appeared over Harwich Harbour during the night of 17th June, 1917 and was picked up by defence searchlights and fired at by high angle naval guns. Flying at 11,000 feet, and rising to 13,000 feet, the raider moved up the coast, pursued by a B.E.12 flown by Second Lieutenant L. P. Watkins and Captain R. H. M. Saundby, M.C. in a D.H.2. Watkins managed to get a burst of machine gun fire into the L.48 when it was at 13,200 feet, without obvious effect, but was luckier with another burst into the stern when it started to burn. Saundby also put in a burst and probably caused additional damage.

Falling down the sky in a roaring cascade of fire, the stricken airship broke into a blazing "V" and crashed into a cornfield at Holly Tree Farm,

Theberton, Suffolk, the commander, Kapitanleutnant Eichler being just alive when the first rescuers arrived, but he died shortly afterwards. The commander of the North Sea Airship Division, Korvettenkapitän Schütze, aboard at the time, was also killed and only a rating and an officer, Oberleutenant Mieth survived, both terribly injured. The latter recovered and died in South Africa just after the Second World War. It is reported that the officer jumped out when the wreckage was near the ground and his greatcoat acted as a parachute and airbrake. The L.48 was on her maiden voyage against England and fate caught up with her high over Felixstowe Air Station.

Mr Millichamp recalls: "During the Zeppelin raid on the night of 16th June, 1917, from our positions on the Air Station we watched one of the Zeppelins caught in the searchlight and a target for many guns. It was obviously disabled and a sitting bird for aeroplanes. It was our privilege as the Senior Air Station to send up the combatting plane and so we started to launch a H.12 flying boat for the job. I was to be the wireless operator and chief gunlayer in charge of two Lewis guns. We, the crew, were all ready to take-off and do battle with the airship, but before we could get off the Zeppelin, L.48, came down in flames at 3.30 a.m., an R.F.C. pilot having 'wiped our eye'."

Also in the dark skies that night was Captain Fane in a B.E. single-seat biplane adapted for night fighting, but the performance of this aircraft was such that it could not gain altitude sufficiently quickly to catch up on the raider. Captain Fane recalls that on that night he was sure that he had glimpsed another Zeppelin, partially hidden by clouds, below him. Banking round swiftly in order to drop his Rankin darts on the raider, being in the ideal position to do so, he could no longer locate the airship. Rejoining the hunt for L.48, Captain Fane gave no more thought to this incident, but only a few years ago, during the course of making a documentary film about the

Sleek and powerful, the Gloster III Schneider racing seaplane taxies past the local dredger and various sailing craft during its brief life at Felixstowe.   *J. T. Hill*

Members of the R.A.F. Far East Flight at Felixstowe during 1927. Front Row, left to right: Flight Lieutenant Wigglesworth, Squadron Leader Livock, Group Captain Cave-Brown-Cave, Flight Lieutenant Maitland, Flying Officer Nicholetts, Flight Lieutenant Freeman. Back Row: Flight Lieutenant Carnegie, Flying Officer Cheesman, Flight Lieutenant Sawyer, Flying Officer Scott, Flying Officer Harwood.   *G. Livock*

Zeppelin raids, Captain Fane came face to face with an ex-Zeppelin commander. To his amazement, the commander stated that he was in command of the other Zeppelin that Captain Fane had caught a glimpse of, and that after seeing his companion fall in flames, had decided to make for his home base. But for the fleeting cloud cover, he too could have suffered the same fate as the L.48.

The Gotha bombers started appearing in greater numbers off the East Coast and on the 4th July, 1917, a number attacked the Orwell Estuary area. As the raiders passed high over the Air Station, bombs rained down and one fell alongside a slipway where a twin-engined Short flying boat was being readied for launching by its attendant crew. Taking refuge under the ramp, the launching crew were unfortunately trapped when the flying boat caught fire and all were killed in the resultant inferno.

Mr Millichamp also recalls this day: "Early in the morning of 4th July, 1917, the klaxon sounded the air raid alarm and we dashed out of our huts to see 13 Gothas flying in from the sea. We had no shelters then, but one of the safest spots was under a slipway used for launching flying boats, so I went full speed for it. Being young, eighteen years or so, I got there first and with seven other later arrivals filled up the available space. It was soon apparent that our Station was the target for the day, and the bombs, including some that burst over the area and scattered shrapnel started dropping. Suddenly, for no logical reason, I felt that I could not stay where I was, although the safest place, and I dashed out along the beach. Within a matter of seconds, a bomb dropped directly onto a flying boat and through the slipway, killing all those I

14

had just left. Many times later that day I had to assure people that I was out and about, and had left the slipway before the bomb fell."

One bomb dropped through the roof of Old Felixstowe parish church of St Peter and St Paul during the Communion Service, bringing down part of the organ, but not exploding or hurting anyone. It is still preserved in a glass case as a reminder of those grim days.

Again on the 22nd July, fifteen Gothas crossed the Suffolk coast, and attacked Harwich Harbour. Fifty-five bombs were dropped during the raid, thirteen people killed and twenty-six injured.

In the 4th August issue of *Wings*, the Air Station's own journal, the famous aviation journalist, the late Mr C. G. Grey, wrote; "Setting aside the Porte boats, Felixstowe is a magnificent station, of which everyone may be well proud, but in the history yet to be written it will go down in posterity, in conjunction with the honoured name of Commander John Porte, R.N. as being responsible for the first ocean going flying machines."

On the 1st October, 1917, a bevy of young pilots took a Porte Baby on a semi-authorized flight out over the North Sea, and straying too far from home, were forced down by German fighter seaplanes near the North Hinder light vessel. With two of the three motors disabled, the Germans circled round the big flying boat and used up all their ammunition in attempting to sink it, finally making off to their base at Zeebrugge. After their adversaries' departure, the crew patched-up the motors, started them up and taxied throughout the night across the North Sea finally beaching at Sizewell Gap, near Southwold, just before dawn. Troops carrying out a coastal patrol assumed they were the enemy and opened fire on the aircraft, adding more holes to the already riddled structure.

When one of the Babys was later dismantled, the hull was used as a hostel for airwomen, four R.N.A.S. drivers living therein in comfort, complete with electric light.

Further paintwork schemes came into being in order to make a "downed" aircraft more easy to spot on the surface, and designs were devised where the hulls were painted in squares and stripes, each aircraft being individual, and charted so that it could be recognised from the air.

With the arrival of the Royal Air Force on 1st April, 1918, many changes became apparent, as the hitherto naval traditions of the R.N.A.S. now took a back seat. Just previously, on the 7th March, a Royal Proclamation announced His Majesty's Will and Pleasure that the Air Force should be styled the "Royal Air Force" and during June a further announcement directed that the Royal Air Force should take precedence after the Navy and the Army.

Ranks were changed and Wing Commanders became Lieutenant Colonels, Squadron Commanders—Majors, Flight Lieutenants—Captains, Flight Sub-Lieutenants—Lieutenants, Petty Officers—Sergeants, Leading

Hands—Corporals, and Ratings—Privates. The naval style officer's uniform was changed to khaki, khaki shirts, brown boots and black tie, whilst all ranks had Army uniform with R.A.F. buttons and badges. Formations were also formed and Felixstowe became part of No. 4 (Operations) Group under the command of Lieutenant Colonel Samson, D.S.O., who made his Headquarters at Felixstowe Air Station. Other units in the Group were Great Yarmouth, Burgh Castle, Covehithe, Aldeburgh, Westgate and the balloon unit at Lowestoft. The Commanding Officer at Felixstowe at this time was Lieutenant Colonel E. D. M. Robertson.

War came very close to home on the 6th July, 1918 when a flight of W.29 floatplanes, led by Oberleutnant Christiansen, attacked a Royal Navy submarine the C.25, off the entrance to Harwich Harbour. With her commander, Lieutenant Bell, R.N. and five ratings dead, and the upper structure badly damaged, the warship had to be towed into harbour by a companion submarine which went to her aid.

During August several flying boat squadrons were formed at Felixstowe,

No. 231 Squadron with F.3 and F.5 aircraft.   Disbanded 9.7.1919.
No. 232 Squadron with F.2A and F.3 aircraft.   Disbanded 5.1.1919.
No. 247 Squadron with F.2A and F.3 aircraft.   Disbanded 22.1.1919.
No. 259 Squadron with F.2A and F.2 and H.12
   aircraft   Disbanded 13.8.1919.
No. 261 Squadron with F.3 aircraft.   Disbanded 13.9.1919.

Saro S.21 Windhover, G-ABJP, "City of Portsmouth" used by the Hon. Mrs Victor Bruce in a record endurance attempt in the district, stands outside "B" Flight Hangars at Martlesham Heath where it was evaluated as a landplane, during August, 1932.

Some special duty Sopwith Camels still resided at Felixstowe and Group Captain Stuart Culley recalls his aircraft: "I kept a Camel at Felixstowe and Martlesham Heath from August 1918 until I left about March 1919 when my unit was disbanded. This was of course to keep my hand in at flying them, for I could do nothing at Felixstowe. On one occasion I took a newly erected Camel off the slipway at Felixstowe to deliver it to Martlesham, that being the simplest way in which to deliver the machine after erection by my Flight. All this was after the L.53 episode, which took place during August 1918."

Another daring experiment carried out by the Royal Navy and the infant Royal Air Force was the flying off of Sopwith 2FI Camels from the foredecks of light cruisers. One such operation was performed on 1st June, 1918 when the Royal Australian Navy light cruisers, *Sydney* and *Melbourne* of the Harwich Cruiser Force flew off a Camel apiece. Their target was enemy seaplanes, one of which was forced down on the sea. This was a hazardous operation as the runway length over the gun turrets was only about twice the length of the aircraft and the cruiser had to steam at speed into the eye of the wind in order to give sufficient airspeed for the aircraft to become airborne.

It was ironical that after the Armistice was signed, the U-Boats which the War Flight had daily sought out in the North Sea, now slipped slowly past the Air Station, with White Ensigns on their jackstaffs, their crews lined up on deck, and escorted by vessels which had hunted them previously. They were interned and lay rusting in long lines in the River Stour near Parkeston Quay, within sight and sound of the Air Station.

With the intense activity of the war years over, the Station settled down to less hectic times and as a sign of the times, the moorings in the river which had been laid down for torpedo boats, destroyers and other naval vessels were now replaced by seaplane moorings.

Zeppelins were seen over the North Sea again and over East Anglia during July, when L.71, the largest airship yet built, arrived at Pulham Market, Norfolk complete with her crew to be handed over under the Peace Treaty conditions. Later in the month, her sister, the L.64, also arrived and both ex-enemy airships resided at the Norfolk airship station for evaluation and trials.

Promotion came for one of the Station's officers, when an assistant of John Porte's in the early days, Captain David Nicholson, became the Air Ministry Chief Production Officer responsible for flying boat construction.

Hulls were still constructed of wood as a form of yacht building, using seasoned elm and mahogany planking, but more and more metal fittings were making their appearance. To give an example of the craftsmanship involved in this work, it was recorded that it took three men and two boys five and a half weeks of forty-seven hours to build a four-seat Supermarine type wooden hull.

New designs and indeed new aircraft of any design were a rarity, as during 1921 several Short 184 twin-float seaplanes were in store at the Station, but were disposed of during 1922.

During 1922, Sir Gerald Geddes made his economic cuts and no orders were placed for any new types of aircraft, and so the work of the Station was one of routine maintenance and jogging along with what they had.

No. 230 Squadron, which had been resident at the Station for the last five years, moved to Calshot and so the aircraft strength dropped even lower.

On 17th March, 1924, the Marine Aircraft Experimental Unit moved from the Isle of Grain to Felixstowe and on the 1st April, 1924, the Marine Aircraft Experimental Establishment was formed, and became the principal unit for testing and evaluating service and civil marine aircraft. Many personnel and much equipment was transferred from the former site, which had been carrying out the bulk of the experimental work, and so now three test centres had been established within a few miles of each other, Felixstowe, Martlesham Heath and Orfordness.

The Station was divided into four Flights, with "A" and "B" in the large No. 1 hangar, "C" in No. 2 Hangar (floatplanes) and "D" in No. 3 Hangar, again with small flying boats. The next set of buildings housed the Engine Repair Section, then the Marine Section and lastly the Aircraft Repair Section. When the High Speed Flight was formed later it was housed in sheds at the Landguard end of the Establishment, always known as the "Old Station".

Ex-Flight Sergeant Middleton recalls memories of the Air Officer Commanding's Parades and their rehearsals: "The tarmac in front of the hangars was an ideal parade ground for 'advancing in Review Order' marched by the whole parade and Band to exactly sixteen paces of the R.A.F. Ceremonial March. This same movement was carried out at R.A.F. Finningley on the occasion of Her Majesty's Jubilee Review of the Royal Air Force during July 1977." So who makes history?

An aviation sporting event, the 1924 King's Cup Air Race was held on 12th August and was unique in that it included both land and seaplanes. The former started at Martlesham Heath, whilst the latter made their getaway from Felixstowe over the course of 950 miles. Turning points were at Leith Harbour, Dumbarton Castle, Falmouth and the finishing point was at Lee-on-Solent. Starting from Felixstowe were two Supermarine Seagull III's flown by Colonel The Master of Sempill and Captain H. C. Biard, and the Fairey IIID, N.9777, piloted by Captain Norman MacMillian, who finished second.

Mr C. H. Barnes, the well-known air historian remembers: "Being a Suffolk 'bor' myself, I used to hang around Felixstowe and Martlesham Heath quite a lot in my school days. I was at the Prep School at Felixstowe with

18

The delicate task of transferring petrol from the refuelling boat by pipes to the upper wing fuel tanks of a Supermarine Southampton.   *Mrs M. Tillyer*

Vincent Drake, (of Boscombe Down and formerly of the M.A.E.E.) and I well remember the Fairey Atlanta arriving at Felixstowe on a Sunday. Vic and I absconded from the school Sunday afternoon 'walk' and ran down Peewit Hill to the Dock to see what all the noise was about. The Atlanta was stuck on the slipway and the capstan had stalled, so they were trying to bring her up with several Caterpillar tractors and the two front Condor motors. It was terrific from the railings on the beach, but of course, I didn't have a camera in those days."

Squadron Leader F. J. French of Felixstowe, an ex-flying boat pilot and now resident in the old Officers' Mess as a Collector for Her Majesty's Customs remembers: "We came to Felixstowe in 1924, when I was five, and at that time there was a small dump of flying boat bits in the middle of the Town where Henley's lock-up garages now stand. I soon cut my knee playing there — I still have the scar. There were other dumps around near the Docks, with a very large one on the east side of the Basin.

Later during 1928 I vividly recall seeing the L-5 Junkers aircraft of Kohl, Fitzmaurice and Hunefeld pass over on its way back to Germany after its unsuccessful trans-Atlantic attempt — they succeeded later.

The best place to see the aircraft at the M.A.E.E. was from the Old Pier near the present Fisher House: Landguard Point was, in general inaccessible, although we were able to get there for fishing and also for the excellent pursuit of recovering bullets from the sand behind the rifle range butts."

A group of Press officials who were at the M.A.E.E. to see the delicate pale blue Gloster III biplane had their attention diverted to a large twin-engined cantilever, all-metal monoplane flying boat coming in to alight. It so impressed the reporters that one of them wrote, that although not very beautiful, it looked very practical both in the air and on the water. The aircraft in question was the Beardmore Inverness, N.183, being ably flown by the builder's German pilot, Herr Landmann, who was conducting the trials.

No. 205 Squadron was reformed on 17th May, 1927, and became the Far East Flight equipped with Supermarine Southampton IIIs. They left for Singapore during October and arrived there after a flag showing tour during February, 1928.

During June 1928, H.R.H. The Prince of Wales and Marshal of the Royal Air Force, Sir Hugh Trenchard, were very surprised when a steward served them tea aboard the Short Calcutta flying boat, shortly after take-off.

In June, the Blackburn Iris II, N.185, was sent from the M.A.E.E. to Plymouth to assist in the search for the submarine H.47 overdue after submerging in the English Channel.

Being on the coast, and in a good position for observation, a Meteorological Section was established and staffed by two civilians, Mr Lamb and Mr Foster, who provided information for the Station and local enquiries.

An officer posted to Felixstowe during the latter part of 1930 was later to be a big name in British aviation, Flying Officer Frank Whittle, now Sir Frank Whittle, K.B.E., C.B., F.R.S. Resident with the floatplane flight, Whittle was attached for a time to Farnborough and H.M.S. *Ark Royal* to carry out experimental work on catapult launching techniques. During the course of this work he performed some 47 launchings and one successful forced landing test in Fairey Seal, S.1325. On returning to Felixstowe, he carried out the duties of test pilot with those of Station Armament Officer, and this included

The 50-ton Titan cantilever crane gently lifts the Saro Severn from the water and round onto its cradle on the Crane Pier. Note the slinger perched on the upper mainplane. *Mrs M. Tillyer*

No. 3 Gantry at the Old Station. On the left can be seen the mooring gantry which allowed moored aircraft to keep a taut mooring line at all states of the tide by means of the sandbag counter-weights. *J. T. Hill*

the armament trials of new flying boats and floatplanes. Although his main "hobby" was the design and theory of the gas turbine aircraft propulsion unit, he was also responsible for other ingenious designs including a method of displaying the field of fire from the gun positions of flying boats, and also a design for an advanced type of enclosed gun turret. Still managing to fly marine aircraft whenever possible, Flying Officer Whittle added eighteen types to his log-book before he was posted to Henlow on an Engineering Officers' Course during August, 1932. Thus it is recorded in the August 1932 issue of the *Foghorn*, the station magazine which replaced *Wings*, "Flying Officer Whittle is leaving us for Henlow where he is due to undergo an Engineering Course. We wish him all success and while at Henlow he must bear in mind that catapults are not permitted in school hours!"

No. 210 Squadron was reformed at Felixstowe on 1st March, 1931, with Southampton III flying boats, and then moved to Pembroke Dock during June.

Mr C. H. Barnes remembers that during the Easter holidays he received an invitation to the M.A.E.E. from Squadron Leader Harry Orlebar, whose old governess was one of his doctor father's patients. This was a memorable event as he was able to sit in the cockpit of one of the High Speed Flight's S.6s, N.247, and he also got a pass to go into Calshot the week before the Contest.

A three-engined flying boat was evident in the district during the first week of August, 1932, this being the Saro A.21 Windhover, G-ABJP "City of Portsmouth" which was attempting an endurance record. Flown by the Hon. Mrs Victor Bruce and crew it was refuelled over the area by a Bristol Fighter Mk. IV, G-ABYA, but the boat was forced to retire after 54 hours, 13 minutes by excessive oil temperature.

21

With the aircraft industry approaching its golden era, many new designs were appearing together with those which had been modified and revised, and the aircraft population steadily increased, the Air Station becoming a mecca for the between wars air enthusiast.

Felixstowe always felt the loss of the ones it loved and the *Foghorn* of August, 1932 recorded: "Since the last issue, our Magazine has suffered an almost irreplaceable loss in the death of Mr D. F. L. Grant-Jones, who after a long period of illness so cheerfully borne, passed away on the 12th June. From the very first number of the *Foghorn* our Whispering Baritone has been the most regular contributor of cartoons and sketches and, whatever the subject, would always be relied upon to produce the goods."

Felixstowe aircraft performed at the 1934 Hendon Air Pageant on 30th June, when a formation of mixed flying boats consisting of a Blackburn Perth, K.3581, Short Singapore II, N.246, Short Sarafand, S.1589, Supermarine Scapa, S.1648, Short R.24/31, K.3574, Saro London, K.3560 and three Saro Clouds. It must have called for a high degree of piloting to hold this motley gaggle in some sort of formation.

A repeat performance was flown the following year, but programmed as No. 209 Squadron, but what must have been the weirdest squadron to take to the air consisted of:

Short R.6/28 Sarafand	S.1589	Wing Commander Livock and Flight Lieutenant Abrams
Short R.24/31 Knuckleduster	K.3574	Squadron Leader Williamson Jones
Supermarine R.24/31 Stranraer	K.3973	Flying Officer L. F. Brown
Saro London	K.3560	Flying Officer Flood
Short Singapore III	K.4577	Flight Lieutenant Lovering
Supermarine Scapa	S.1648	Flying Officer Walsh
Saro Cloud		Flying Officer Chadwick

On the way home from Hendon, the formation took a very good photograph of Lords Cricket Ground where England were playing South Australia. Wing Commander Livock presented a copy to the M.C.C. who hung it in the Pavilion. Here it must be pointed out that he was a well-known cricketer and played three times for Middlesex at Lords in 1925. He also played that year for the Gentlemen against the Players and some years later for the Gentlemen of England against Australia.

Group Captain Crosbie, O.B.E., recalls that when he joined No. 209 Squadron at Felixstowe, it was officially equipped with the large Blackburn Perth biplane flying boats, but for some reason or other they were all out of action and therefore the motley assortment of marine aircraft were pressed into service as No. 209 Squadron.

A new landmark appeared during 1934, when the 50-ton Titan cantilever crane took shape on the Crane Pier which had been completed during 1932. The crane, of Stodart and Pitt design, worked regularly lifting and lowering all types of aircraft and boats, and throughout its life was always operated by a civilian crane-driver. One of the sayings of the Station was, "Ask the crane-driver", used as the reply to questions regarding almost anything.

On 6th June, 1936 a Unit Badge was authorised for the M.A.E.E., the badge symbol being a balance and the motto "Trial by air and sea".

During 1936, the giant Short Sarafand, S.1589, was dismantled and scrapped at Felixstowe, the process taking some time and various items and pieces of the once proud flying boat were carefully hidden and kept as relics. It was a tribute to the designers and makers that this large aircraft was right from the start and only the pace of development which overtook it caused its demise.

Sport was always well represented at the Station and during July 1937 the Station brought home three Team Championship Cups from the R.A.F. Championships at Uxbridge, these being the Tug-of-War, the Hurdles and the High Jump. Corporal Bishop cleared 5 feet 6 inches in the last event, only twice equalled before, in 1929 and 1931. Three months previously, Aircraftsman Hewitt had become the Flyweight Boxing Champion of the R.A.F.

The August 1937 *Foghorn* recorded that the Felixstowe Air Station Old Comrades, those who had served at the Station during the War, paid a visit on Sunday, 20th June, 1937, and thoroughly enjoyed themselves.

Three Singapore IIIs of No. 209 Squadron which had left Felixstowe, revisited their old home and carried out formation flying in the district. One of these aircraft lived on for some years serving with No. 4 Operational Training Unit until it was scrapped during 1941.

One of the attractions on Empire Air Day, 1938, was the Short Knuckleduster, K.3574, which the public were allowed to inspect at close range. Unfortunately this hard-worked prototype was near the end of its working life and shortly afterwards it was taken to the R.A.F.'s Cosford No. 2 School of Technical Training to become 1154M, an instructional airframe.

The Boom Defence Depot which had left its site alongside the Air Station during 1925, returned to the Dock in 1938, and a new slipway was constructed near the M.A.E.E.'s slipways.

A sign of things to come happened on 17th July, 1938, when a Hawker Hurricane from R.A.F. Debden, Essex, crashed into the sea, four miles off the coast. The pilot had parachuted into the sea and was picked up by a Felixstowe-based flying boat.

With the Munich Crisis just around the corner, on 31st March, 1939, Mr Neville Chamberlain, the Prime Minister, announced that Great Britain and France would back Poland if she was attacked. The prospect of the coming conflict was evidenced on 24th August, when Billeting Notices were served on

The long serving M.A.E.E. resident, Short Sarafand, S.1589 at her moorings showing the six Rolls-Royce Buzzard in-line engines in their tandem pairs mountings. *Mrs M. Tillyer*

residents living in the vicinity of the Air Station to accommodate troops of the No. 409 (Suffolk) R. A. Battery, who moved in the same day. Members of the National Defence Corps also arrived to guard the nearby dock installations.

Germany invaded Poland on 1st September, 1939, and war seemed near as on that Friday three paddle steamers arrived at Felixstowe New Pier, laden with women and children evacuated from the Dagenham area of Essex. Spending the night in the town, they were dispersed the following day for billeting throughout county. On 3rd September, 1939, at 11 o'clock, a fine Sunday morning, the announcement of the Prime Minister told the country that the worst had happened and the conflict had begun.

By virtue of the M.A.E.E.'s position on the East Coast, at the outbreak of hostilities it moved to a safer location in order to carry on the now even more important testing and evaluation of marine aircraft. Its new home was at Helensburgh, on the River Clyde, and only a few aircraft remained at Felixstowe for patrol work and air sea rescue duties. No. 209 Squadron which still had aircraft resident at Felixstowe moved them north to Invergordon, Scotland.

After the departure of the M.A.E.E. the tarmac rang to the sound of marching feet as recruits marched up and down the now empty spaces on the "Seafront". Other recruits were pigeons which had been handed over by their local owners and trained for use aboard aircraft as emergency messengers. No. 85 Maintenance Unit came along shortly afterwards and continued to store and maintain flying boats which arrived for modifications and repair. A unit not seen before in the area was No. 928 Balloon Squadron who had their "aircraft" displayed around the locality, whilst the launches of No. 26 Air Sea Rescue (Marine Craft) Squadron carried out valuable services in that role.

On the night of 20th November, 1939, Heinkel 115 floatplanes of the Köstenfliegerstaffel 3/906 (Coastal Reconnaissance Squadron) of the Luftwaffe laid magnetic mines in the approaches to Harwich Harbour, and returned again the following night to repeat the operation. The next night, H.M.S. *Gipsy* was moving out of the harbour, the Harwich base now being named H.M.S. *Badger*, in company with the Polish destroyer *Burza*, when it struck a mine sown by one of the seaplanes. The *Gipsy's* captain attempted to beach the stricken warship and made "the ground" near the Air Station, with fifty of his crew dead.

Nature seemed to be against the Station on 28th June, 1940, when one of the defence balloons was struck by lightning and fell, blazing, onto one of the buildings, setting it on fire.

Not only the enemy fell foul of the barrage balloons. On 22nd May 1940 a Whitley bomber returning from a raid was engaged by anti-aircraft guns and, after miraculously dodging the gasbags as it flew through their lines, managed to make off out to sea again. Tragedy came the following week when a No. 44 Squadron Hampden struck a cable and dived into the River Orwell with the loss of its crew, whilst on the 11th June, another Hampden belonging to No. 144 Squadron hit a cable and dived into the East Anglian Flour Mills on the dockside. All the crew and a member of the mill staff died, whilst several railway trucks and small vessels were damaged in the ensuing inferno.

When the Germans over-ran the Low Countries during May, 1940, the Dutch Forces put up a strong fight against overwhelming odds, but on the 14th all the serviceable aircraft of the Netherland's Marine Luchtvaartdienst (M.L.D.) took flight and made for France. Their residence there was short lived and they moved on to England, twenty-six aircraft eventually arriving on the South Coast and collecting at Calshot.

Fastest of the pre-war biplane flying boats, the Supermarine Stranraer served during the early months of the Second World War. Several were produced in Canada and one of these is fortunately preserved in the R.A.F. Museum at Hendon. *Vickers Limited*

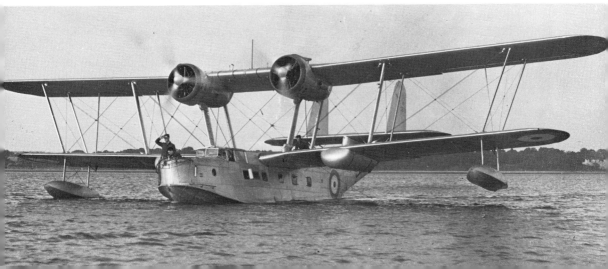

One of the aircraft types which escaped was the comparatively recently constructed Fokker T.VIII.W twin-engined monoplane floatplane powered by British built Bristol Mercury radial motors. On 1st June, 1940 the best of these aircraft moved to Pembroke Dock in South Wales where they became No. 320 (Dutch) Squadron of the Royal Air Force. Manned by Dutch personnel it operated within the framework of the R.A.F. Coastal Command.

The Dutch built aircraft were brought up to R.A.F. operational standards and serialled AV.958 to AV.965 and commenced sea patrols over the Western Approaches. Two aircraft were lost on these operations whilst the ravages of wartime service and lack of spares resulted in two more being reduced to spares in order to maintain the remainder.

On 28th November, 1940 the four survivors, AV.958, AV.960, AV.961 and AV.965, left Pembroke Dock for Felixstowe for North Sea duties, but one of their number, AV.958, suffered fuel starvation whilst near Middleton, Sudbury, Suffolk, miles from any friendly water surface. A colleague of the author who witnessed this incident recalls that the aircraft made a normal landing but in a somewhat dry field and although the aircraft was a total write-off, the pilot, Sergeant De Borst, and his observer escaped with injuries. The remaining three aircraft carried out "specified duties" until June 1941 when they were scrapped at Felixstowe.

One other T.VIII.W arrived during the autumn of 1942, and this was R-25 which after being constructed in Holland under German supervision for use by the Luftwaffe was secretly prepared by Dutch patriots, and then two escapees managed to fly it to England where it also served at Felixstowe.

A pre-war visitor returned when the Short Mayo upper component "Mercury" G-ADHJ, flew into Felixstowe, piloted by Captain D. C. T. Bennett, later to be known as "Pathfinder" Bennett. It was handed over to the Dutch unit for use as a trainer. It was broken up by its makers at Rochester during the autumn of 1941, and for the interested, the lower component, "Maia", G-ADHL, was destroyed by enemy action in Poole Harbour on 11th May, 1941.

On Sunday, 16th June, the beaches and foreshore were mined as a defence measure against enemy landings, whilst three nights later, two aircraft were heard engaging each other off the coast. One crashed into the sea, on fire, about two miles offshore, and at daybreak a British parachute was picked up presumably from an R.A.F. Blenheim which had been shot down by a Heinkel bomber. With the threat of invasion ever present, more defence measures were put in hand, two of them being novel. The first was an armoured train which ran between Westerfield Junction, north of Ipswich, down the single branch line to Felixstowe and operated mainly at night and during air raids. More unusual were the two 12 inch howitzers weighing some 80 tons each, of No. 9 Super Heavy Battery which were stationed on the railway track at Levington, near Felixstowe. Firing shells weighing 750 lbs at a maximum range of 16,600 yards and an altitude of 16,000 feet, they were positioned to shell the War Channel from the Cork Light Vessel to Harwich Harbour. In the other direction they were able to shell Martlesham Heath airfield or Bawdsey Radio Location Station if the need should arise. The large shed constructed to house these guns still stands alongside the railway track near the level crossing gates at Stratton Hall Lane.

Barrage balloons downed another victim on the night of 9th September, 1940, when an unidentified aircraft became entangled and dived into the river. The threat of invasion seemed nearer, as the Local Defence Volunteers were called out to standby during September, greater security was imposed and the beach areas and river banks were out of bounds to all civilians.

A deed worthy of the best spy thriller stories was performed by one of the Fokker T.VIII.Ws during October 1940, when at midnight on the 15th it took off from the Air Station and set course for the Tjeukemeer Lake in Friesland in order to pick-up four Dutch agents. Flying through low cloud and rain it was extremely difficult to locate the pick-up point and being unable to obtain any recognition signals the mission was aborted and the aircraft returned to Felixstowe, arriving back at about 04.30 a.m.

The same evening, the T.VIII.W set out again on the same operation and, after an uneventful flight over the North Sea in better weather conditions, the lake was located and the correct recognition signals received. Turning gently through the dark skies, the pilot, Lieutenant Schaper, made a smooth touch-down and taxied towards the shore with his motors quietly ticking over.

Out of the darkness appeared the anticipated small boat, but, when it was still some 30 yards from the aircraft, the occupants opened up with small arms fire on the machine. Ramming his throttles forward the pilot raced the floatplane across the lake and took-off, beating a hasty retreat for base which he reached at 05.00 a.m. His troubles were not yet over, as a group of Local Defence Volunteers, not too familar with the silhouette of the Dutch aircraft, decided attack was the best form of defence and pumped another load of small arms fire into the already riddled machine. After the matter had been resolved the T.VIII.W was found to have collected over 40 holes—from both sides!

It was later learned that the four agents whom the aircraft had set out to collect had been captured by the Germans, who had then set a trap to capture the aircraft and its crew.

Of interest is the fact that the same squadron, No. 320, still existed in 1978 as a unit of the Dutch Kon Marine and operated American-built Lockheed Neptune maritime patrol aircraft from Valkenburg, Holland engaged on Atlantic patrol duties with N.A.T.O.

At about 8 o'clock on the evening of Saturday, 12th October, a Junkers 88 was illuminated by searchlights over the Station, and diving, it crashed into

The Armstrong Siddeley Tiger radial motor of the prototype Blackburn Shark, K.4295, screams as it is "run-up" tethered by ropes and held down by ground handling crew. Note the upward inclination of the elevators in order to keep the tail down. *Hawker Siddeley Limited*

the river near Landguard Point, the wreckage being discovered the next morning. Four nights later, a Heinkel III ran into the balloons at 23.20 hours and crashed on the foreshore across the river at Shotley, where it caught fire and the crew of six perished. Two parachute mines on board failed to detonate, whilst eleven days later another enemy aircraft gunned the area, but local defence guns scored a hit and it crashed offshore. Two days later another enemy bomber crashed in the river and one of the crew was captured. With now only a few aircraft at Felixstowe, the emphasis was on the small fast motor boats which lived for maintenance purposes in the hangars, and the Luftwaffe were opposed to their residence. On the night of 24th February, 1941, they made a heavy attack on the harbour and its installations at Harwich, but fortunately, once again, Felixstowe escaped their full attention. The Station had a lucky escape on 12th May, when a large high explosive bomb exploded up against the wall of a building which contained seven tons of explosives, which did not detonate. Seven days later, a Junkers 88, flying near the harbour entrance was hit by heavy machine-gun fire from the converted paddle steamer mine-sweeper, *Princess Elizabeth*, and set on fire. It crashed into the sea and the next day the body of the pilot, Pilot Sergeant Herbert Lindemann, was landed at Felixstowe.

The balloon barrage still claimed victims on both sides, as on Wednesday, 28th January, 1942, a Whitley bomber from Croft, Yorkshire, hit one of the

28

balloons, and badly crippled, crashed into the sea on fire, the crew all perishing.

Evidence of enemy air activity was shown on 9th April, when the body of a Luftwaffe airman, N.4325/40 Heinrich Fischer, was taken from the water near the Station, whilst later the body of Feldwebel Franz Zwesler came ashore, followed the next day by that of Warrant Officer Roggenbrick.

From 1942 until 1944, when winds were favourable, small balloons carrying incendiary devices and power and communication cable interference gadgets were launched from the area towards the enemy or enemy occupied territory.

Squadron Leader F. J. French of Felixstowe, who had joined the R.A.F.V.R. during 1938, flew from the Air Station on 21st June, 1943, when he took Catalina IB, FP 222, for a test flight around the area, and then to Sullom Voe in Shetland. Prepared and radar checked at the Felixstowe Maintenance Unit, he had to wait until the barrage balloons were lowered before taking off.

One of these balloons was sited in the Dooley Fort, where there was a lighting installation devised to confuse enemy aircraft at night. Squadron Leader French came back to the area again on 12th August, 1944, in another Catalina, this time a Mark IV, JX.268 of No. 210 Squadron, which had come south to have a Leigh Light fitted at Felixstowe.

The Mayo Composite aircraft, "Maia", G-ADHK and "Mercury", G-ADHJ. The latter served with No. 320 (Dutch) Squadron as a seaplane trainer.   *Short Brothers*

On Friday, 10th June, 1943 a shell from a local anti-aircraft gun struck a nearby gas-holder, exploded, and holed it. Escaping gas caught fire and some 150,000 cubic feet were lost before the gas could be shut off.

A new Luftwaffe aircraft type, the Messrschmitt 410, met its doom on 23rd August, at 18,000 feet near the Station, when it encountered a Mosquito night fighter and crashed up river near Chelmondiston. One of the crew died in the wreck, whilst the other, Obergefreiter Neurer, aged twenty-two, baled out and landed at Stratton Hall.

Situated under the nightly bomber streams, the Air Station received many unexpected visitors, as machines which had received the full attention of the defences of the Third Reich limped home and ditched off shore to be picked up by the rescue services. Some came from further afield, such as the Halifax V, LL.119 from No. 138 (Special Duties) Squadron based at Tempsford, Bedfordshire, which had been on a very long haul to Eastern Europe with resistance personnel and supplies on the night of 17th December, 1943, and only just managed to make an off-shore ditching where the crew were picked up by the local A.S.R. launches.

On Sunday, 1st April, 1944, Felixstowe was declared a Protected and Regulated Zone, whilst from the 24th of that month until 28th September, the area became a Byelaw Controlled Area and special military or police passes were required to enter the area. The Landguard Fort district was further restricted with entry only by a special pass. On 1st May, all roads were closed to the public for military reasons and all civilians with telephones were instructed by the police not to allow unknown persons to use them.

The invasion of Europe seemed very near when troops embarked on naval vessels off the Station on 1st June, and, as a further security measure, the main road from Ipswich to Felixstowe was closed at Trimley.

Felixstowe appeared to attract Miles Martinet target tug aircraft down to the ground as on 26th May, 1944 and 19th January, and again on the 9th February, 1945 aircraft of this type operating from Ipswich Airport crashed in the district. They were engaged in target towing duties for gunnery practice by R.A.F. fighters and local anti-aircraft guns.

During September 1944, the A.A. defences and balloon barrage were strengthened with the advent of the V.1 flying bombs. A feature of this new scheme was a dive bombing barrage in which the guns fired at an approximate height of 3,000 feet and formed a "Fire Curtain" from each gunsite.

With the gigantic daylight offensive being mounted by the American Eighth Air Force, many calls were made on the rescue services to pick up the crews of ditched B.17s and B.24s, often far out in the North Sea. Others, having struggled all the way home, losing altitude with knocked-out motors and dying crews, passed over the Station, but then turned to ditch in the sea, rather than crash-land, with the terrible risk of fire, on the East Anglian countryside.

Some were fortunate, like the crew of an R.A.F. Lancaster from Mepal, Cambs, which on the night of 7th/8th December, 1944, ditched in the River Orwell. The crew were able to take to their dinghy, set sail and reach the shore safely.

A new visitor arrived on 10th October, 1944, when a V.2 rocket exploded in mid-air high over Harwich Harbour, scattering pieces of debris over a wide area. The enemy did not seem so far away, when in clear weather conditions, a distinct white condensation trail from an ascending V.2 rocket was observed at a bearing of 84 degrees from its Felixstowe sighting.

About four or five minutes later, a loud mid-air explosion over the district announced that the missile had exploded prematurely. A repeat performance was experienced again the next day. These missiles were fired by the Lehr und Versuchs Artillerie Batterie 444 from Staveren, in Friesland, Eastern Holland, and captured German records reveal that the missiles were aimed at Norwich and Ipswich.

With the light of peace coming up over the horizon, the M.A.E.E. returned to its old home from its exile in Scotland, and started to re-organise the testing of marine aircraft. As described in a later chapter a great deal of work was carried out with captured Luftwaffe marine aircraft at this period.

A Marine Training School was established, and new buildings being erected were to house a Link Trainer system for the training of marine aircraft pilots in blind and instrument flying.

One of No. 210 Squadron's pilots, Mr C. B. White, became a Felixstowe test pilot, before joining Hawker Siddeley Aircraft. Squadron Leader French returned again to the Station from the Shetlands and, during January, 1946, he flew with Squadron Leader F. (Squib) Squire, D.S.O. in the Short Seaford prototype MZ.269 for a series of take-off and alightings, but unfortunately the work was to no avail, as the day of the large flying boat was near its end.

Postwar activity on the M.A.E.E's return to Felixstowe from Helensburgh. Sitting on the tarmac are Short Sunderland Mk V., ML.765 and ML.758, and an unidentified Consolidated Catalina with an airborne lifeboat under its starboard wing.   *E. Graystone*

Big and beautiful, the B.O.A.C's Short Sandringham Mk 5, G-AHZA "Penzance" sits high and dry on her beaching gear.   *Short Brothers*

It was the swing of the pendulum on 1st June, 1946, when R.A.F. Martlesham Heath came under the control of R.A.F. Felixstowe with Group Captain Welch in command of both stations.

Last of the Supermarine biplane amphibians, the Sea Otter developed from the famous Walrus, served at the postwar M.A.E.E. as a general utility runabout and A.S.R. aircraft, and also participated in many experiments.

September 14th, 1946 was Battle of Britain Day and many R.A.F. stations were opened to the public so that they could inspect the aircraft and equipment, and this was the only occasion when the U.S.A.F. participated.

The growth of aircraft designs was extremely slow in the immediate post war days and this especially applied to marine aircraft which, in the main, only embraced modifications to existing types, with the exceptions of the giant Short Shetland and the jet powered Saro SRA/1.

The Marine Training School left the Station during 1948 and moved to Pembroke Dock, South Wales, and from this time the activity at the Station steadily decreased. The strength was cut by half, and another reversal of procedure occurred when the Accounting Branch which dealt with Martlesham Heath moved there and became self-accounting.

One of the ex-R.A.F. Short Seafords, NJ.200, was converted for civil use and registered to Mr R. L. Whyham, as G-ALIJ, but for some unknown reason, the aircraft was not collected from Felixstowe and was eventually scrapped on site.

When members of the W.R.A.F. arrived during November, 1949 this was the first time that members of this branch of the service had served at the Station, and although they were involved with radar at Trimley Heath, they were billeted at Felixstowe. The Station Diary for this month bears this

32

comment — "Felixstowe ceases to be an all male station". They remained at the station until the 1953 floods when they were moved to R.A.F. Bawdsey.

There was a brief spell of activity during 1950, when accounting was carried out for R.A.F. Bawdsey, but this was short lived when that station became self-accounting.

At the end of 1950, British Overseas Airways Corporation terminated all flying boat services and several Solents were flown into Felixstowe to await disposal instructions. Sitting on their beaching trolleys, they rested behind the hangars and looked gigantic from the road alongside. As the months passed, dirt collected in the various control surface gaps and slots and grass and weeds sprouted from the once proud machines.

Work loads gradually decreased, no new aircraft appearing for test, and the death of the flying boat was only just around the corner. The few which remained only carried out limited flying and the once busy station was almost on a Care and Maintenance basis. The accommodation at the Station was used during 1952 by other units in the district, and Mr John Langford of Ipswich remembers residing there at this time. Working on the G.C.I. radar equipment at Trimley Heath, he travelled each day to and from his work site by the local Eastern Counties omnibus. His unit's 15 cwt Bedford truck was left in the Felixstowe hangar in order to conserve petrol! Later the radar personnel moved to a hotel, Kersey Towers, in Tomline Road, and they once again travelled by bus to Felixstowe Ferry and then by Mr Charles Brinkley's ferry across the River Deben to Bawdsey. The 15 cwt Bedford truck was parked behind Felixstowe Police Station, in a very cramped position, and the police force usually turned out to see the R.A.F. endeavour to move it out on its infrequent trips.

Early on Saturday evening, 31st January, 1953, the Great Flood occurred when a strong north westerly gale gusted to over 50 m.p.h. and at 20.00 hours a gust of 81 m.p.h. was recorded. At 23.30 hours the authorities warned the Air Station of the impending danger as an exceptional tide mounted. The waters burst through the river walls upstream from the Dock and passed through the Station, along Carr Road, over the tops of the quays and on along Langer Road towards the town. Residents of the Married Quarters were rescued by boats and taken over the river to Parkeston Quay by H.M.S. *Mull of Kintyre* and naval launches. They were then taken to quarters at R.A.F. Wattisham, near Ipswich. The water around the Station rose to around seven feet and when it eventually receded, a vast trail of destruction was revealed. Thirty-nine lives were lost around the Station, one of the casualties being Warrant Officer Raymond Pettitt, who was home on leave, together with his wife Sheila and their two children. A platoon of the Suffolk Regiment with landing craft assisted the Royal Navy in the rescue work, and the Station's A.S.R. launches ferried personnel across to Harwich.

Developed from the famous Walrus, the Supermarine Sea Otter was used for the same Air Sea Rescue duties. The tractor mounted Bristol Mercury radial motor gave this aircraft a better performance than the Walrus's pusher Bristol Pegasus.   *Vickers Limited*

The local paper reported that twenty-four people were rescued from a Martello Tower on the sea front where they had been marooned for thirty-six hours. They owed their lives to Coastguard John Dobson who carried them to safety from their roofs at the height of the flood. He found a drifting rowing boat and using a couple of shovels as oars, ran a one-man shuttle service. The rescued people lived on the pre-fab estate where most of the town's casualties occurred. Soldiers in assault craft and collapsible dinghies searched the area for bodies and for any families still marooned there. A dog which had floated out of a bungalow on a mattress in Levington Road was rescued but its owners were drowned. The R.A.F. base was completely cut-off and a party of airwomen were saved in their night attire. The River Deben's banks were breached in thirty places between Felixstowe Ferry and Woodbridge and the pattern of the river changed considerably. A large number of farm animals were swept away.

In its last days, Felixstowe was used as a diversion landing base for the R.A.F. Stations, Calshot and Pembroke Dock, and later as a practice base for U.S.A.F. amphibious aircraft based at R.A.F. Manston, Kent, and used for Air Sea Rescue operations. Mr and Mrs Grace recall standing by the Felixstowe Control Tower and watching a Grumman twin-engined amphibian of the U.S.A.F. start its take-off run on the far side of Harwich Harbour. With its Pratt and Whitney engines snarling it raced across the harbour at speed but still on the water disappeared behind the East Anglian Flour Mills. Everyone watching braced themselves for the expected crash and black smoke, but miraculously it appeared, just airborne, on the other side of the Mill, much to the relief of the observers.

A tragedy of a different kind occurred off the Air Station when a Royal Navy and a Royal Dutch Navy motor patrol boat collided with the loss of several lives including some boy-sailors from the nearby Royal Navy Training Establishment at Shotley, H.M.S. *Ganges.*

Mr James Arnott Hamilton, who was the Principal Scientific Officer at the M.A.E.E. at the end of its time, eventually became one of the top men in the later Anglo-French Concorde supersonic airliner project.

April 1954 saw the arrival of two "stranger" units, No. 63 and No. 194 Squadrons of the Royal Air Force Regiment who were billeted at the Station together with their vehicles and equipment. Hangars were used for stores and garaging the trucks and the apron outside rang to the crunch of marching feet. The firing butts at the Landguard end of the Station were active again as the marksmen perfected their art, and camouflaged vehicles, draped with netting, trundled in convoys along the roads at all hours of the night and day. Others left the Station laden with fearsome looking men with black faces, whilst the trunks returned empty. The men, in straggling weary groups, returned along the road on foot very much later. At this time, Felixstowe was transferred from No. 11 Group, Fighter Command to No. 27 Group, Technical Training Command.

Mr K. D. Wickenden, Chairman of European Ferries and the Felixstowe Dock and Railway Company recalls his days during 1956-7 as an R.A.F. Regiment officer with No. 194 Anti-Aircraft Squadron, which later became No. 194 Field Squadron:

The 50-ton Titan crane was a landmark for many years and it is seen here with two A.S.R. launches which it lifted from the water as well as the marine aircraft.   *F. V. Powell*

Westland Whirlwind XJ.435. These aircraft of No. 22 Squadron effected many notable rescues whilst stationed in the district, and are remembered with affection by many.

"I owned an old B.S.A. Bantam motor cycle which I had bought for the princely sum of £5. The Station Adjutant owned a Vespa scooter. Along the length of the Officers' Mess there ran a wide corridor and after particularly successful dining-in nights it was not unknown for us to ride our machines up and down the corridor. I also remember a very new U.S.A.F. Colonel who had been posted to nearby Bentwaters never, presumably, having served in the United Kingdom before. He was soon invited to one of our Guest Nights and was firstly astonished by the formality of the dinner proceedings, and even more surprised by the R.A.F.'s habit of playing boisterous, not to mention dangerous, games immediately after the formal session. He was a short, round man with rimless glasses, and to his credit after a few minutes he joined in. Although during the following events he lost his jacket and his shirt was half ripped off his back, I have an everlasting impression of him continuing the 'game' with the cigar still in his mouth!

While I was at Felixstowe our sister squadron, No. 63 Field Squadron, went to Cyprus and, I believe, on to Egypt during the 1956 Suez Crisis. No. 194 Squadron was on stand-by for Suez but did not go. A month or two later we were sent to Northern Ireland to guard the R.A.F. installations because of an outbreak of I.R.A. troubles."

Some time later they were replaced by No. 33 Wing, R.A.F. Regiment, which consisted of Nos. 2, 16 and 48 Field Squadrons of the Regiment and they remained until midsummer, 1962.

As a reflection of the feeling of the people of Felixstowe, on 26th September, 1958, the Urban District Council granted the R.A.F. Station, Felixstowe, the Freedom of Entry. On the previous day at a ceremony in the Officers' Mess, a ceremonial chair made by a local craftsman and bearing the

R.A.F crest and a plaque was presented to the Council by the Air Station. A highlight of the proceedings was the landing of a Whirlwind helicopter on the car park of the Pier Pavilion, watched by a large gathering of townsfolk.

New aircraft of a different kind descended on the station during May, 1956, when the Westland Whirlwind helicopters of No. 22 Squadron, "B" Flight, took up residence, leaving their recent home at nearby Martlesham Heath.

Whilst the Westland Whirlwinds were still based at Martlesham, they used Felixstowe as a "forward base" when carrying out the rescue of the crew of the tug *Rumania* which had run onto the sands off the Essex coast. In terrible weather conditions the crew were all hoisted from the wreck and brought ashore safely.

An impressive display in the hangar of A.S.R. and survival equipment. Among the exhibits are airborne lifeboats, A.S.R. launches, tenders and protective clothing.   *E. Graystone*

Ceremony at the Pier Pavilion, Felixstowe when the Chairman of the Council, Mr Yetton Ward, accompanied by his wife, presents the Freedom of Entry to R.A.F. Felixstowe. 26th September, 1958.

Tragedy struck again on Thursday, 15th May, 1958, when a Whirlwind crashed into the sea off Felixstowe and the winchman, Sergeant D. W. Frampton of Manor Park, London was killed. The pilot, who suffered a fractured leg and spinal injuries, was Flight Lieutenant K. Alderson of Felixstowe, whilst the third member of the crew, the navigator, was unhurt.

The value of No. 22 Squadron's helicopters was illustrated on 12th November, 1956, when two Whirlwinds from the Station picked up two Norwegian seamen from the s.s. *San Miguel*, 35 miles off Orfordness after an engine room fire on the vessel. The two men were flown to Ipswich hospital for urgent treatment, one being critical and the other in "moderate condition". Four years later, on 22nd August, 1960, two yachtsmen, Mr Baker and Mr Fair of Ipswich, were picked up by a Felixstowe-based Whirlwind when their craft capsized off the Air Station. Within ten minutes of the call being received, the two men had been landed at the Air Station where they received hot baths and a tot of rum apiece.

Many notable rescues were effected whilst they were stationed at Felixstowe, and the local residents remember them well as on the more pleasant days they cruised along the sea-front, the holiday makers waving to them and their crews waving back. Another change of command occurred during 1958 when the Station was transferred from No. 26 Group to No. 22 Group.

In a farewell demonstration on 20th May, 1959, High Speed Launch 2688 of No. 1103 Marine Craft Unit and a Whirlwind roared along Felixstowe front, much closer inshore than usual to give the many spectators a close up view of rescue operations. After 46 years association with the town, this was to be the last run. A ceremony at the Station followed when the Unit Commander, Squadron Leader R. N. Dennis presented the Station Commander, Wing Commander J. T. O'Sullivan, with a scroll recording the Unit's record. Among those present was the Chairman of the Council, Mr Stanley Bradbeer, and his Clerk, Mr R. W. Harvey, who went for a short run in one of the launches. Later the launches roared out of the harbour for the last time en route for Bridlington, Yorkshire, their new home.

The Felixstowe Dock and Railway Company hired from the Air Ministry, with a view to eventual purchase, the 50-ton Titan crane on the Crane Pier, and a shipping firm, Messrs James Fisher and Son, commenced a heavy lift service between Felixstowe and Rotterdam.

With its days numbered, the Station was visibly running down, and the last inspection was made on 27th April, 1961, although a reprieve came through at the eleventh hour, postponing the closure until October of that year. On 29th May, the Whirlwind helicopters of the "B" Flight. No. 22 Squadron took off on their last sortie from Felixstowe and departed for their new base at Tangmere, Sussex. This was the last day of flying of any description from Felixstowe.

Early during 1962, No. 33 Wing of the R.A.F. Regiment left Felixstowe and the final closure came on 21st June, 1962. At the closing down ceremony held at the Station, one of the oldest serving R.A.F. officers was present, the late Air Chief Marshal Sir Arthur Longmore, holder of Royal Aero Club Certificate No. 72, the oldest held by any R.A.F. officer. Also as part of the ceremony, the Schneider Trophy was brought to the Station and displayed, a unique exhibit indeed.

Finally the Air Station was handed over by the Air Ministry to the War Office, and units of the 1st East Anglian Regiment took over.

Felixstowe's oldest aircraft relic left the district on 11th October, 1967 when the wooden hull of a 1925 Supermarine Southampton was taken by road on a "Queen Mary" aircraft transporter lorry for refurbishing and exhibition to the R.A.F. Museum, Hendon. The hull, which had been used for many years as a houseboat at Felixstowe Ferry, is believed to be the only wooden flying boat hull still in existence. Taken to the Ferry during the 1930s, the hull was originally bought by a Mr Kemp, who later sold it to a Mr Keith Coombs, who then returned it to the R.A.F. An Ipswich airman, Chief Technician C. D. Allen, stationed at R.A.F. Leconfield, was in charge of the six man crew who prepared the hull for its journey by removing it from the mud and then accompanied it to its new home. After minute examination, the experts stated that although a little rotten in places, the hull was in wonderful condition.

The last building of the Air Station to be used in any connection with aviation is the old Guard Room and adjacent building. These are now the Headquarters of No. 356 Squadron, A.T.C. under the command of Flight

Lieutenant A. Cowan. Formed on 10th February, 1941, under the late Flight Lieutenant Walter Dallow, the Unit has passed 610 lads through its hands between 1941 and 1966. The first Felixstowe cadet was Mr Ronald Vernon Lee, who still lives in Felixstowe and who graduated to fly Hurricane, Spitfires and Typhoons.

Although the hangars still stand proud and erect as they have done for the last six decades, only the ghosts of flying boats now alight on the windswept waters of the Estuary. New monster cranes stand tall on the new quays built far out into the stream, over the old aircraft mooring, slipways and launching ramps. Giant container vessels berth on the "Seafront" and the Control Tower remains, but far from the water which it knew well, now surrounded by gaily coloured containers from the four corners of the earth, and their attendant roaring lorries. This building which controlled the movements of giant aircraft, now houses the Waterguard (Customs) Service, whilst the Officers' Mess, since February 1972, has been the Long Room for Her Majesty's Customs, and it is here that ex-Squadron Leader French, an ex-Felixstowe pilot, has in his office the "No Treating" notice of 1941, found behind the ante-room fireplace. It is also reported by reliable sources that the Officers' Mess Bar is still kept in full operational working order!

Married Quarters and administration buildings remain busy with the chatter of shipping personnel and the constant jangle of hastily answered telephones, all components of the now tremendous centre of activity known as Felixstowe Docks, the second busiest container port in Europe.

Standing white and erect among the hustle and bustle of dockland, the Little Ships Hotel, under the command of Mr "Sandy" Powell, has its Beehive Room, where a wonderful collection of photographs and mementos of the little ships of H.M.S. *Beehive* are displayed, and cherished by the ex-coxswain /landlord, within a stone's throw of his wartime departure point.

If ever the large maritime aircraft should stage a comeback, and the coastal seadrome replace the acres of landborne concrete of the modern airport, Felixstowe will have been at the birth of it and would have laid the keel for this operation.

40

The Deed of Freedom of Entry conferred on Royal Air Force, Felixstowe on 26th September 1958.

Urban District Council
of
FELIXSTOWE
(in the Administrative County of East Suffolk)

Whereas

The Royal Air Force Station, Felixstowe, was established as a Royal Naval Air Service Station on 5th August, 1913, and as a Royal Air Force Station on 1st April, 1918, and is one of the oldest Stations in the Country

And whereas

The Urban District Council of Felixstowe are desirous of perpetuating the close bonds of friendship and mutual respect which have existed through the years between the Local Authority and the People of Felixstowe and the

Royal Air Force Station
Felixstowe

And

Wish to record pride in the achievements and the honourable record of the Station and to give expression to the admiration and high esteem in which the Station and the Personnel serving thereat have always been held And also to show appreciation of the great services which they have rendered to the Community over a long period and especially during the Flood Disaster of 1953

Now therefore the Council do hereby

Confer upon the Commanding Officer and all Ranks of the Royal Air Force for the time being and from time to time stationed at Felixstowe

THE FREEDOM OF ENTRY

And thereby the privilege, honour and distinction henceforth and for ever of marching through the streets of Felixstowe on all ceremonial occasions with bayonets fixed, colours flying, drums beating and bands playing

Dated this Twenty-Sixth day of September, One thousand nine hundred and fifty-eight

In witness whereof

The Common Seal of the Council has been hereunto affixed in the presence of :—

Stanley Bodbun.
CHAIRMAN OF THE COUNCIL

J. H. Bodru
VICE-CHAIRMAN OF THE COUNCIL

R. Sturway
CLERK OF THE COUNCIL

CHAPTER TWO

War Flight

FELIXSTOWE in its unique position on the eastern shores of Harwich was due to play a major part in the battle against the German Navy's U-Boats* during the First World War.

The flying boat which was beginning to come into service with the Royal Naval Air Service was deemed the tool to carry the war to the enemy over the North Sea. Twin float seaplanes which had been in service with several R.N.A.S. units around the coast of the British Isles were not really able to carry the load of bombs and fuel over the required patrol range, and were also of less substantial construction than the flying boat with its more seaworthy hull. Seaplanes had been taken to sea by vessels of the Royal Navy, lowered onto the water surface for take-off and retrieved again after their flights, but even these were regarded with reservation by the Senior Service.

The development of the British flying boat had been mainly in the hands of one man, John Porte, who, at Felixstowe, designed and built the F. series of aircraft, the first of each type being built and flown from the Air Station. In the main, his aircraft were large biplanes, mostly accommodating a crew of four in the hull, and with the usual twin engines mounted between the mainplanes. Before going further in the story it is worthy of note that none of the Porte designed boats were lost through unseaworthiness, nor were any lives lost either.

Porte's main difficulty lay in designing an efficient hull form with a seaworthy planing form providing the minimum adhesion to the water at take off and capable of alighting in most sea conditions. He was further hampered by the lack of engines of sufficient power for his machines which were reliable enough to carry the aircraft on its errands in all weathers out over the ever-changing North Sea.

The German Navy was stepping up its U-Boat campaign during the summer of 1917, and the big ship-building yards at Bremen, Vagesack, Kiel, Weser, Danzig and Hamburg were working ceaselessly round the clock turning out the long lean sea wolves. Naval Intelligence had an idea of the odds against them when, on 27th April, 1916, the UC-5, a mine-laying U-boat, had run aground on the Shipwash Sands, 18 miles off Felixstowe. It had been salvaged and towed into Harwich Harbour for detailed examination by experts of the Royal Navy.

*Unterseeboaten. Submarines developed by the German Navy during the First World War. Whilst U-Boat indicated a German submarine the word was also used to indicate all enemy submarines of countries hostile to the Allies in the Second World War.

When setting out on their patrols from the north German ports, the U-Boats hugged the Continental coast as far as the Hook of Holland, and then turned out into the North Sea to make their way down the middle of the English Channel. As the distance between the Hook of Holland and Felixstowe is approximately 110 miles, it was thus only one hour's flying time from the Air Station to the enemy's passage area. This stretch of Continental coastline from the Hook of Holland ran northwards to Scheveningen, passing the off-shore islands of Texel, Vlieland, Terschelling and Ameland. Further along and just round the corner was the scene of the action, the Bight of Heligoland, home of the German seaplanes and Zeppelins, operating from their bases on Borkum, Norderney and sheds at Wittmundshaven, Ahlhorn and Hordholz. Southwards of the Dutch ports lay the German-occupied Belgium ports of Zeebrugge and Ostend with their seaplane and naval establishments. The reader will now have gathered that the opposition facing Felixstowe was quite formidable, and apart from one or two stations on the south coast, and Great Yarmouth to the north, it stood alone to face the enemy.

Harwich Harbour was the base for the Light Cruiser Force and a flotilla of destroyers, all under the command of Rear-Admiral Tyrwhitt. The destroyers were known among the Force as "Tyrwhitt's Hot Stuff Mob" and indeed their score of successes was impressive.

Squadron Leader T. B. Hallam, a Canadian from Toronto, who had seen action in the Dardanelles during March, 1915, became the flying boat commander during March, 1917, with Lieutenant Partridge, R.N.V.R., as his lieutenant.

Members of the establishment at this period recall the watch-dog which virtually ruled the Guard-Room, and which delighted in the name of Joe. A bitch in all respects, she hated with untold venom all civilians, but it is rumoured that she supplied her keepers with additional pocket money when her puppies were sold off at regular intervals.

Although an R.N.A.S. establishment, the Air Station was run on strict Royal Navy lines with a bell striking the passing watches, a liberty boat, in the shape of a requisitioned omnibus, for shore runs and in general, all ship-shape and Bristol fashion. Not least among the Station facilities was the Quarter Deck with its raked gravel square and white mast where the White Ensign fluttered during the hours of daylight. On the waterfront stood the three large camouflaged sheds or hangars for the aircraft, and these were of massive proportions, being some 300 feet long by 200 feet wide, and in front of each a slipway down into the water. In between each of these a jetty ran out and these were utilized as mooring places for the various small marine craft used by the Station.

Short Type D seaplane fitted with a 225 h.p. Sunbeam engine, and it was with this type of aircraft that the R.N.A.S. went to war during 1914. *Short Brothers*

During this period the Station's first magazine, *Wings*, was published as and when the Editor had the time and the paper, and these are now valued by those fortunate enough to possess copies of them.

Out on the heaving grey North Sea, 55 miles from Felixstowe and also 55 miles from the Hook of Holland, swinging to wind and tide, rode the Dutch maintained light vessel, North Hinder. Streaked with rust, her once all-red hull carried the large white letters identifying her role, and the solitary steel mast carried the lantern which gave warning of the nearby shoals to shipping of all nations. This vessel may seem a long way from the history of Felixstowe, but in actual fact it played a tremendous part in the work of the Air Station, as will be seen later.

In addition to the previously mentioned U-Boats, the Imperial German Navy sent its Zeppelins on daylight patrols over the North Sea from their north German bases. Ranging across the Bight of Heligoland they were able to keep an eye on any intruding movements of the Royal Navy and guide, by means of wireless messages, fighter seaplanes to the Felixstowe flying boats patrolling off the Dutch coast.

Up to the beginning of 1917, the flying boats had not engaged to any great extent in operations against the U-Boats which were mainly of the U-B, U-C and U types. Varying in size from 225 feet in length down to a mere 90 feet they were forced by necessity to travel considerable distances on the surface, their underwater endurance being only some 75 miles, and two hours at their top speed of 8 knots drained their batteries flat. Thus at every opportunity a U-Boat commander ran on the surface, where he was then at peril from aerial and surface craft. An additional hazard encountered was that when approaching the southern end of the North Sea, returning submarines signalled by wireless their homing position, and these signals could be picked up and pin-pointed by wireless stations at Hunstanton, Norfolk, Lowestoft, Suffolk, and Birchington in Kent.

In order to capitalize on these wireless plots, an ingenious plan was devised, code-named the "Spider's Web". Using the North Hinder light vessel as the base point, an octagonal figure was drawn with eight arms radiating out for a distance of 30 miles from the base. A set of circumvential lines then joined the radial arms at 10, 20 and 30 miles making eight sections, each sector divided into three sections. As the patrolling aircraft flew up and down each sector line, the area was surveyed twice on any patrol, and two sectors, or a quarter of the "Web", could be surveyed in under five hours. A flying boat would take-off at Felixstowe, make for the North Hinder, proceed down one of the radial arms by previous instruction, and then along the patrol lines of the sector. The time that could be used for patrol depended on the wind conditions, a south-easterly making it more difficult to reach the base point and thus cutting down the sector patrol time available.

The "Man of the Cloth" attached to the Air Station, the Reverend W. G. Litchfield, was also a mathematician and it was he who worked out a simple table which enabled a pilot, who knowing the wind force and direction, to compute compass corrections and allowances for drift.

The plan was thus inaugurated with Squadron Commander Hallam as the War Flight Commander, although he had not flown either of the H.12 flying boats (No. 8663 and No. 8661) which were to be used, whilst Flight Sub-Lieutenant Hobbs had flown the aircraft, but had no operational experience.

Operations were commenced on 13th April, 1917, when No. 8661, four and a half tons of flying boat, slid into the water with her crew of four. Carrying 4-100lb bombs and sufficient fuel for six and a half hours, she could cruise at 60 knots, or if necessary, burn up more fuel in order to roar along at 80 knots. The captain was Flight Sub-Lieutenant Hobbs, with Squadron Commander Hallam as second pilot, the wireless operator and engineer being ratings. Leaving her base, No. 8661 made for the North Hinder, with the other light vessels spaced around the "Web", Shipwash to the west, the Haaks to the south-west and the Schouen Bank Buoy to the south-east. When sufficient height had been attained, the wireless operator wound down his copper aerial wire, and established communication with base. Low level communication with surface vessels was still carried out with an Aldis signalling lamp.

Flying the patrol pattern to plan, No. 8661, its duty completed, at the appointed time set course for home and finally, with only 18 miles to go, passed the Shipwash which was to be a welcome sight for many a crew over the coming months.

It was No. 8661, again flown by Flight Sub-Lieutenant Hobbs who on the 16th April, sighted the first U-Boat in the "Web". Surprising the enemy, Hobbs made a low pass, but the bombs failed to leave the aircraft, so the pilot brought the aircraft round in a steep bank for another run at the now submerging enemy. At the vital time, when the bombs should have been thudding down on the hull of the U-boat, they were still attached to their bomb-racks, because the bomb-aimer had pulled the wrong wires. It must have been a very relieved U-Boat commander who slid beneath the waves to fight another day.

Another U-Boat was not so fortunate a week later when Flight Sub-Lieutenant Aplin caught the enemy on the surface and delivered 4-100lb bombs onto it, hopefully sending it on its way to the bottom of the North Sea.

Further success came on the 23rd April when Squadron Commander Hallam in the hard-worked No. 8661 found his first enemy craft. Having carried out a routine patrol towards the Dutch coast, the flying boat's crew spotted a U-Boat on the surface, obviously charging up its batteries as it ran on one diesel motor. The U-Boat's lookout however, was not caught napping and before No. 8661 could get into a bombing position, the submarine disappeared beneath the surface in a welter of foaming water, and all the aircraft's crew could do was watch. Continuing the patrol No. 8661 flew up along the hostile shore and eventually approached the area again where they had seen the enemy. To their amazement, there it was again with some of the crew taking the air on the after deck. Approaching out of the sun, Hallam brought No. 8661 roaring down and the bomb-aimer in the front cockpit released the 4 100 lb bombs at the correct time. Too late the enemy sprang to their anti-aircraft gun and attempted to fire at their attacker, but it was a lost cause as the bombs crashed down across the steel hull which then disappeared in a mass of heaving water. When it cleared, the U-Boat, one of the U-B class, was seen to heel-over, with the men who been on deck, washed or blown into the sea.

No. 8661 was in action again on 30th April when she ran into four German destroyers north of the North Hinder light vessel. These resented her presence and they filled the air with anti-aircraft fire, but the flying boat was able to avoid the barrage and rumbled home to Felixstowe to report the whereabouts of the destroyers, the wireless equipment having gone unserviceable.

On the same day Hallam and Hobbs sighted a U-Boat 20 miles south-east of the North Hinder and bombed it. Although they observed their bombs bursting all around it, they did not claim her as sunk.

This was the day when the War Flight lost their first flying boat, No. 8659, crewed by Aplin and Rees with two crew ratings. Having set out for the "Web" they were in the middle of their patrol when No. 8659 suffered engine failure in one power unit and the remaining one began to burn up more than its fair share of fuel. Drifting to the north, the stricken aircraft finally put down in a 30 knot wind on a very choppy sea near a group of trawlers off the Haisboro' Bank. The seas played havoc with the frail machine and she soon began to break up as one of the trawlers attempted to tow her towards home. With the aircrew aboard the trawler, No. 8659 succumbed to the waves, lost on her first patrol to the "Web".

May saw the action stepping-up for the War Flight as the log-book recorded seven U-Boats sighted, five bombed and the first anti-Zeppelin patrol flown. Also, during this month, a protective patrol was mounted for a convoy routed from Harwich to the Hook of Holland. It was commonly alleged that the convoy was bringing back Dutch beef to the beleagured British Isles and so it became known as the "Beef Trip". The convoy comprised sixteen merchantment, escorted by the Harwich Force. Flying boats from the Air Station flew out in relays to cover the convoy on its eleven hour passage, which passed without event.

The peculiarities of operations from Felixstowe are well illustrated by an episode which occurred on 5th May. Two aircraft, captained by Hallam and Martin, were on patrol and sighted a U-Boat which was bombed by Martin,

Not all homecomings were of the smooth kind, as portrayed by the sorry condition of this Felixstowe flying boat which suffered considerable damage when it dived into the water whilst alighting. The crew escaped with shock and a soaking.

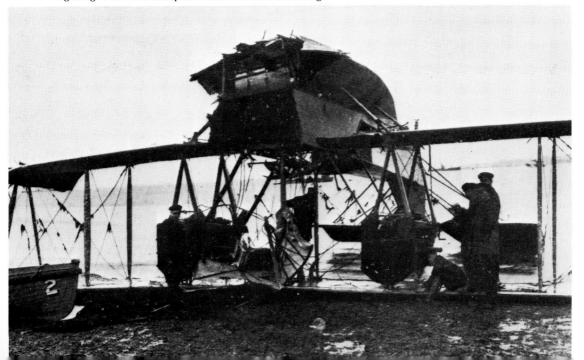

who, when pulling up from his bombing run, went into a steep bank, followed by a dive, and only just managed to pull out of it before making a a fast landing on the surface. Hallam then alighted also and enquired what was wrong, receiving the reply that a metal casting had fractured and it was impossible to mend it. To ensure safety from surfaced U-Boats, the two H.12 flying boats taxied into a known mine-field where they would be safer, and then anchored. Martin's machine was no longer airworthy, but its engines could be run, so Hallam advised Martin to taxi down-wind, which was now blowing at 30 knots, whilst he took-off and made for home. Martin progressed down-wind, and after making several stops to cool the motors was eventually taken in tow by a patrol boat, arriving back at base several hours after his companion.

Another aircraft suffered engine failure whilst off the Dutch coast and having managed to stay airborne for one and a half hours on the remaining engine, was forced to alight some distance off the North Hinder light vessel. Luckily a destroyer was at hand and she towed the flying boat the rest of the way across the North Sea.

An outstanding rescue was effected on 29th May, 1917, and this is fully described in the next chapter.

The Zeppelins which ventured out from their bases were a thorn in the flesh of the British forces and so steps were taken to put a stop to their spying activities. On 14th June, Flight Sub-Lieutenants B. D. Hobbs and R. F. L. Dickey, and Air Mechanics Davis and Goody, took off in H.12, No. 8677, which had been fitted with extra petrol tanks, and set course for the Dutch islands. When approaching their objective, mist settled in, but pressing on, Hobbs eventually made a land-fall off Vlieland. Suddenly, only some five miles away, hovering over the sea and glistening in the early morning sun rode a giant Zeppelin, L.43. Flying boat and airship saw each other at the same time and both went into immediate action. Thrusting the throttles hard forward, Hobbs roared up after the monster gasbag, whilst Dickey, who was the gunner, managed to get a short burst of machine-gun fire at it from one of the aircraft's guns. This was a fortunate burst as when the aircraft passed by the Zeppelin, its crew observed that it was beginning to burn, and, in a matter of seconds, it broke in half and fell, a roaring inferno to the sea below, leaving an immense pillar of oily black smoke. The L.43 was almost consumed by the flames before it reached the surface, taking her Commander, Krausbaar and his crew to their doom. No. 8677 flew home in gay mood, and when she arrived over the Air Station, the crew fired off the remainder of their Very signal cartridges to announce the good news.

Mr Milward of Heacham recalls this day; "We had a 'buzz' and got off an H.12 in a hurry. After a while she came back, and as I was on stand-by watch, I checked up on her ammunition. The only shortage was a few rounds

The burnt out wreckage of the LZ.48 lying in a field at Theberton, near Leiston, Suffolk on 17th June, 1917 after encountering aircraft of the R.F.C. and the R.N.A.S. The initial pursuit started over Harwich Harbour and proceeded up the coast towards Orfordness.

J. S. Waddell

from the main hatch gun. We always mounted in each gun tray a tracer followed by a Brock and a Pomeroy — two explosive types used for anti-Zeppelin work. They did their job as the Zeppelin had gone down in flames, but the H.12 only had one bullet hole in her lower port wing. The engineer on board 'cussed uphill and down dale' — he never meant to risk his life in a plane! Some weeks later all four men in the crew were decorated."

Success came again on the 23rd July, when five flying boats from Felixstowe, one of them being a new experimental type, the F.2C crewed by Commander John Porte, the designer, and an experimental test pilot named Cooper, set course for the "Web". On that day, the formation was carrying a new weapon, a heavy 235 lb bomb under each wing, and that was most unfortunate for Commander Mildenstein of the U-Boat, UC-1. Having left Zeebrugge the previous day, the 111 foot long mine-laying submarine had placed her deadly cargo of twelve mines in the channel off Harwich and was now on her way home past the North Hinder. Too late he tried to dive, as two of the new bombs hurtled down on him from one of the aircraft, followed by those from the F.2C. All that remained of UC-1 was a large patch of oil, a mass of bursting bubbles and a large chunk of wreckage several fathoms down on the bed of the North Sea.

A few days later another flying boat crewed by Mackenzie and Dickey surprised another Zeppelin off the Dutch islands. Both spotted each other at the same time and both raced to gain height, but the airship, having the edge on the heavily laden aircraft, outstripped it in the climb to safety. The H.12 was exhausted at eleven thousand feet, whilst the Zeppelin was two and a half thousand higher when the chase was reluctantly abandoned.

49

One aspect of the flying boat's capabilities was that, as in the case of our now homeward bound aircraft, it could alight on the water if things went wrong. Mackenzie ran into petrol pump trouble, a common fault on these machines, and after repairs which took half an hour, took off again and arrived home none the worse for the adventure.

The first day of July was another good day as two H.12s flown by Mackenzie and Ball and Young and Barker met up with a surfaced U-Boat near the North Hinder. A large submarine of the ocean type, she was surprised by the two aircraft and the first 230 lb bomb crashed down on her stern, ripping it off. Two more bombs put paid to U.20, which went out of control, reared up, and then dived straight down with Commander Glimpf and his crew.

It was also the last day for another ocean type U-Boat, U.66, under the command of Commander Muhle on the 3rd September when she was surprised by two machines flown by Hallam and Dickey and Cuckney and Clayton. Running on the surface with some of her crew on deck, the first indication of danger was the whistle of descending bombs which hit on the after deck. Heeling over under the impact of further bombs, it is doubtful if she ever made her home port. Ten days later another U-Boat, lying in wait for prey, was herself surprised by two Felixstowe machines and bombed, large masses of oil coming to the surface, and the vessel claimed as a victory. Two days later and another large U-Boat received a load of bombs, but the results were not confirmed.

Luck continued, when on the 28th September, Hobbs and Dickey were patrolling in the "Web" in No. 8676 and they sighted a large U-Boat, UC 70, running in the surface. The two adversaries saw each other at about the same time, the enemy putting up a heavy barrage of anti-aircraft fire, but the aircraft dropped its bombs which hit the vessel on the stern. Rolling on the

Felixstowe type flying boats resting in their pontoon lighters prior to setting out on an operation off the Dutch coast. These lighters were semi-submerged to allow the aircraft to float in from the stern and then the tanks were blown to raise the aircraft to the position shown.

surface for a few minutes, she then put her stern skywards and slid beneath the waves, leaving a mass of oil and wreckage on the surface. Two other U-Boats and three destroyers which had been accompanying the ill-fated UC.6 made off at high speed, but not before a signal had been made to Felixstowe reporting their presence. When this was received several other aircraft hurried out to the scene, but thickening fog hid the escaping enemy from the searching aircraft.

A Porte Baby aircraft left Felixstowe on 1st October, 1917 under the command of Flight Commander E. Sholto Douglas for a "Web" patrol, but was set upon by three German fighter seaplanes. Two of the enemy aircraft were hit and disabled, as well as a crew member of the Baby, and it was put down on the surface. Repairs were effected to the aircraft, the crew member given first aid, and then the motors were restarted and the slow taxi westwards towards Felixstowe began. After some hours landfall was made on the Suffolk coast, and the boat was then towed back to its base.

Another casualty was an elderly H.12 which had set out with a crew of five for a North Sea patrol and off the Suffolk coast encountered five enemy seaplanes from Zeebrugge. It was promptly shot down and turned turtle after hitting the water, the crew which included the Commanding Officer, Lieutenant Colonel Robertson and Major Galpin, clung to the upturned hull until they were rescued by another Felixstowe machine. The German aircraft which had shot them down landed alongside and enquired if they needed assistance. Those were the days of chivalry.

The North Sea on a dirty autumn day was no place for a fragile flying boat, and the 23rd October 1917, was no exception, when two Felixstowe boats were on their usual patrol. After becoming parted, the first aircraft searched for its companion which was crewed by Perham and Gooch, but without success, and as fuel was running low, made tracks for home, but not before releasing two carrier pigeons carrying messages asking for help. At this time a large carrier pigeon loft was located in the grounds of a large Felixstowe cliff top hotel. Each flying boat operating on patrol work took with it a basket of these homing carrier pigeons and they were released, if necessary, at intervals in order to ensure that at least one bird would manage to get home with its message.

After the first aircraft had returned home, two more aircraft, crewed by Hodgson and Wilson, and Gordon and Fauz, took-off into the worsening weather to search for their lost companions. Some time later, but unbeknown to the searching boats, a pigeon returned to its loft with a message from the missing aircraft stating that it had suffered a broken crank-shaft on one engine and had alighted safely a few miles from the North Hinder.

In the now terrible weather conditions, the two searching flying boats had eventually made the North Hinder, but they had not been able to sight

A Felixstowe flying boat is towed behind a warship at speed across the North Sea. It is worth noting the punishment these machines took before they even became airborne.

Perham's aircraft. The crew of four in the downed machine were now suffering real hardship, the wind was gusting to forty knots and big seas were running, and the aircraft, with its large wingspan acting as a lever, rolled violently. Drifting downwind, away from home, the boat eventually reached the Schouen Bank Buoy off the Dutch coast, and in the shallower water the seas were even steeper, and all the crew were forced to bale at a frantic pace in order to keep the aircraft's hull buoyant. During the next morning, after the terrible ordeal of the previous night, they were sighted by a Dutch vessel, which approached the stricken machine.

When the vessel sent over a boat, three of the crew members went aboard, but the captain, Perham, took steps to sink his craft so that it would not fall into unauthorised hands. This he successfully carried out, and then went aboard the Dutch vessel to be interned with the rest of his crew, for the duration.

Serving as a coxswain in the Motor Boat Section at Felixstowe during 1917 was Mr Frank Woolley, now living in Chester, Nova Scotia, and remembered by many in latter days as Frank Woolley, the Kent and England cricketer. Too old for service in the Second World War he joined the Fire Watching Patrol at Dover and helped in the evacuation of Dunkirk.

During eight and a half months in 1917 the War Flight had enjoyed moderate success having carried out 554 offensive patrols and flown over

77,500 miles, mostly over the North Sea. They had bombed 25 U-Boats, sighted 45 more and had definitely destroyed one Zeppelin, the L.43.

Two events marked the New Year of 1918, the first being the arrival of the first American pilots to the War Flight, and the second an incident with a new type of flying boat. When taking off in a strong wind and choppy sea, Gordon, flying an experimental machine, lost engine power and plunged down into the rough water, where the flying boat quickly sank, but the crew were all rescued.

At this time, the Felixstowe aircraft were encountering in increasing numbers a new menace in the shape of fast, single-engined monoplane seaplanes operating from Zeebrugge and the North German ports. Fierce battles now became the order of the day between the flying boats and the seaplanes. At first the enemy appeared to have the upper hand and several aircraft were lost, with well-loved crews such as that of Young's, off Borkum, all sadly missed.

Ensign Potter, United States Navy, was lost with Captain Major in H.12, No. 8677, when it was shot down in flames on 25th April. In order to avenge the loss of this aircraft and crew, a joint force ventured forth from Felixstowe and Great Yarmouth, eight flying boats from the former and landplanes from the latter. They returned without seeing the enemy, although H.12, No. 8683 flown by Captain MacLauren and Captain Dickey, gave the Zeebrugge Mole a "good going over". Another similar force went out searching the same area the following day, but without any success.

Earlier on, the veteran aircraft, No. 8661, was out on patrol when she was intercepted by five enemy seaplanes which attacked it from all quarters. Returning their fire, one of the H.12's gunners managed to hit an enemy seaplane's engine which caused it to side-slip into the water, whilst its companions broke off the engagement and made for home. Ten days later on the 15th February, 1918, it was a sad Air Station when Purdy and Sturtevant and their crew were shot down in flames by enemy seaplanes 25 miles the other side of the former position of the North Hinder, which had been taken "off station" by the Dutch maritime authorities. The accompanying aircraft, although attacked by five seaplanes, managed to get down near the surface and hold the enemy at arm's length until it was able to turn into a fog bank and make good its escape.

Better weather came with March, and on the 12th, three boats were patrolling off the Dutch islands when five enemy seaplanes roared onto the scene. The boats turned for home, chased by the enemy as far as the Outer Gabbard Buoy where they broke off the fight. On arrival back at Felixstowe they reported the action, and three more aircraft hurried out to the area and found the five enemy aircraft resting on the surface. Spotting the flying boats, the enemy took-off to do battle, but the boats by dint of their heavier armament were able to bag three of them, the remaining two making off for home at high speed. One of the boats involved in the second action was, once again, the veteran No. 8661.

The Zeppelins still carried out their spying patrols over the Heligoland Bight, and plans were formed to close their eyes. The range was too great for the flying boats, so a joint operation with the Royal Navy was planned. Submersible lighters were constructed with specially designed hull prows so as not to create too large a bow wave when being towed at speed. Hollow tanks along the sides allowed the lighters to be flooded and the aircraft floated in. When they were secured, the tanks were blown by compressed air stored in bottles, and the aircraft lifted clear of the water ready for its towed journey.

The first foray was mounted on 2nd March, 1918, when three flying boats crewed by Major and Potter, (both later lost), Webster and Fallon, and Clayton and Barker, each with two ratings as crew, were readied and put in position on their lighters. The engines were slowly run-up to warm the oil and then electric heaters were fitted to them, and cover-muffs to keep the power units ready for starting.

Taking up the tow, three destroyers gradually worked-up to eighteen knots and set course for Texel and the scene of action. As dawn broke near the Haaks light vessel, the lighters floated off their charges, and with roaring engines the aircraft rose into the early morning sky. Flying into the Heligoland Bight, they photographed enemy shipping, but were intercepted by two German seaplanes, one of which was shot down in flames by Major's crew, and the other turned for home, chased by Clayton. Major's aircraft suffered machine gun fire damage, and flew for an hour with only one motor

Over sixty years later, a derelict pontoon lighter lies on the mud at Ipswich, after its varied career at Felixstowe and Ipswich. *Courtesy of The East Anglian Daily Times*

functioning, but after stalwart work in mid-air by the engineer, the captain was able to start up the damaged motor and all three boats arrived safely back at Felixstowe.

On 21st March, a second expedition was mounted to the same area, three aircraft on three lighters, the crews being Webster and Rees, Galpin and Rhys-Davis, and Barker and Galvayne. Encountering several enemy seaplanes during the course of their reconnaissance, none of them gave serious battle and the boats turned onto their homeward leg. Webster had trouble with his engines and was forced to alight several times on the way home to make temporary repairs, all the aircraft eventually returning to base.

The famous Saint George's Day raid on Zeebrugge Mole was made on 22nd/23rd April, 1918 and this had sorely stung the enemy, stirring up a real hornet's nest, resulting in a call for revenge from the opposition camp. Two days later Oberleutnant Christiansen leading a formation of seven fighter seaplanes ranged over the Felixstowe boat's haunts and fell upon H.12, N.8677, flown by Captain Major and Ensign Potter, U.S.N. No match for the opposition, the H.12 was set on fire and in attempting to alight, crashed into the sea on fire and all the crew were lost. The following day it was the turn of the new Royal Air Force, but the enemy were not to be drawn out and no battles ensued.

Early in June it was decided to have a go at the Zeppelins which now appeared to be cruising a lot further to the west over the North Sea. Two Great Yarmouth boats joined up with three from Felixstowe on the 4th June, and set out across the sea to a position near the Haaks light vessel. The three Felixstowe boats were No. 8689, Lieutenants Duff-Fyffe and Pattison and Ensign Eaton, U.S.A., No. 4533, Captain Dickey, Captain Paull, Lieutenant Hodgson and N.4302, Captain Barker, Lieutenant Galvayne and Ensign Keep, U.S.N., each with a crew of two non-commissioned crew members.

When off the Dutch islands, N.4533 was forced to alight with a petrol pipe fracture, and owing to the rough seas could not get off again. A short time after this, five German seaplanes turned up but did not join in the battle, although one of them raced back to base to bring up reinforcements. In the meantime the other four boats circled N.4533, and kept the enemy at bay, until the new force of about 15 German seaplanes appeared and attempted to sink the downed flying boat. They were taken on by the three flying boats, as No. 8689 had pursued the original attackers and running out of fuel had been forced down off the Dutch coast and interned.

In the ensuing conflict and as a result of it the enemy lost six seaplanes and the Felixstowe force two of its flying boats, both interned. Lieutenant Galvayne was shot through the head and was the only casualty when the three remaining boats arrived back at Great Yarmouth late in the evening from the greatest aerial battle of the First World War over the North Sea.

A Sopwith Camel 2F1 scout, as used on lighters from Felixstowe, hangs on display from the roof of the old Spa Pavilion, Felixstowe.   *Stuart Culley*

It was decided to have another show on 11th August, 1918, but this time it was to be in greater numbers and with the full backing of the Royal Navy. The object was two-fold — to carry out an armed reconnaissance and to attack any Zeppelins that were lurking in the area.

For the first phase, six coastal motor boats were to be carried to the scene by light cruisers of the Harwich Force, and when launched, would proceed to make themselves a nuisance in the Heligoland Bight. With their forty knots and torpedoes, and the element of surprise, they would indeed be a headache for the Imperial German Navy. Another surprise which had been worked out for this operation had called for previous preparation before it could be implemented.

One of the flying boat lighters had been fitted with a thirty foot long sloping deck and to this was secured, by quick-release clamps, a Sopwith Camel single-seat landplane scout, fitted with two machine-guns as armament. The scheme was for the lighter to be towed to take-off position, headed into wind and towed at speed, the securing latches released, and the Camel would lift off after an extremely short take-off run, aided by the towing head wind.

The first experimental attempt was carried out off Orfordness on the 30th May, 1918, when the lighter was towed by H.M.S. *Truculent* and the Camel was flown by the veteran, Lieutenant Colonel Samson D.S.O., the Officer Commanding No. 4 Group, R.A.F. Although towed at 30 knots this experiment was a failure as the Camel did not attain enough flying speed and stalled off the end of the lighter to fall into the destroyer's wake and be run down by the lighter. Fortunately both the pilot and plane were salvaged.

56

Captain Fane of Feering was also involved with these experiments and after the first unsuccessful attempt made the recommendations that if the skids on the aircraft's undercarriage were to be replaced with the more orthodox wheels it would enable the Camel to make a cleaner getaway.

During these experiments the Camel was supported in flying position on trestles with the tailplane supported in a long rail to which it was secured by a quick release fitting. The erratic movements of the lighter in the towing vessel's wake gave the somewhat frail aircraft a terrific pounding, and on one occasion, the aircraft which Captain Fane was to fly was found to have broken fuselage main structural members as a result of this treatment. If the aircraft had been launched it would most certainly have suffered complete structural failure whilst banking sharply to clear the towing vessel.

A second attempt was made with the same pilot but a different aircraft, this one being fitted with wheels instead of skids as the first one had been. The lighter's deck was also given more elevation to assist forward speed, and this time the Camel soared into the air and landed safely near Felixstowe.

This was to be the other surprise, for whilst the Zeppelin was climbing away from the heavily laden flying boats attempting to get up to it, it was hoped that the unseen Camel would be able to deal it a deadly blow.

All was assembled for the sortie, cruisers, destroyers, lighters, flying boats and the Camel which was to be flown by Sub-Lieutenant Stuart Culley, a Canadian with a great deal of experience.

The naval stages of the scheme went according to plan, the coastal motor boats launched, and the flying boats from Great Yarmouth rendezvoused with them. Owing to a long swell, the Felixstowe machines, N.4302, N.4533 and No. 8689, could not become airborne and had to return to their lighters, but joy was unleashed, when, glistening in the early morning sunlight, a giant Zeppelin appeared, flying some 30 miles away, at about 10,000 feet, and apparently watching the Coastal Motor Boats (C.M.Bs).

Carrying a Sopwith Camel on an improvised lighter, towed behind a warship, and flown off when a Zeppelin was sighted, far out in the North Sea. The engines had to be started, lashings removed, and when airborne it had to bank sharply in order to avoid the towing vessel.

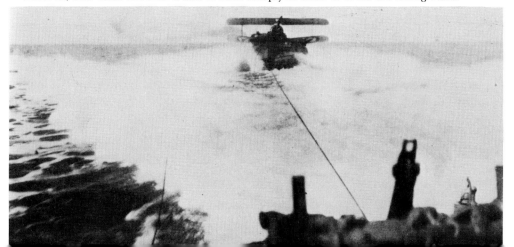

The destroyer *Redoubt* towing the Camel lighter opened up to 30 knots, the Camel's Bentley rotary motor started, and Culley in N.6812 zoomed off the sloping deck and settled down for the long climb upwards. The Zeppelin, L.53, under the command of Zeppelin Commander Proells, had wirelessed back to Borkum the news of the Naval force and fifteen German seaplanes appeared on the scene. Attempting to bomb the warships, they met with no success at all, and lost one of their number. Having witnessed its destruction they departed, but fate overtook the C.M.Bs on their way back as the seaplanes again bombed them, three being quickly sunk and their crews picked up by the surviving craft. Not being able to return to their parent ships, they struggled to the Dutch coast where they gave themselves up to the authorities and were interned.

Meanwhile, off-stage as it were, Culley was still gaining height and creeping up unseen on the L.53, now at 18,000 feet. Unaware of the Camel, the airship turned towards the North Sea, and one hour after he had taken off, Culley fired both his guns at the monster 640 feet long airship. Passing alongside, Culley thought that his bullets had not done much damage, but then with a terrible roar the Zeppelin gushed vivid flame as two million cubic feet of hydrogen gas ignited. Breaking in half and dropping down the sky, it left only a train of black smoke as evidence of its former existence. Losing altitude, Culley glided down and at first could only see a Dutch fishing boat which he decided to alight alongside, but then at the last moment saw the parent fleet and ditched near them. He was promptly picked up, the Camel retrieved, and the force set course for home.

The Camel involved can still be seen in the Imperial War Museum, London, where it is displayed to this day, a reminder of tenacity and courage, over sixty years ago.

A recorded reminder of the operation is the signal made by Admiral Tyrwhitt on the homeward journey. Calling for his Flag-Officer, he ordered him to make the signal, "Flag-General. Your attention is called to Hymn No. 224, Verse 7." This read,

> "O happy band of pilgrims,
> Look upward to the skies,
> Where such a light affliction,
> Shall win so great a prize."

So ended the War Flight, with its daily excursions out across the face of the grey North Sea, the crews of the flying boats with names like North Hinder, Maas, Terschelling, Texel and Shipwash forever implanted in their minds, and the roar of Rolls-Royce Eagle engines still in their ears.

CHAPTER THREE

An Airman Remembers

AN EX-AIRCREW member of the First World War who flew from Felixstowe, Mr Millichamp of Ludlow, recalls his days at the Air Station in a vivid manner:

"We went on patrol at 7.30 a.m. on Tuesday, 24th April, 1917 and flew east until 8.20 a.m., when one engine failed and we force-landed on the sea with such a hefty bump that I hit my head on the top of the hull. So far as I can remember we were only drifting about half an hour before the destroyer F.59 turned up and took three of us aboard her, leaving Lieutenant Galpin, the pilot, on board our H.12 flying boat, which was taken in tow.

I was just settled down in the Petty Officers' Mess, about to start on a meal of, I think, ham and eggs, when there came a call for me and I was told to join Galpin back in the flying boat. My transfer was effected at full, and dangerous, speed because a destroyer does not like hanging about hove-to at sea in wartime, and I found the reason for my recall. The speed at which the plane was being towed had forced the sea up the copper tubing through which the aerial wire is let down through the bottom of the hull and the cap had broken away. Consequently when we were pulled forward the sea just fountained in through the pipe of about 2 inches diameter.

My job was to stop it, if possible, and for a time I managed by alternately using each hand pressed tightly on top, but as I had to lie in a cramped position on the decking and exert a lot of pressure it was too exhausting to keep up for long. I then had a brainwave. I took off my shoes and stood on the top of the tube after finding that it didn't work so well with my shoes on.

It was still uncomfortable and cramping, but I was able keep it up until we arrived back at Felixstowe Air Station about 11.20 a.m.

At 8 a.m. on 10th May, 1917, we went on a routine submarine patrol in flying boat No. 8667 from Felixstowe over the North Sea. During the flight we were mystified to see in the sea a funnel protruding and from it smoke belching as though a submerged vessel was proceeding full steam ahead.

After a short conference we decided it must be a new steam driven submarine or submersible vessel about which we had heard rumours. Although to the best our knowledge the Royal Navy had no such vessel I challenged it with Very lights of the colour of the day, but there was no response, so we decided to bomb it.

A flotilla of destroyers enters Harwich Harbour, watched over by the Sopwith Bat Boat No. 1, Serial No. 38, during 1913. *Richard Crier*

The second pilot did the bombing, releasing three of our four bombs, one sticking in the rack. It was not good aiming as we could not claim even a near miss, so we continued our patrol. The vessel, whatever it was, seemed completely indifferent — did not submerge or alter course or speed, and continued on its way with just a short wake behind it.

Soon afterwards we came on four British warships going at full speed in line ahead towards the Belgian coast. The ship at the rear of the line signalled in Morse by searchlight to us, 'Can you see the enemy?' I, the wireless operator, read and reported the message, and as we could not see any other ships I replied, 'No, but just bombed a submarine, (at whatever position it was).' This I did by Aldis Lamp and got the 'message received' acknowledgement as the warships carried on.

A minute later I happened to glance up and there above and behind us was a German plane. It was the first time I'd seen the black crosses of a German aircraft at such close range and my heart turned over at the prospect of my first air engagement, especially as it was a small land machine which could easily outmanoeuvre our clumsy flying boat. If he kept on our tail it meant that the engineer and I had to climb out and stand on the bottom wing to operate the two Lewis guns which swung loosely on a bar between the back struts. The only safeguard against our being blown off was a wire to secure to our belts, but neither of us wore a belt! Another snag was that we could cut off our own tail with the bullets from our guns as we followed round in the excitement of the fray.

However, we were relieved to find that the enemy did not intend to attack but was turning away towards the Belgian coast. We too, decided that it was time to continue our patrol.

Shortly afterwards the officer who had been piloting handed over the wheel to the second pilot, and took his place at the main hatch. Within a short time he turned to me and said, 'Look, Wireless, here's a Jerry sub right on the surface and we've no bombs left.' I jumped to the hatch and saw the submarine beginning to submerge. 'But there is one bomb left,' I said, 'the second pilot only dropped three. There's one left in the rack that may go this time.'

He immediately clambered forward to the front cockpit but by the time he got there and was able to look out, he could see nothing—the sub had gone under. I knew the exact spot because I had my eye on the small streak of oil from the periscope, but all I could do was to direct the pilot straight. Being away from the bomb-sight I couldn't say when to drop the bomb, so that was that, and we went home to base.

The sequel is rather amusing, as we learned later that the mystery vessel we bombed was a round smoke cannister dropped by one of 11 German destroyers which were being chased by four of our light cruisers—the warships I have mentioned.

On the 29th May, 1917 we set out on patrol at noon in an H.12 flying boat, a twin-engined craft with a three-ply wooden hull covered with canvas. Our cruising speed was about 60 knots and the maximum about 80 knots, although we never used the maximum if it could be avoided as it caused too great a strain on the structure and involved white hot exhaust pipes only about 3 inches from the doped canvas of the top wing.

Our job was to hunt submarines, and the crew consisted of pilot, Hodgson, second pilot, Gordon, wireless operator, Millichamp and engineer, Anderson. I was the wireless operator.

We were returning to base because of bad flying conditions when at about 2 p.m. Lieutenant Gordon, who was looking out of the main hatch, called to me and said, 'Here, Wireless, look at this.' I joined him and saw a float from a floatplane with two figures on it—one moving and one recumbent.

Gordon said 'Well, what about it? Are you prepared to have a go?' Being only eighteen at the time I'm afraid I said 'Yes' without waiting to think how foolish and hazardous it was to attempt to land and take-off at sea, especially as it was pretty rough. Our boat was only intended to get off from smooth water in harbour.

All agreed to have a go, but before going down I sent a message to Felixstowe on my spark-set to say we were landing. Actually because of bad atmospherics the message was not received—only completely unintelligible fragments.

Down we went, hitting the sea with an inevitably heavy wallop, and taxied straight for the float. One man jumped on to the nose of our boat and was pulled in by Gordon, whilst the other jumped and clung to the landing wire which runs from the nose to the wing-tip. He was thus suspended a couple of yards from the hull, and I hopped over the side to stand on the bulge below the main hatch and by stretching to the utmost just reached his outstretched hand. I naturally expected to drag him through the water as he let go, but it is a strange but true fact that although such a feat seems physically impossible I just lifted him straight on to the bulge beside me.

Imagine my surprise when his first words were, 'Hullo, Milli, fancy meeting you.' He was G. L. Wright, a friend of mine at the Cranwell Wireless School. I did not recognize him at first because, understandably he looked much older than his eighteen years.

After Wright and his companion, Flight Sub-Lieutenant H. M. Morris, had been given some brandy from Gordon's pocket flask, Wright told us that they had been adrift for six days after a forced landing in a Short floatplane. He said that the plane broke up after the first day and they were forced to take refuge on the float, which was only a fairly small metal box, just a few feet in length. All the food they possessed was a tin of Horlicks Malted Milk Tablets, emergency rations. They each had one tablet a day, half in the morning and half at night. When I asked what they had to drink Wright told me, 'sea water'. I expressed my surprise at this and said that I understood that it would drive them mad. 'Perhaps it did a little,' said Wright, and to prevent suicide they ditched Morris's pistol after three days. So now we had a second physical impossibility, seemingly, of two people living for six days on salt water.

By this time Morris had passed out completely and Wright was just about to do so, but he was conscious enough to feel our bouncing on the waves and said, 'It's rough flying today, isn't it?' I let him think so as it would have been heartbreaking to tell him that his position was very little better than before we picked them up.

Next, Anderson, the engineer, drew my attention to the fact that when we landed we had knocked a hole in the bottom of the hull and that the three-ply bulkhead had collapsed. This meant we had to bale, and I crawled through the wires to his place by the petrol tanks and together we tried baling with his tool-box from which he'd torn the lid. It was a ghastly business with no room to move, one bending down to fill the box and the other emptying it, head high, over the side.

However, this didn't last long as poor Anderson soon became very seasick and my sole puny efforts had no effect so I clambered forward to Gordon, who was then at the wheel and asked what he proposed to do. He said the only thing was to taxi towards the shipping channel and trust to contacting a ship as we all knew it was not possible to get off in that sea. When I pointed out that if we did not get off we would probably go under as baling seemed useless he replied, 'O.K. We may as well have a smack at it. Drop the bombs and let's go.'

So we went, throttle right down, biff-bang, wallop, water and bits flying but no lift for what seemed a lifetime. Then — cheers — we were airborne, but only for a few seconds, and down we crashed again, smashing a float and the tailplane. That was that—we could only taxi from now on. So long as our engines kept going we felt we would not sink but would we sight a ship in time. We certainly couldn't reach land.

We continued on, over a mine-field, to find a mist coming down, which seemed to seal our fate, but Providence was kind and we reached the shipping channel. How our spirits soared when we saw the smoke of three vessels, and when we were near enouh to see their hulls I fired them green Very lights from my Very pistol—the distress signal.

All three immediately altered course—away from us. It was horrid hard luck but you couldn't blame them, as it could have been a submarine ruse to lure them.

Better luck followed as later we came on the tramp steamer *Orient* which hove to and threw us a rope when we taxied alongside. The rope fell over the tail portion of the aircraft and so anxious was I to get hold of it that instead of waiting for it to be withdrawn for a second cast, I just hopped onto the body and ran along to the tail. This was a fish-shaped hull that was being violently thrown up and down on the waves. I mention this as just another instance of something happening that day that would normally be impossible. It wasn't a question of being brave, but just an easy way to do it, at the time.

Morris and Wright, both unconscious, were drawn up by rope and we, the crew, followed by rope ladder. Later that day we were all transferred to the steam drifter *White Lilac* and eventually reached Felixstowe at 10 p.m.

Felixstowe F.2.C flying boat sits on the tarmac outside the Air Station. Developed from the F.2 types this type was not too successful and the design was dropped.

As I salvaged my crystal set receiver, which very seldom received anything, and some other gear, I was instructed to stand guard over it at the quay until transport arrived. I was forgotten for 1½ hours but eventually got to my hammock. I was expected to go on early morning patrol next day but managed to get myself excused.

Morris and Wright were taken to the Sick Bay and completely recovered as evidenced that Morris later became Cricket Captain of Essex and Wright a pilot. After the War I heard that Wright made seven trips in one day to look for me when I was adrift during October 1917."

Mr Wright, who still lives at Birchington-on-Sea, Kent, recalls his time on the float:

"On the 24th May, 1917, I was detailed for the early morning patrol from Westgate Seaplane Base from there to the Tongue Light Vessel, the Edinburgh Light, Kentish Knock Light and the West Hinder Light off the Dutch coast when we had trouble and made a very bad landing on the sea. Shortly after this we turned over and Morris was swept away. However, I pulled him back and we stayed there for six days. The water-logged float was taking in water all the time and getting lower in the water, every wave covering us both.

As far as sleep was concerned we had to take it in turns to hold each other on sitting astride the float. All the food we had was a small tin of Horlicks Malted Milk Tablets which had been issued to each aircraft when on patrol, and we had one tablet each per day.

During this time on the float we saw a squadron of German aircraft, the leader firing a Very light, but they continued on their way. On the sixth day we saw the H.12, but the sea was too rough for them to make a decent landing and they had to taxi over us to take us off. Millichamp caught hold of me and hauled me aboard. Unfortunately the H.12 broke its back on landing and could not take to the air so we had to taxi to the shipping lane where we were taken off by the *Orient* of Leith, and later transferred to a drifter and taken into Felixstowe. After 3 months leave I was posted to Eastchurch and thence to the Grand Fleet flying off the deck of H.M.S. *Furious.*

I first met Millichamp at Cranwell in 1916 when we were training together so we were well known to each other and he was most surprised when we met again."

Mr George Hodgson, the pilot who now lives in Montreal, Canada, and who before joining the R.N.A.S. had won two Gold Medals at the 1912 Stockholm Olympic Games for the 400 and 500 metre free style swimming events, and had set up World Records for the 400, 1,000 and 15,000 metres and one mile titles, recalls the events of that day. "Lindsay Gordon, who was a cousin of mine, and myself enlisted together in September, 1915, in the R.N.A.S. and on completion of our training were posted to flying boats and seaplanes at the Felixstowe base on the East Coast of England.

On 29th May, 1917, we left Felixstowe in an 'F' flying boat on a routine patrol over the North Sea in search of German U-Boats. Having left our base around 11.00 a.m. we would normally be back about 3.00 p.m. We carried an engineer, Anderson, and a wireless operator, Millichamp, making a crew of four. These flights were carried out at an altitude of 1,000 feet. I was at the controls and Lindsay was in the observer's cockpit in the nose of the boat. The other two members of the crew were in the back of the plane, between the mainplanes.

After about an hour in the air our view was partially obscured by low-flying clouds just above the sea, which were called 'scud'. Being unable to see, we decided to return to base and set our course accordingly. A few minutes later, Lindsay signalled to me to go down because he had seen something of interest on the water through a break in the scud. This I did and we spotted two men hanging onto the upturned float of a seaplane. We then went up, let out our wireless aerial, and Millichamp sent a message in Morse to Felixstowe that we were about to land in such and such an area to pick up these men.

I did not anticipate any problem, as there was very little sea running, and a light breeze blowing from the south, but neither of us had ever landed a boat in the open sea before. What we did not see from the boat was a sea swell and the light breeze caused us to hit the water very hard.

We then taxied to pick up the two men, Lindsay pulling up one through the nose cockpit, and we asked them how long they had been down and they replied, six days. We gave them a shot of brandy and they both passed out. At this point we were about in the middle of the North Sea or some 50 miles from the coast of England. We then had a conference as to what we should do, and we only had two choices: try and take-off or taxi to the English coast. Conditions for take-off were not good because of the sea swell and the light wind and now we had six men on board. Our decision was to taxi to England which, if all went well, would take us about five hours.

So we started but in a few minutes Anderson told us that on landing we had broken a hole in the boat and we were taking in water. We then decided the only chance of getting out of our predicament was to attempt a take-off even though we were quite a bit heavier due to the sea water taken in. Our attempt was a failure owing to the conditions described but worse still, we broke our tail plane, which made flying impossible.

We then set out on the only thing left — a taxi run to the west. We alternated our positions at the controls and in the nose, as the man at the controls was protected from the spray thrown up by the boat's bow, but the man in the nose was drenched to the skin. We estimated we were making 10 m.p.h., and at the end of about one and a half hours, we encountered a fairly thick minefield — British or German we never knew — but the mines were

Lindsay Gordon, Captain of Felixstowe War Flight aircraft and the captain of the aircraft which effected the dramatic rescue of Morris and Wright. After the war he rose to be Chief of Staff of the Royal Canadian Air Force.
George Hodgson

floating on the water and we knew if we touched one that it would be it. The field was perhaps 10 miles wide and having crossed this slowly and safely in about an hour and a half, we came to what was called the 'shipping channel'. This channel was some 20-25 miles off the coast of England and was swept of mines daily to permit small English cargo vessels to pass safely north or south.

A fog now came down and visibility was perhaps a quarter of a mile. During the taxi run the water was coming into the boat faster than Millichamp and Anderson could pump it out and the boat was gradually getting lower in the water.

Now the miracle happened. Through the fog we saw a small cargo vessel coming south. What a sight that was! We had no trouble attracting their attention with Very lights, and they stopped and we taxied alongside. The crew members of the vessel took all six of us safely aboard and put a line on the flying boat. We started down the channel to Felixstowe, a trip of about 30 miles, where we arrived after one or two more adventures. The rescued men, or should I say boys, one was eighteen and the other seventeen, were unconscious throughout all these activities. On arrival at our base, the top plane of our boat was about two feet out of the water, whilst the Medical Officer who examined the boys said he did not expect either of them to live the night. Both did and both flew again.

Lindsay and I were awarded the Silver Sea Gallantry Medal which in due course we had pinned on our left breast by King George V at an investiture at Buckingham Palace."

Lindsay Gordon died during 1940 at the age of forty-six, whilst the other members of this event are in their eighties.

Mr Millichamp further recollects: "On the 9th June, 1917 we took off from Felixstowe in company with another H.12 flying boat piloted by Lieutenant Galpin, who was to accompany us as escort for a convoy. We went across to the Dutch coast and having found our ships began flying round over them.

Suddenly, to the great alarm of the crew of my plane, Galpin's aircraft flew directly over us at about 100 feet or less, which meant we stood a very good chance of being brought down by his trailing aerial which had a lead weight at the end. The copper wire could tangle with our propellers or the weight could smash our wood and canvas mainplanes. Fortunately this did not happen, but no sooner had we cooled off than Galpin flew over us again, even closer.

This was too much for Morrish, our pilot, and he left the control wheel, letting the plane fly itself, stood up in the main hatch, shook both fists at Galpin's plane and let loose a steam of invective that was a masterpiece of impassioned oratory worthy of a much larger audience. After a minute or two he cooled off, resumed his place at the wheel, went down to about 250 feet and just swung right away from the convoy in order, as he said violently, to get away from that asterisk maniac in the other boat. Within a matter of minutes we found we were heading straight for a German submarine, fully surfaced, a perfect target.

George Hodgson, War Flight pilot, Olympic Gold Medallist and World Record swimmer. Was also involved, with his cousin, Lindsay Gordon, in the Morris/Wright rescue. *George Hodgson*

Unfortunately we were only 250 feet up and if we had bombed we should have blown ourselves up. Even at 1,000 feet we always got a hefty bump from the explosions. Before we could gain height and get back into position the sub had submerged.

Soon after this it was realized that none of us knew our position, as when Morrish had swung away from the convoy no attention had been paid to navigation and all that we could ascertain was the direction we were flying as shown by the compass.

I can't remember how long it was before we sighted land but when we did the second pilot asked me if I recognized it. I couldn't, but said I felt sure it was the coast of France or Belgium, so we decided to fly north until we thought we were north of the English Channel and then due west, but we were worried about our petrol supply which was only enough for a five hour flight. After following our proposed plan we found that we were just about at the end of our petrol and no land in sight. Once again Providence was kind and just in time we spotted the white cliffs of Deal.

The engines were actually packing-up as we landed, near the monitor *Marshal Ney*, anchored off Deal. We were taken aboard by motor launch, and one of the crew enquired, 'How many did you bring down?' 'How many what?' we said. 'Why Jerry planes, of course,' he replied and explained that 17 enemy planes had just finished a raid and gone out to sea in our direction. He said we must have met them, but I was glad we had not seen them.

During the afternoon many two gallon tins of petrol were brought by launch and we emptied these into our tanks, and then cast off and attempted to start the engines. Unfortunately the choppy sea and the petrol fumes had made the engineer so groggy that he hadn't the strength to turn the starting handles strongly enough. The second pilot and I also failed to do so, and so we just drifted out to sea accompanied by a school of porpoises playing merrily around our bow. This did not suit Morrish who showed us what a tough guy could do — apparently he had quite a reputation as a boxer in Australia. He almost lifted the plane out of the water, the engines started with a roar and cloud of exhaust smoke and we eventually arrived back at base without further incident.

On Thursday, 14th June, 1917, I was detailed for patrol over the North Sea in an H.12 flying boat and we set out at 9.30 a.m. In place of the second pilot was a Brass Hat from the Royal Navy, Commodore Henderson, who wanted to see how it was possible to improve communications between the R.N.A.S. and ships at sea.

For a time I sent messages by spark-set and tried, unsuccessfully, to receive them on my crystal set, and then we continued our patrol towards the Dutch coast.

Not far from Ijmuiden we came across a submarine right in the middle of a Dutch fishing fleet, and it started to submerge and did not answer my challenge by Very pistol with the colour of the day. Here let me diverge for a spell to explain that a submarine is challenged by a colour changed each day and that if it was British or Allied it replied by a letter in the Morse code spouted up, with long spouts for dashes and short ones for dots. There was a snag about this as by the time the submarine could see whether or not the plane was friendly he had very little, if any time to dive. So I guess the submarine always dived, I only remember one that didn't, and we always bombed.

This was no exception, the Commodore did the bombing and straddled the sub with our four bombs. We thought we had got it but there was no great quantity of oil. Rumour had it later, but I hope that it was untrue, that a British submarine limped home in a damaged condition a day or so later.

We had gone out with another H.12 and soon after it had left our company it came upon a Zeppelin, L.43, low down, and without opposition they had shot it down in flames with a pan which included Brock bullets.

While returning on Sunday, 23rd September, 1917 from submarine patrol in an H.12 flying boat, the second pilot went forward to the front hatch with the intention of doing some firing practice with the Lewis gun mounted there. I saw him lift a full pan of 97 rounds and realised instinctively that he was not going to hold it streamline, i.e. narrow edge forward. He didn't, but just exposed the full flat surface and the force of the wind tore it from his hand and hurled it straight for the port propeller.

Now it would take only a very small part of a second to reach the fast revolving propeller, yet to me it seemed ages. I saw every inch of that pan's flight as though in slow motion, as it went straight for the prop about a foot above the bottom of the circle of its rotation and then, miraculously, when only a couple of feet from it, dipped suddenly and missed by not more than two inches. Just another episode.

Now this is a true account of what happened on 23rd October, 1917, to H.12 flying boat on anti-submarine patrol over the North Sea from our base at Felixstowe. The crew comprised pilot, Perham, second pilot, Gooch, wireless operator, Millichamp and engineer, Sivyer.

On this particular day the weather was so bad that in normal circumstances there would have been no flying, but as it had been reported from or Radio Direction Finding (R.D.F.) Stations that a submarine was to be located at a certain spot, two H.12 flying boats were detailed to try and find it.

My boat was to be the second one to be launched, but as its operator was late I took his place in the first one. How I regretted that in the next 24 hours! We got off very bumpily and were flung all over the sky for about two hours, when, about noon, the boat began vibrating violently and spinning to starboard. Something had happened to the starboard engine, and nothing could be done about it but to try and make the best forced landing possible. We hit the sea with a tremendous wallop and bounced, with no doubt help from the engines, up to about 200 feet. The pilot shouted, 'Pull the rope, Wireless,' and I did. We immediately nose dived in and I, half way along the hull, went a long way under the water.

I should explain that 'the rope' was a Heath Robinson device that it was hoped would help to keep the aircraft from spinning for a short time if one engine failed. Actually it consisted of two ropes, one to each side of the rudder and they were brought forward along one side of the hull. They were, however, so twisted together that it would have taken me quite a time to ascertain which one I should pull. So, having only a split second to decide, I trusted to luck and pulled the nearer. Apparently it was the wrong one, hence the nosedive, but I have since thought I was right as one clean nosedive was better than a succession of crashes on and through the largest seas I had ever seen.

As we went under I pulled the handle of my 'water wings' to inflate them by means of the compressed air cylinder inside but nothing happened as someone had already used the cylinder without replacing it. However by nosediving we had gone under so rapidly that the three open hatchways were covered practically instantaneously by the sea and imprisoned air inside the hull so that we popped up again to the surface. We saw our companion boat disappearing in the distance.

What a mess it was inside the hull. It will give an illustration of the force of the impact when I say that my Aldis Lamp batteries which were housed inside a closed box had been completely scattered in the water inside the hull although they were originally wired to each other. We, the crew of four, had escaped injury except for Gooch who had rushed forward just before we dived to try to drop the bombs. He hadn't time to do it and as we struck his head was in the front hatch. The Lewis gun there was torn from its steel Scarff mounting and cut his face, not badly, as it carried away. The two pigeons in their wicker basket also appeared to be unharmed, but we then noticed that one blade was missing from the starboard propeller.

The waves were really mountainous, there was a 40 knot gale blowing, and Perham said to me, 'Well, Wireless, what do we do now? (I was experienced as I'd been adrift three times before.) I replied that we should tie on the sea anchors. These were like canvas buckets with no bottom and we carried two, which Perham and myself tied to each wing.

Frankly the position looked so absolutely hopeless that I, and I'm quite sure all the others, did not think it was possible to survive even for an hour. The hull was made only of three ply covered with canvas and it was so bashed about that our lives depended entirely on the canvas holding. There were no rubber dinghies in those days. When the sea anchors were tied Perham told me to send off a pigeon with the message, 'Crashed 8 miles S.W. of North Hinder Lightship'. This I did and shortly after he told me to send off the second pigeon, and when I asked what the message was to be he said I was to repeat the first. I suggested that we wait awhile, having in mind a farewell message, but he insisted and off it went. Later he regretted this action.

Apart from the great quantity of water in the hull which necessitated constant baling, the float on the starboard wing had been carried away in the crash, and this meant that the engineer and I had to stand out on the port wing to neutralise its buoyancy. Often during the long night which followed we were clinging at full stretch to the cross wires while the waves tried to wash us off. Occasionally we came into the hull to help with the baling, and I suggested to Perham that I should try to rig up an aerial along the top wing and attempt to transmit a message to Felixstowe but he wouldn't agree. I still think that it might have worked.

Later I suggested that I might recover the scattered accumulators of the Aldis Lamp from the water and get it working, if possible, as a light would cheer us up, provided, by some miracle, we were still floating when darkness fell. It would also naturally be useful for signalling too, if we did see a ship. Perham vetoed this too, but when darkness did fall he told me to fix the lamp.

Now what would have been a comparatively easy task of improvisation in daylight was a vastly different thing in total darkness. However I groped around in the water and collected all the seven accumulators. Then I tore wire from the wireless set to make the necessary connections. By the Grace of God the positive and negative terminals were marked with impressed signs but where I got the delicacy of touch with frozen fingers to distinguish them by feel I do not know. The ticklish part was to avoid making a 'short' as a spark would probably ignite the petrol fumes in the hull, at least so I thought.

With great pains I connected about four cells when the inevitable happened but the spark was not followed by an explosion. Eventually I had them all connected and pressed the trigger. It worked, and how that light cheered us up, me at any rate.

The long night passed, baling and out on the wing, the waves so huge that from the crest to the trough they seemed three times the length of the hull. It was bitterly cold and of course we were all saturated. I was dressed in tunic, short duffle coat, breeches and putties but my legs were so cold that I tore the linings from my tunic and put them under my putties.

How the boat kept afloat and nose on to the seas I cannot understand, as once only during the night did we go askew and it seemed the end when a wave swept right over us. In the morning it was discovered that the sea anchor tied on by Perham had carried away, and this emphasised the miracle of our riding nose-on. Once during the night I came in from the wing and sat at my seat to offer up a silent prayer. Actually I'd been praying on and off the whole time but this was a special one, I was dog tired and miserable so I thought that I would dodge the buffeting on the wing for a spell and pretend to be asleep. Before long Perham shouted to me to get back on the wing but I pretended not to hear and Gooch said to him, 'Oh, let the poor kid alone. He's only eighteen and lucky to be asleep and free from worry for the time being'. However we were all very 'British', and I'd bet that all four of us were putting up silent prayers but at no time did any of us have courage to admit we were frightened and suggest that a combined petition to Providence seemed more than justified.

During the night we saw only one light and that for a few minutes only but the phosphorescence of the sea was something to be wondered at.

The following morning at about 7 a.m. I was on the wing when I saw a wave top in the distance that didn't seem to move. Each time we rose to a crest I looked harder and harder and finally decided it was no mirage, but land. I shouted 'Land Ahoy' in the approved manner, but it was some time before I could convince the others and get their eyes focussed on it.

We drifted nearer and nearer until we could see houses on the shore, and I then had horrible recollections of two other airmen who had drifted near to

A distinctively painted Felixstowe flying boat on patrol over the North Sea. The black object in the top right corner is a bomb under the wing of the photographer's aircraft.

France and then drifted away again because the tide turned. I mentioned this and it was decided to try to start the port engine. We didn't really think that it would start but it did.

Unfortunately it was a wasted effort as we couldn't keep the boat straight and so we shut it off. Thinking that we were near enough for distress signals to be seen I got my Very pistol, to find there was a cartridge in it, saturated and jammed. It wouldn't fire and the only way to get it out was to ram something down the muzzle and knock it out. This meant that apart from another miracle it would explode and the effect of a Very cartridge exploding in the hull can be imagined. So with a prayer and a screwdriver from the engineer I jabbed it out. It didn't explode. I then found some green cartridges which did fire and I let off as many as I could.

It wasn't long before we saw a torpedo boat bouncing over the waves towards us. It was a Dutch one and we were in the mouth of the River Scheldt. We then ditched our 4 Lewis guns and the pilot's pistol, also my code books in their weighted container and were then, we hoped, in a position to be treated as shipwrecked mariners, not subject to internment.

The torpedo boat launched a small boat manned by a Javanese officer and 2 sailors. I admired their courage in that sea, and one at a time we were taken aboard. During this operation the port wing, which was being flung violently up and down by the waves, descended unseen by the Javanese officer right on to his head. He leaned forward at the crucial moment and the back of his neck was struck by the trailing edge of the wing. Still another miracle — it collapsed in a neat semi-circle round his neck and he did not even notice it. Of course it was only wood and canvas, but it should have knocked him out at least.

I was the last but one to be taken off and while we waited our turn Perham said that we had better sink the boat, so we did. He and I jumped on the hull, that was sufficient. It didn't keep up long enough after Perham was taken off for the torpedo boat to attempt a tow.

We were taken into Flushing where our plea to be shipwrecked mariners was duly considered but, not unreasonably, rejected. We spent the rest of the war in Holland where we were well treated.

Whilst prisoners and living in The Hague, it was a common sight to see Queen Wilhelmina walking through the city followed by a liveried footman, perhaps carrying her coat. All the passers by when they drew level would doff their hats, if male, and receive in turn the royal bow to them in general.

One day as I was walking along near what we called the Peace Palace, I saw Her Majesty approaching on my side of the street. There were not many pedestrians about so I fell back to get a nice clear space to myself. On reaching the Queen I doffed my hat and achieved my object of getting the Royal bow all to myself.

Another unimportant incident in The Hague that gave me pleasure and which I frequently recall was the sight of the Generalissimo, General Snijders, of the Dutch Military Forces around on his push bike with his sword clipped to one side of the front forks."

Heligoland from 10,000 feet. This tiny island in the Heligoland Bight was the centre of many operations in both wars.   *Mrs M. Martin*

CHAPTER FOUR

Boats and Floats

IN ORDER to gain an insight into the varied testing work carried out both before the arrival of the M.A.E.E. during 1924, and during its two periods of residence at Felixstowe, a review of some of the aircraft and their equipment is desirable.

The earliest residents were the French-built Farman biplanes on floats, so often referred to as "box-kites" and these flimsy and not too airworthy machines were launched from the beach and flown over the district: also of French design and construction were the Borel monoplanes with their 80 h.p. Gnome rotary motors.

General marine aircraft experimentation was carried out at the R.N.A.S. Station, Grain, on the Isle of Sheppey, where aerodynamic testing was combined with armament development for marine applications.

During 1914, before the advent of the metal-hulled flying boat, the R.N.A.S. had ordered two American designed and built Curtiss wooden hulls, the first one, No. 950, arriving at the Air Station during November. This was minutely examined by John Porte who then made many proposals for improving its performance. A new hull was constructed at Felixstowe incorporating Porte's recommendations, but this too was found to be unsuitable, and so it was decided that the hull form of the Curtiss "America"* flying boats needed radical re-design. The first two American built boats were serialled No. 950 and No. 951, and became known as the H.4, "Small America."

Always interested in aircraft design, Porte had built a two-seat glider during 1908, and had then joined the British Deperdussin Company during 1911, but his interest turned to marine aircraft during 1913. Joining the Felixstowe staff just after the outbreak of hostilities, Porte set about his experiments, one of which involved research into mainplane incidence angles; the aircraft used for this work was a Curtiss H.4, No. 3546.

Research was carried out into all aspects of aerodynamic and hydrodynamic performance, although several different types were "on the strength for treatment". In those early days the Felixstowe Seaplane Development Flight was commanded by Squadron Leader R. B. Maycock, O.B.E.

Work carried on apace and another Curtiss boat, No. 1231, was fitted with an experimental Saunders-built hull, and this aircraft carried out a considerable amount of experimental flying at the Station.

*The name was derived from Rod Wannamaker's flying boat, designed by Glen Curtiss and intended to fly the Atlantic. The boat was named "America".

David and Goliath. The Bristol Scout C No. 3028 sits high on the upper mainplane of Porte Baby No. 9800 before taking off for the first ever air release experiment on 17th May, 1916.

For several weeks during 1915 the long-winged Short 184 seaplane was tested in the role of torpedo bomber and, although giving good service, was not particularly liked and Felixstowe reported that it was difficult to get up on the float step, but when it eventually did at about 46 knots, it took off easily, climbed to 600 feet at 2,200 r.p.m. and just managed to keep level flying trim at 50 knots. Anything below this airspeed caused it to become soggy. The report then ended, "Very satisfactory, and a great improvement on all previous torpedo carrying aircraft."

Faireys had now entered the field of marine aviation with their Hamble Baby, whilst Short Brothers had their Type 320 in service. Next in appearance, and advanced in design, the Norman Thompson NT.2B flying boat carried out extensive trials.

The hydrodynamic trials tank at Felixstowe was used a great deal for water performance research and Mr G. S. Baker, Head of the National Physical Laboratory's William Froude model-testing unit, made frequent visits in connection with hull designs. He was particularly interested in the Felixstowe/America flying boats and their water behaviour which was causing many problems, especially at take-offs.

Porte's assistant in this experimental design work was Lieutenant R. D. Rennie who was the Chief Technical Officer.

Other early residents were the Sopwith Schneider and Baby seaplanes, small, reasonably fast and used in a scouting role, whilst unusual machines like

76

the unsuccessful AD.1000 twin fuselage seaplane and the Wight Twin arrived but only carried out very limited flying.

As might be expected of an experimental station at this period, Felixstowe gathered together many expert carpenters in the wood-working shops, and the hulls built were of the very highest standard. When a team of experts from Boulton and Pauls of Norwich visited the Station preparatory to manufacturing their own hulls, they commented on the excellence of the local work.

Another Norwich firm, Mann Egerton Limited, undertook seaplane manufacture and the first Short 184 Type B produced by them, No. 8349, was flown to Felixstowe during June, 1916. It was test flown from there by the well-known aviator, Sidney Pickles.

An experiment carried out on 17th May, 1916, was repeated in essence many years later over the same airspace. A Porte Baby flying boat, No. 9800, which had been designed and built at the Air Station by Porte, was fitted with a cradle on the upper wing surface, and attached to it by quick release catches was a Bristol Scout C, No. 3028, on loan from the seaplane carrier *Vindex* based at Harwich. The flying boat was piloted by its designer, Squadron Commander Porte, assisted by Flight Lieutenant Hope, whilst upstairs in the Scout was Flight Lieutenant M. J. Day.

Taking off from Harwich Harbour the pair climbed up to 1,000 feet, whereupon the Scout's pilot released the catches and zoomed up to fly away and land locally. The object of the exercise was to carry a fighter out over the North Sea and patrol around until a Zeppelin was sighted, when the small

Felixstowe designed and built, John Porte's Felixstowe Fury, N.123, a giant triplane with five engines which recorded several weight lifting feats before crashing in Harwich Harbour. Note the dazzle painting on the wrecked H.12 hull in the foreground, and on the aircraft in the background.

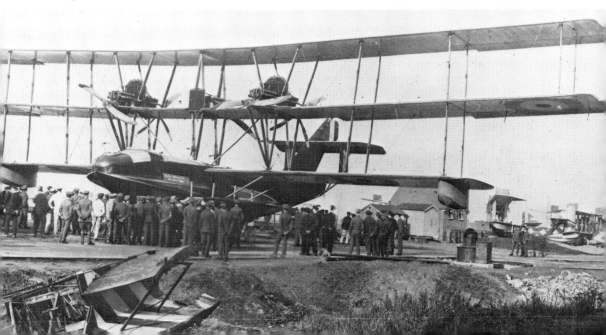

Unorthodox methods in use when the Felixstowe Fury was built — builder's scaffolding was employed for the erection of the massive mainplanes.

aircraft would release and hopefully, shoot down the enemy. The experiment was not repeated and Flight Lieutenant Day was unfortunately killed shortly afterwards in France.

A large three-engined design, the Porte Baby spanned 124 feet, and ten of these aircraft were built at Felixstowe, but were not used extensively on operations due to their poor manoeuvrability and low speed of 78 m.p.h. When they did venture forth they were usually escorted by an H.12 or "F" flying boat. Another fault was that they wallowed a great deal whilst taxi-ing, but this was rectified by adding three feet to the bows of the hull.

An early flying boat was the twin-engined Norman Thompson NT.4 named the "Small America", which led to a great deal of confusion with the imported American Curtiss boats. Powered by two 200 h.p. Hispano Suiza motors driving 4-bladed airscrews, they were used for coastal patrols and later as training aircraft.

One of the aircraft used for hull form experiments, Curtiss H.4 No. 1230, was lost over the North Sea during 1916. This boat had a modified hull which did not prove too successful, creating excessive suction, which made take-off almost impossible in some conditions — its strength was also suspect. A further developed hull was fitted to No. 3569, but this was beset with take-off difficulties and the planning step was moved to various positions to help improve take-off performance. The final development was No. 3580, later named the Porte I, and then Felixstowe F.I, this becoming the production type aircraft.

A massive triplane flying boat of American design and build was erected at Felixstowe during 1916, this being the Curtiss-Wannamaker Model T, No. 3073, powered by four 250 h.p. Curtiss motors, later replaced by those of Rolls-Royce manufacture. The performance of this giant was not impressive and all orders for further aircraft were cancelled. One interesting feature was the control surfaces which were so large that servo power in the form of windmill-driven drums and cables were used in order to assist the pilot to operate them.

Another Short Brothers product, the 320 seaplane, was also tested in the torpedo carrying role, but its 320 h.p. Sunbeam Cossack motor was hard pushed to haul the 75ft span biplane weighing 7,000 lbs along at 71 m.p.h.

Not satisfied with the water performance of the H.12, or Large America flying boats, Porte decided to do the same with these aircraft as he had done with the earlier H.4. Consequently, No. 8650, the first H.12, was rebuilt at Felixstowe with a new Porte-designed hull and this proved extremely successful. As a result, production was given the go-ahead and the modified version, named the F.2A, had a top speed of 96 m.p.h. and an endurance of 6 hours, no mean achievement for so large an aircraft. One fault, fractured petrol pipes caused by vibration, persisted throughout their life and in service it was common to alight far out at sea and effect repairs before resuming patrol.

Further modifications to the F.2A resulted in the F.2C, with open cockpits, a more streamlined hull form of lighter construction, and no gun

A large wash impinges on the Fury's lower wing as it taxies past the Air Station, showing a defect in the hull design which may have in some way brought about its final demise.

A competitor in the 1920 Air Ministry Civil Aeroplane Competition, the Fairey III amphibian, G-EALQ gained the third prize, and is seen here at Martlesham Heath undergoing land trials.

J. F. Brown

positions aft of the mainplanes. Not reaching production status, the F.2C, N.65 did valuable service with the Felixstowe War Flight and was often flown by its designer, Porte.

Not as successful as its predecessors, the Felixstowe F.3 was not well liked, although it was produced in larger quantities than the F.2s. The prototype, N.64, appeared early in 1917, and served with the War Flight. Capable of carrying twice the bomb load of the F.2s but with an inferior performance, it was used mainly as a patrol bomber, not having the fighting capabilities of the F.2s.

Not everyone was completely satisfied with the Porte type of hull construction, as one school of thought maintained that the Linton-Hope type of stressed skin hull was stronger weight for weight. One report stated, "The Curtiss boats, built in the U.S.A. are probably the worst example of boat building that can be imagined. However, many were built and did arduous service during the war years, although the first hulls proved too weak for operational service and were reinforced with planking by Porte. In tribute it must be recorded that as a result of Porte's modifications, over its development period, the Curtiss type flying boat was enabled to lift six times its original payload".

Porte was very biased towards the flying boat and although Felixstowe was there to test and evaluate all marine aircraft, it is recorded that he stated that he would not have a Short seaplane on his station. Of course, Porte was not able to carry out this threat, but nevertheless, it did not make the lot of the seaplane designers any easier knowing that their products were almost damned from the outset. Commander, now Wing Commander, Porte was in trouble at this time due to his association with the American Curtiss Company, being

80

accused at Bow Street Court, London, of accepting monies in respect of contracts with the United States firm. Contracts valued at 11 million dollars had been placed, and it was stated that commission of £64,000 was paid as a result of these orders. During the hearing, Porte was taken ill with chronic tuberculosis and although the case proceeded without him, it was ruled that the case against him be adjourned sine die.

Porte's last operational Felixstowe design was the F.5, and the prototype, N.90, appeared during 1917. Similar in appearance to the F.3, the prototype was assessed as an excellent machine, but alterations were incorporated in the production aircraft including a different wing section which created a greater all-up weight and loss of performance. This aircraft represented the turning of the circle as it was also produced in America, where the original Curtiss-designed boats had originated.

Developed from the Curtiss Wannamaker Model T triplane of 1916, Porte's last Felixstowe design was the Fury, N.123, sometimes called the Super Baby. A large triplane of 123 feet span with a hull length of 63 feet, it was powered by five 334 h.p. Rolls Royce Eagle VII motors mounted as two tractors, and three pushers. The original design motors, three Rolls Royce Condors of 600 h.p., were not available so the five smaller motors were used. Employing servo-motor actuated power operated controls, the Fury was the first R.A.F. aircraft to use this device. Top and centre wings of equal span

Front view of the Felixstowe F.5, N.178, fitted with Saunders Patent Ventilated Hull bottom. Note the large launching trollies with buoyancy tanks at the top ends. *J. T. Hill*

The large single seat Fairey Fremantle seaplane, N.173 with which it was hoped to establish long distance records, but the aircraft suffered various troubles and remained at Felixstowe. The Norwegian wooden house, still standing in 1978, is visible on the right.

Westland Aircraft

with a shorter span lower wing, whilst too different types of tail unit were used during the aircraft's life. Water trials showed that the Fury made excessive wash when running fast, this impinging on the lower surface of the bottom wing. After flight trials, the tailplane was modified into a cleaner unit, and in this form Major Hallam, D.S.C., took off with 24 passengers, 5,000 lbs of ballast and fuel for seven hours. On another occasion the Fury was airborne at a gross weight of 33,000 lbs.

An aircraft unusually stationed at Felixstowe at this time was the specially modified Sopwith Camel 2FI which incorporated a sturdy steel tube "V" undercarriage structure and twin Vickers 0.303 inch machine guns. This aircraft was basically developed for use from the towed launching platforms described elsewhere.

A propaganda flight was undertaken during 1919, when an F.5 left the Air Station and flew for fourteen and a half hours non-stop, cruising as far as Brighton one way and Lowestoft the other. No attempt was made to alight until all the fuel was used, and no modifications were carried out for the flight. Average speed was 55 knots and the take-off weight was 13,710 lbs. Wireless communication was kept with base throughout the flight.

A defect manifested itself in some of the Felixstowe-designed Porte boats in the fabric covering of the four-bladed airscrews stripping off and causing excessive vibration. This necessitated complete engine shut-down and a resultant long drift to await pick-up if the boat was on a North Sea patrol.

Before leaving the Porte-designed boats it is worth noting that the manufacturing cost of the F.2A was £6,738, and this included the launching trolley.

A small fast single seat flying boat came along too late for the war, this was the Supermarine Baby, N.I.B. No. 59, and the 30 foot wingspan boat attained a speed of 117 m.p.h. with its 150 h.p. Hispano-Suiza motor. Only two machines were built but they proved that the design was sound and capable of further development.

Another late comer was the English Electric (Phoenix Dynamo Company) P.5. Cork Mk.1 flying boat, N.86, with its sleek Linton-Hope wooden hull so distinct from the wide flared Porte-type of construction. Used for experimental work it gave solid service, and the second prototype, N.87, differed in that it was powered by two 450 h.p. Napier Lion motors instead of the original 352 h.p. Rolls Royce Eagle VIIIs.

On 22nd October, 1919, Colonel John Cyril Porte, C.M.G., died after a lengthy and painful illness. He had only recently retired from the Royal Air Force, the reason being that he wanted more time to devote to the development of large civil flying boats. The historian Sir Walter Raleigh summed up Porte's work: "The shortest possible list of those who served the country in its hour of need would have to include his name", whilst another historian C. F. Snowden Gamble, stated: "In this work, Wing Commander John Porte and his staff at Felixstowe Air Station must be remembered always."

During this year, Porte's huge Felixstowe Fury stalled on take-off and crashed into Harwich Harbour, breaking up and killing the pilot and two crew

The wreckage of the Supermarine Sea Lion III which crashed on 8th July, 1924 after porpoising and plunging beneath the surface.   *J. T. Hill*

Of large proportions, the 4-engined Fairey Atlanta N.119 with its polished wooden hull caused many a raised eyebrow when it arrived for testing and it remained for a long time conducting various trials.   *Westland Aircraft*

Sister to the large Atlanta, the 4-engined Fairey Titania, N.129 also remained at Felixstowe for several months on trials as the requirement for its Service use had become outdated.

H. F. King

members. It was later suggested that the boat had been loaded with the centre of gravity too far aft and this had caused a stalled condition as soon as the machine was airborne. However, Major R. D. Rennie who had assisted Porte in the Fury's design, found that when a metal model of the hull was tested in the N.P.L.* tank it porpoised at low speeds, and this is what apparently happened to the unfortunate crew of the Fury.

On 29th April, 1920, the F.5, N.4044, which the previous year had made a survey flight to Norway and back, went into a flat spin when approaching the Station from the Harwich direction. Desperately struggling with the controls, the crew almost had the aircraft under control, when it hit the water with a terrific impact and broke up immediately, four of the crew dying and two surviving. Among the dead was Squadron Leader Edwin "Rolly" Moon, a much respected man at Felixstowe, both on and off the Station, who had survived the Fury crash of the previous year.

During 1920 the Air Ministry announced that a Civil Aeroplane Competition would be held during the year, the venue Martlesham Heath, and the amphibian machines would be tested at both the land and marine establishments. The latter comprised:

Vickers Viking III	G-EAUK	450 h.p. Napier Lion
Supermarine Seagull	G-EAVE	350 h.p. Rolls Royce Eagle VIII
Fairey IIID	G-EALO	350 h.p. Napier Lion

As a result of the trials the following statement was made on 11th October, 1920: "The Air Ministry announces that the Judges' Committee consider that the results achieved in the competition for amphibians, conducted at Martlesham Heath and Felixstowe, show considerable advance has been achieved. The Committee are of the opinion that the proportion of the monetary awards does not adequately represent the relative standards by merit of the first two machines and recommend an increase in the amount of the second prize. The following sums have therefore been awarded;

1st Prize	£10,000	Vickers Viking III
2nd Prize	£8,000	Supermarine Seagull
3rd Prize	£2,000	Fairey IIID

The Fairey entry, G-EALQ, was remarkable in that it had been handed over to the R.N.A.S. during April, 1917, and served with this service for the rest of the War. Demobbed during May, 1919, the makers bought it back and used it in an experimental role, flew it in the Schneider Trophy Race during September, 1919, and then used it for the above Competition. The Vickers Viking was later taken on R.A.F. charge during January, 1921 and became N.147.

*National Physical Laboratory.

An early experiment to achieve better control on flying boats was carried out during 1920, when F.5, N.4838, was fitted with auxiliary aerofoil aileron balances which it flew with for several months. An attempt to improve water handling was also carried out with another F.5, N.178, which was fitted with a Saunders hollow-bottomed hull, aimed at reducing water friction.

Two very similar floatplanes paid brief visits during their testing stay at the Isle of Grain, these being the Parnall Puffin, N.136, and the Fairey Pintails, Mk.I., N.133, Mk.II., N.134, and the Mk.III., N.135. Both types suffered from the same defect, ineffective water behaviour of the single main float and longitudinal instability.

An improved version of the Felixstowe F.5, the Short Cromarty, N.120, was evaluated by the Seaplane Development Flight during July, 1922, and received a good report. Designed and built by Messrs. S. E. Saunders for Vickers Limited, the one and only Vickers Valentia, N.126, made a few short visits, but the 112 foot biplane was not accepted for the R.A.F. Supermarines kept up the biplane amphibian theme with their Seal II, N.146, and Seagull I, N.158 types, a configuration which was further developed during the years until the Second World War. These were followed by a cross between the Seagull and the Sea Eagle, resulting in the Scarab, a 3-seat bomber reconnaissance amphibian; and although it never saw service in the R.A.F., twelve were sold to the Spanish Naval Air Force.

At the same time the Seagull II, N.158, was being evaluated at both Felixstowe and Martlesham Heath, but the majority of its pilots stated that they preferred twin-float seaplanes.

Looking very much like an F.5 the Phoenix P.5 Corks, N.86 and N.87, had beautiful polished Linton-Hope hulls, two Rolls-Royce Eagle VIII motors of 350 h.p. mounted at midgap between the 85 foot span wings. Unfortunately too late for operations, they carried out a great deal of test flying and development work until 1924.

Larger aircraft appeared for testing and one such example was the four-engined Fairey N.4 Titania, N.129, which arrived during 1923. Spanning 139 feet its handsome wooden monocque hull was 66 feet in length, and the motors were fitted as tandem pairs between the mainplanes. With a loaded weight of 31,610 lbs the Titania was an excellent performer, but once again arrived too late for war service and also at a time of extreme economic pressure, and thus only the one aircraft was built. Greatly liked by all the Felixstowe pilots, the Titania remained at Felixstowe until 1927. Another unusual machine at this time was the English Electric Ayr, N.148, a three seat flying boat which attained water stability by means of a heavily dihedralled lower wing. The 450 h.p. Napier Lion gave the Ayr a good airspeed, but a great deal of trouble was experienced with excessive wash on the lower wing or

Squadron Leader Rae puts the De Havilland D.H.15 G-EAWW down onto the surface of the River Orwell, just off the Air Station, in an experiment carried out to ascertain the buoyancy of civil aircraft. Pulled ashore the remains of G-EAWW sit forlornly on the foreshore after the experiment which ended her life in the cause of aircraft safety. *J. T. Hill*

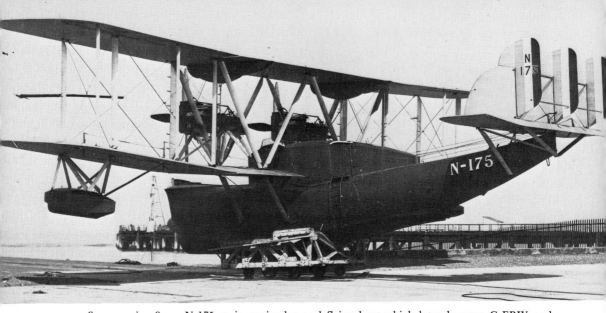

Supermarine Swan N.175, twin-engined patrol flying boat which later became G-EBJY and from which was developed the Southampton. *S. D. Snell*

The prototype Supermarine Southampton, N.9896, first of a series which gave yeoman service to the R.A.F. This particular aircraft carries the crest of the City of Southampton on the bow, and of interest is the elderly ambulance in the background. *S. D. Snell*

Short Cockle, G-EBKA, N.193, a tiny twin-engined single seat flying boat which paid several visits to the M.A.E.E. The large wheels are for beaching purposes only, and one of the small airscrews is still preserved by an ex-Felixstowe serving airman.   *S. D. Snell*

Always known as "The Tin Five", the Short modified F.5, N.177 was used for a considerable period as an experimental aircraft with an all metal hull.   *Short Brothers*

sponson, and the Ayr remained at Felixstowe for some time carrying out useful hydrodynamic research.

Ill-fortune came to the Station on 20th April, 1923, when the English Electric Kingston Mk.I, N.9709 ran into trouble whilst on official trials. Just after take-off, with Flight Lieutenant Carnegie at the controls and Mr Baker as Flight Observer, the engines broke away from their mountings and the whole wing structure collapsed. The flying boat dropped back onto the water and sank, the crew escaping and being able later to report on the demise of their mount. This aircraft was the first of five wooden hulled pre-production models and re-design was hastily instituted for the remainder of the batch. The fourth machine, N.9712, was constructed with a duralumin hull and became the Kingston Mk.II.

The 1923 Schneider Trophy contender, the Supermarine Sea Lion III, G-EBAH, which had been flown into third place by Mr H. C. Biard, was transferred to the R.A.F. and serialled N.170. Used as an experimental aircraft it was useful in assisting with problems associated with the higher speeds of the newer flying boats.

The cost of testing was always high and added to during 1924 when Flying Officer Smith was killed near the Air Station when the Fairey Flycatcher he was flying broke up in the air. He was buried with full military honours, the service taking place at St John's Church, Felixstowe, of which the Chaplain to the Station, Canon Cox, was rector.

Carrying out its dual role of military and civil testing, an experiment was carried out on 2nd May, 1924, and reported thus:

"An interesting experiment was carried out at the Air Station, Felixstowe, today when an ordinary land aeroplane was brought down on the surface of the sea in order that information might be obtained as to what happens in the case of the forced landing of an ordinary passenger machine in the sea.

The machine chosen for the test was an old De Havilland 18, a four seater enclosed cabin machine, the forerunner of the present D.H.34. The experiment, which was not altogether conclusive, showed that it took half an hour in this instance before the aeroplane had gradually sunk at the head until it assumed an upright position in the water. It had then about one third of its length above water: and at this point the nose of the machine was resting on the bottom. The machine had taken off from Martlesham Heath experimental station, and R.A.F. motor and rowing boats were waiting at the landing stages to go to the machine as soon as it alighted. A small company of officials assembled, chief of whom was the Director of Civil Aviation, Air Vice Marshal Sir Sefton Brancker, and Wing Commander Cave-Brown-Cave of the Directorate of Supply and Research, and also Mr Walker of the De Havilland Aircraft Company.

The aircraft was flown by Flight Lieutenant Rea and the aircraft bore the registration letters, G-EAWW, and this was the first experiment to be carried out in the interests of civil aviation."

One of the then fastest aircraft, the Gloster Schneider seaplane, ex-Bamel I, G-EAXZ, arrived during 1924 and was used as a high speed trainer. Supermarine's designer Mr R. J. Mitchell's first twin-engined design also arrived during August, 1924, the Swan, N.175, later G-EBJY, and was favourably received by the test pilots. As a result of its trials a specification was drawn up for a similar design, for use on military duties.

Martlesham Heath and Felixstowe both tested the Vickers Viking VII amphibian for fleet spotting duties and later as the Vanellus, N.169, it carried out comparison trials with the Seagull III. An unsuccessful design tested was the Parnall Plover floatplane, N.9610, the pilots all registering their dislike of the type, the landplane version of which had already crashed at Martlesham Heath.

Early during 1924, the Aircraft Experimental Unit moved from the Isle of Grain to Felixstowe and was re-named the Marine Aircraft Experimental Establishment, or M.A.E.E., the name by which it was always then known. Responsible for the testing and evaluation of all British constructors' marine aircraft, engines and equipment, Service and civil, it also incorporated the Marine Craft Experimental Unit which had been formed at Felixstowe just prior to the M.A.E.E. This latter unit's responsibilities were to carry out development of high speed marine craft for aircraft servicing and rescue duties. One of its first assignments was the testing and evaluation of a lightweight rubber buoy which had been designed and made by Short Brothers of Rochester, this later becoming standard equipment. One of the pecularities of this device was that for overseas use they were coloured bright red to dissuade crocodiles from using them for food!

One ex-Felixstowe serving member, Squadron-Leader L. P. Coombes, remembers his days at the M.A.E.E., "I went to the M.A.E.E. from the Royal Aircraft Establishment, Farnborough during August, 1925, as a Scientific Officer. I was the first scientist and the first civilian officer on the Station and despite my R.A.F. background as a Sopwith Camel pilot with the D.F.C. the Commanding Officer regarded me with the greatest suspicion. Later a Chief Technical Officer, Mr Cowlin was appointed as my superior and he was followed by Major Lediboer and then H.M. (later Sir Harry) Garner. Mr E. Robinson was attached to the staff as Senior Technical Officer during my time and the staff of service draughtsmen under Sergeant R. K. Cushing were made civilians a year or two later. By the time of my return to the R.A.E. to establish the Seaplane Testing Tank in October, 1930, the civilian scientific and technical staff were highly regarded by the R.A.F. personnel — both the later C.Os, Group Captains Maycock and Bromet, were very well disposed to us.

A design for an exacting requirement. The small 2-seat Parnall Peto, N.181 was designed to be accommodated in the hangar of a M Class submarine. The aircraft was lost when the parent vessel sank in the English Channel.   *S. D. Snell*

We carried out many scientific experiments and I collaborated with the late Sir Harry Garner in writing a review of scientific work on seaplanes. which was published in Aircraft Engineering before World War II.

One of the burdens which flying boats had to carry were heavy anchors and chains which reduced the pay load. Mr B. C. H. Cross invited me to research the problem which fell into two parts, (a) the drag of the moored flying boat due to winds and the pitch angle caused by waves, and (b) making anchors lighter and more efficient. We fitted recorders in moored aircraft in order to amass the relevant data.

I commenced this work of testing the holding powers of various anchors and after my departure this work was carried on by Squadron Leader Lucking. A contribution I was proud of was the use of models under controllable conditions. Professor Sir Geoffrey Taylor visited the M.A.E.E. and saw a scale model demonstration of the instability of stockless anchors, and this inspired him to invent the famous C.Q.R. single fluke anchors. The M.A.E.E. work culminated in the Felixstowe Mark XII anchor, a great advance on existing ones and this was then standard equipment for many years.

The scale effect between wind tunnel tests and the actual flying machine was a great concern in those days. Lift and drag were deduced by power glides and in the case of land aircraft, the propeller was stopped by stalling and re-started by diving; calculations with stopped propellers/s were more accurate than with a rotating one. It was, in those days of manual starters, not practical to stop the 'props' of flying boats or large seaplanes, and McKinnon Ward of the R.A.E. had suggested using a 'Zero Thrust' intregating pilot tube to allow the engine revolutions to be adjusted to zero thrust. I was the first scientist to take up this suggestion and it was used to measure lift and drag on a Fairey IIID and the Blackburn Iris II.

There were other facets of research, water resistance of hulls, porpoising characteristics and the water pressures on hulls during alighting and take-off. Measurement of the centre of gravity position was difficult and I invented a device to determine this on aircraft fitted with special slinging gear."

New equipment was installed to carry out the test work, many of the instruments being of quite large proportions to deal with the flying boats now coming along for trials. These were gradually increasing in size and all-up weight and in the main were generally larger than their land-based counterparts being tested at nearby Martlesham Heath.

The usual material for the construction of marine aircraft up to 1924 was, in the main, timber and fabric but metal construction was making great advances and a large all-metal monoplane flying boat made its appearance during 1925. Messrs William Beardmore, the famous Clydeside shipbuilders, had secured Air Ministry contracts for two flying boats and one landplane, built to the German all-metal Rhorbach system. The first of these two boats, N.183 and known as the Beardmore Inverness, was built by Rhorbach at their Copenhagen works since Germany, under the terms of the 1918 Peace Treaty, was not allowed to construct aircraft there; it was flown to the M.A.E.E. in September. A high wing, cantilever monoplane, the wing consisted of a box girder built of channel sections with top and bottom plating, and unstressed fairings at the leading and trailing edges. It had a flat bottomed hull and two long floats mounted well in board below the wing to give it water stability. The two Napier Lion water-cooled engines were close mounted on struts above the wing, this arrangement assisting assymetrical flight in the case of one engine failing. A unique feature of the design was that if the aircraft was forced

Blackburn Blackburn, N.9833 floatplane is moved into the hangar by a well wrapped-up handling party, the tarmac always being a draughty place.   *S. D. Snell*

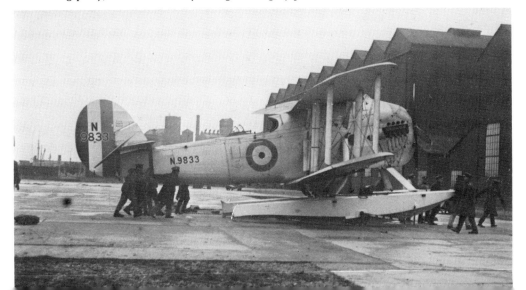

The unusual German built Dornier Dolphin III, N.176, acquired by the Air Ministry for evaluation into metal construction. *S. D. Snell*

down, masts could be erected, sails bent on to them, and the aircraft sailed to the nearest point of land.

Tests showed that the British-designed hulls were more stable and ran cleaner in water although the German-designed construction had many merits. As a large scale exercise in all-metal stressed skin construction, the Inverness was very successful. The methods pioneered by Rhorbach, and taken up by Beardmore, were basically those in general use today, although improvements in engineering methods, structural test facilities and materials available now enable a much lighter structure to be designed. In 1926 Dr Adolph Rhorbach gave a lecture in the United States of America which attracted a lot of attention and led to widespread use of stressed skin construction by Douglas, Boeing and other American aircraft constructors.

The Air Ministry had now decided to accept metal hull construction as its advantages over the water-absorbing wooden hull outweighed the additional cost. Short Brothers received a contract to construct a Felixstowe F.5 with a metal hull, retaining the wooden mainplanes and tail unit. Always known as the "Tin Five", N.177, arrived at the M.A.E.E. on 14th March, 1925, for evaluation, flown by Mr John Lankester Parker. The 44 foot duralumin hull incorporated a multichine "V"-bottomed, fluted planing surface and as a test of its durability it spent all its non-flying time anchored out in the river. After one year's service it was found to be completely satisfactory, its performance ringing the death knell for wooden hull construction. Among the many exhaustive tests carried out on the hull was a series of stalled drops onto the water surface from various altitudes in order to prove the rough water capabilities of its construction.

In later years several flying boats were used in a series of tests which involved their being lifted out of the water by the 50-ton Titan crane, and then swiftly dropped down from gradually increasing heights. Between each drop full examination of the structure was carried out in order to assess how much punishment the craft could take.

As the economic crisis gradually passed so the ordering of new aircraft types proceeded and consequently fresh designs arrived for testing. Not only the airframes, but quite often the power units were also new and many innovations involved both sides of the aircraft.

One of the oddities tested at the M.A.E.E. during 1925 was the diminutive Short Cockle, G-EBKA, a tiny high winged monoplane flying boat powered by two Bristol Cherub motors of 32 h.p. each, although these were replacing two 696 c.c. Blackburn motor cycle type motors. Only on a few occasions was the grossly underpowered Cockle persuaded to leave the water, usually in the hands of Parker, the renowned Short test pilot. Returning later as R.A.F. N.193, the Cockle remained until August, 1926, an interesting but unsuccessful attempt at a small, simple flying boat. A relic of this tiny aircraft still exists, as an ex-Felixstowe serving airman still proudly possesses one of the airscrews from the Cockle, and it is cherished and regularly polished, a reminder of days long past.

Many aircraft, after evaluation at Martlesham Heath as landplanes, went back to their makers to be fitted with floats for trials at the M.A.E.E. Typical examples were the civil Vickers Vixen II, G-EBIP biplane, and the Hawker Hedgehog, N.187, hopefully submitted for a contract, but in the case of these two aircraft, their performance was no better than the existing Fairey IIIs, so they fell by the wayside. Also in many instances the requirement had become obsolete by the time that the aircraft were ready for trials. The makers then tried to upgrade their designs further by making the aircraft an amphibian,

Gently down, the three engined Blackburn Iris, N.185 patrol flying boat settles onto the surface with the Dock buildings in the background.   *Hawker Siddeley Aviation*

One of the last of the wooden hulled flying boats which appeared too late for Service acceptance, the Saro Valkyrie, N.186, prepared to alight with her 3 Rolls-Royce Condor motors throttled back. *British Hovercraft Corporation Ltd*

examples being the Fairey Flycatcher, Hawker Hedgehog, Avro Bison and the Short Gurnard.

Developed from the successful Swan, the Supermarine Southampton, N.218, prototype caused quite a stir when it arrived on 15th March, 1925, with its beautiful mahogany planked hull, equal span biplane wing layout and triple fins and rudders. Immediately noted for its case of control and fine rough water performance, it was much sought after by the M.A.E.E. pilots. The ground crews and handling parties soon christened it the "Swampton", a name which it lived with for many years. Later in its Mark II version with metal hull and uprated 500 h.p. Napier Lion VA motors it carried out successful trials and the type served for many years at both home and overseas stations.

During May, 1926, the Blackburn Blackburn Mk.I, N.9833, was evaluated as a twin floatplane, but the floats were deemed unsuitable by the M.A.E.E. and this was followed by N.9828 fitted as a twin float amphibian. The M.A.E.E. Report F/17 on the former imparts the information that the twin floats could be used for carrier deck landings as well as on the water, and that the pilot for the trials was Flying Officer A. R. Wardle.

When the Secretary of State for Air, Sir Samuel Hoare, visited the Station on 29th September, 1926, Flight Lieutenant Sawyer flew him on a tour round the East Anglian coast in one of the resident flying boats, the Blackburn Iris Mk.I, N.185.

Blackburns sent the second Ripon I, N.204, in its seaplane form, for evaluation and performance trials during December, 1926, whilst Short's Singapore I, N.179 did its service trials. Of all metal construction, and powered by two Rolls-Royce Condor IIIs, the design was a great advance on previous types. Other residents at this time were the Handley-Page Harrow, N.205, and various ageing Fairey III Ds.

A most unusual diminutive floatplane appeared for trials during 1926, in the form of the Parnall Peto, N.181, a two seat folding wing reconnaissance biplane to Air Ministry Specification 16/24. Designed to reside inside the 8 foot wide hangar of an M Class submarine, it was a most difficult design requirement to fulfill and, because of its environment, stainless steel was used for its structure. Successful in that it was able to perform its exacting duties, it went down with the submarine M.2 when it was lost with all hands off the south coast of England. The report of the M.A.E.E. tests was that the performance of such a small aircraft was acceptable, but that on other than a smooth sea it tended to bounce off the surface before flying speed was attained. Squadron Leader Coombes issued the Test Report for the Peto and said "The Peto has an exceptionally robust undercarriage". Just after this was published Flying Officer Worsley, a Schneider Trophy pilot, landed the Peto heavily and badly bent the struts of the undercarriage. A cartoon appeared in the Station Book, illustrating the incident with Worsley saying "I'm the guy who put the bust in robust".

The aircraft manufacturers always heeded what the M.A.E.E. had to say about their products and during 1927 the Blackburn Iris RB.I, N.185, which had been at Felixstowe for some time carrying out performance trials under Flight Lieutenant Sawyer, A.F.C., returned to its builders at Brough, E. Yorks, for modifications. It was fitted with a new all-metal hull in place of the wooden one, and a new tailplane in order to provide an extreme tail gunner's position, recommendations which had stemmed from Felixstowe. Another innovation was a five man metal dinghy for crew ferrying purposes, and in this form it returned to the M.A.E.E. as the Iris, Mk.II.

Long distance flights were always part and parcel of aircraft testing and several such excursions were mounted from Felixstowe. Apart from the cruises around the British Isles which always followed the coastline, others crossed stretches of open water. One of the first was during 1919, when the Felixstowe F.5 Nos. N.4041 and N.4044, flew to Norway to demonstrate the possibilities of commercial flying boat operations in the fiord coastline of that country.

The large 3-engined civil Short Calcutta, G-EBVG shows her fine hull lines and majestic appearance. Aerial masts for wireless communication are shown erected and the two pilots can be seen in the open cockpit.   *Short Brothers*

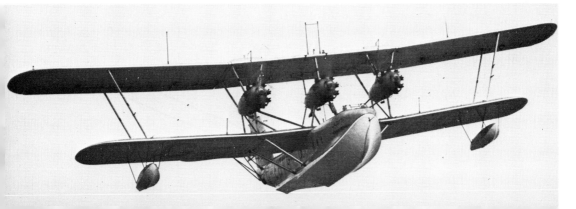

The civil registered Supermarine Air Yacht G-AASE, specially built for the Hon. A. E. Guinness and used as a private aircraft for travelling between England and the Irish Lakes.

via Paul Leaman

First stop was Dundee where they refuelled and then crossed the North Sea, during which time they ran into terrible weather and No. 4041 returned to Dundee. The other F.5, N.4044, commanded by Major J. Galpin and Captain C. Scott, dropped down below the fog and made landfall only two miles from their objective, Kristensand. The flight took 7¼ hours and covered 430 miles, an extraordinary feat of navigation for those days.

During 1926 two Supermarine Southamptons, S.1037 and S.1038, made the journey to Egypt and back, a cruise of 7,000 miles and this was concluded without incident. The purpose of the exercise was to test the ability of the flying boat to operate from remote sites. The aircraft were captained by Squadron Leader Livock and Flight Lieutenant Carnegie.

Group Captain G. E. Livock recalls the Southampton in which he flew many thousands of miles: "It was a most excellent flying boat in every way. It went through its acceptance tests and service trials straight away and went into service without modifications, a very unusual thing. It was easy to fly, and manoeuvre on the water, was robust and easy to maintain and very reliable in every way. It was however very noisy, open cockpits, especially in the second pilot's seat, and over the years I came to have a great deal of experience with it."

Another flight began on the 12th August, 1927 when the Blackburn Iris II, N.185, the Short Singapore I, N.179, the Supermarine Southampton I, N.218, and the Saunders Valkyrie, N.186, left Felixstowe to carry out a 3,000 mile goodwill tour of the Northern European capitals. The Iris II, piloted by Squadron Leader Scott, A.F.C., had on board Sir Samuel Hoare who was to visit Copenhagen to attend the Air Traffic Exhibition. Encountering engine trouble, the Singapore returned to Felixstowe but the next day made a non-stop flight to Oslo, to catch up with the other three who had stayed overnight at Esberg. Encountering gale conditions the four flying boats continued their cruise until the 24th when the Iris flew the Minister back to Felixstowe and then returned to Gdynia and rejoined the squadron. Temporarily held up with mechanical trouble the Southampton stayed over at Danzig for a day or so, and on the 30th the Valkyrie was forced to alight on the open sea near Königsberg with engine trouble, and was towed into port. After further adventures the four aircraft arrived back at Felixstowe, this cruise proving that the metal hulled Iris and Singapore were better suited to sea work than the water soaking hulls of the other two.

On 27th September, the Iris II, piloted again by Squadron Leader Scott, set out for another long distance cruise, eventually reaching Karachi, and arrived home again, without incident, on 14th November having covered a total of 11,360 miles at an average speed of 92 m.p.h.

Again on 17th October, four Southamptons, S.1149, S.1150, S.1151 and S.1152 under the command of Group Captain H. M. Cave-Brown-Cave, set out on a twelve month cruise to the Far East. Eventually reaching Australia, having covered 24,000 miles, the Far East Flight as it was known, visited the principal cities and then took up residence at Seletar, Singapore during September, 1928, where it became No. 205 Squadron.

Two more Southamptons commanded by Squadron Leader Scott carried out another goodwill cruise to Norway on the 7th October and returned on the 14th.

The Air Ministry had decided during 1926 that the flying boat represented a practical means of transport to places in the then far flung Empire and ordered Short Brothers to design two civil flying boats based on the successful military Singapore I. These two graceful boats, named Calcutta, appeared during February, 1928 and caused quite a stir. The first to arrive was G-EBUG during March, and it successfully passed its sea worthiness and airworthiness trials, gaining a full Certificate of Airworthiness (C. of A.) on 27th July, the first large commercial flying boat to do so. Shortly afterwards, John Lankester astounded Londoners by landing on the River Thames in front of the Houses of Parliament in the Calcutta. The following take-off was hair raising but a pilot of the calibre of Parker had fully calculated the odds, and although close, it was successfully carried out. The sister boat, G-EBUH, arrived at the M.A.E.E. on 22nd May, 1928 and differed only in that it was fitted with Handley-Page slots on the upper mainplanes. Fully evaluated for its civil role,

Another Blackburn Aircraft design which carried out lengthy trials at the M.A.E.E. but was not accepted for production, the Blackburn Sydney, N.241, General Reconnaissance flying boat to Specification R5/27.   *Hawker Siddeley Aviation*

Seaplane version of the carrier borne torpedo bomber, the Blackburn Ripon II, S.1271, taxies towards the Crane Pier during 1931. *Mrs M. Tillyer*

A frequent visitor to Felixstowe in various forms, the Short Gunard N.229, seen here as a single float seaplane, being launched off the "Seafront" during 1931. *Mrs M. Tillyer*

Hawker Nimrod, S.1578, single seat seaplane fighter i handled along Crane Pier. *Mrs M. Tillye*

it was assessed for R.A.F. use and then returned to Rochester during September.

On 30th November, 1926, the second Beardmore Inverness, N.184, made its first flight, this being at Dalmuir on the River Clyde where it had been built. It then came south for testing at the M.A.E.E., but the type did not go into production.

Civil aircraft were becoming more evident, and the Supermarine Solent G-AAAB, derived from the Southampton, was certified for its C. of A. and used by the Hon. A. E. Guinness as a private air yacht. The same maker's Seagull III amphibian, G-EBXH, also underwent trials, together with their Seamew, N.212, but these did not go into production. An unusual version of the Blackburn Iris Mk.IV was N.185, with three Armstrong Siddeley Leopard III radial motors, two mounted as tractors and one as a pusher. Not a successful installation, it was not proceeded with, but the Southampton in its Mark III version was enjoying an extended life and further development. Smaller floatplanes were the Short Sturgeon, N.200, and the Avro Buffalo II, N.239, the former with a metal monocque fuselage, deemed by the authorities as difficult to repair. The latter was reported as not sufficiently advanced to warrant production and remained at the M.A.E.E. as a trials and "hack" aircraft.

Unsuccessful in meeting the specifications laid down in Air Ministry F.9/26, the Hawker Hawfinch, J.8776, was rebuilt with single bay wings and twin floats and in this form carried out a series of trials, together with the Vickers Vireo, N.211 and the Gloster Goring, J.8674, which also failed to gain a production contract.

A Felixstowe resident, the Short Singapore I, N.179, was loaned by the Air Ministry to its builders, Short Brothers, who in turn loaned it to Alan Cobham to carry out a 23,000 mile survey flight round Africa. The money for the venture was put up by Sir Charles Wakefield of Castrol, Short Brothers and Rolls-Royce. Bearing the civil registration, G-EBUP, the journey was successfully completed and the Singapore returned to Felixstowe during November, 1929, where it remained as a Buzzard engine test bed.

A feature of the experimental establishment was the comparison trials which were held to assess various designs to an Air Ministry specification, (A.M. Spec). Participating in A.M. Spec 5/24 for seaplane trainers were the Blackburn TR.I Spratt, N.207, the Vickers Type 120 Vendace I, N.208, and the Parnall Perch N.217, all powered by the same type of Rolls-Royce motor, the Falcon III. Later they were all fitted with land undercarriages and evaluated at Martlesham Heath, the Vendace being the eventual winner. This did not profit it much as the requirement was cancelled and no further aircraft to this specification were built.

Test pilots' remarks regarding their mounts were always enlightening and a report on the Hawker Hoopee, N.237 a contender for the N.21/26

101

specification read: "It merely hopped from one float to the other rather than made an attempt to fly."

With the success of the Blackburn Iris II, the R.A.F. ordered a new version, and this arrived at the M.A.E.E. during 1929 as the Iris III, N.238, carried out extended trials and then left for No. 209 Squadron at Mount Batten, Plymouth, during May, 1930. The same maker's Ripon II, S.1268, also spent some time on trials, and although meeting the requirements of the specification, it was not ordered. Newcomers to the Seaplane Flight were the Westland Wapiti, J.9084, the Hawker Hoopee, N.237, and the Vickers Vildebeest, N.230. Civil representation was the Short Mussel II, G-AAFZ, for C. of A. certification, the third Calcutta G-ADDN for brief trials, and another air yacht for the Hon. A. E. Guinness, the Supermarine Air Yacht, G-AASE.

Some aircraft spent a considerable time at the M.A.E.E. carrying out extended trials and one such machine was the Blackburn Sydney, N.241. A large three-engined monoplane, it arrived on the 9th December, 1930, and caused a stir with its then new monoplane layout. Armament was advanced with three 0.303 inch machine guns and two 850 lb Whitehead torpedoes and, although trials continued until 1934, it was decided not to proceed with the design.

A light civil biplane, the Blackburn Bluebird IV, G-AAUT, arrived for civil certification for long distance overseas flights, but sank off the Station after making a heavy landing during January, 1931. Another light biplane used for experimental work was the De Havilland 60M Gipsy Moth, K.2235, fitted with a single main float and wing tip floats. The 25 foot main float provided valuable hydrodynamic data. Also completing floatplane trials was the civil Spartan Arrow biplane, G-ABBE, owned by Captain Harold H. Balfour, the Member of Parliament for Thanet. After trials it was shipped to New Zealand and registered ZK-ACG. Looking very similar, the Simmonds Spartan, G-AMMG, carried out the same tests but then reverted to a landplane in which guise it later crashed. A De Havilland high wing monoplane, the D.H. 80A Puss Moth, G-AAVB, fitted with Short floats and owned by Colonel The Master of Sempill, was certified and on the 4th September, he flew it 1,040 miles non-stop from London to Stockholm, in 12 hours.

Another trials competition was staged for twin float seaplanes, the prototypes being the Hawker Osprey, J.9052, and the Short Gurnard, N.228, and although the Osprey gained the contract, many sets of Short-built floats, as used on the Gurnard, were supplied for the Hawker machine.

Unusual for its size and configuration, the Short Valetta was a large, three-engined twin floatplane, the largest built up to that date. Like the Singapore from the same stable, the Valetta was loaned to Alan Cobham for an African survey flight. On its return, it was converted to a landplane,

The Saro Cloud amphibian trainer receives attention to its Armstrong Siddeley radial motors.   *Mrs M. Tillyer*

Blackburn Iris with three Armstrong Siddeley Leopard radial motors, two as tractors and the centre one as a pusher.   *Mrs M. Tillyer*

John Lankester Parker, Suffolk born at Barton Mills, became one of the best known flying boat test pilots. He visited the M.A.E.E. for a number of years as Short Brothers Chief Test Pilot.

103

The civil 4-engined Short Kent, G-ABFA, later named Scipio, which served for a number of years, with its sisters, on the Mediterranean routes. The white spots on the illustration were caused by water damage during an enemy air raid on the Rochester Works. *Short Brothers*

evaluated at Martlesham Heath, and finally sent to R.A.F. Henlow, Bedfordshire, as a radio trainer during 1933. Short Brothers also presented the their Singapore II, N.246, for evaluation flying in the capable hands of John Lankester Parker, who brought the machine from Rochester to the M.A.E.E. in a time of 32 minutes. Graceful, reliable and an efficient performer, this flying boat was liked by the M.A.E.E. pilots and developed into the long serving Mark III version.

Even in 1930, exports were necessary, and a British built flying boat for service in Japan was tested at the M.A.E.E. On 22nd October, the Short Kawanishi KF.I arrived for trials; looking like a cross between a Singapore and the Calcutta, it was distinctive with its all-white finish and red disc national markings of the Japanese Navy. Certification was unusual in that although it was a military aircraft it was granted a civil C. of A.

Another "foreigner" at the same time was the American-built, Sikorsky S.39A single-engined, four-seat amphibian, for civil registration as G-ABFN, and residents at that time remember its very noisy 300 h.p. Pratt and Whitney Wasp Junior radial motor.

More long distance work again during 1931, when the Flying Boat Development Flight despatched two Singapores captained by Flight Lieutenants H. Davies and C. H. Cahill on a cruise to the Middle East and back. Taking approximately four weeks, the boats covered 6,500 miles without mechanical trouble.

Three Short Rangoons, S.1433, S.1434 and S.1435, led by Group Captain W. L. Walsh left Felixstowe during 1931 and flying by easy stages reached Basra where they re-equipped No. 203 Squadron. This was the first time in the history of the R.A.F. that a squadron had flown out to its new station as a unit.

Of all-metal construction with fabric covering, the large three-engined Saunders-Roe A.7, Severn, N.240, joined the other inmates of the large hangar. Spanning 88 feet, its three 485 h.p. Bristol Jupiter IX radial motors gave it a top speed of 130 m.p.h. at an all-up weight of 22,000 lbs. Like so many before it, the Severn remained at the M.A.E.E. for the rest of its days, carrying out useful research work.

The following year saw several new types, both service and civil, as well as modified types such as the Blackburn Iris II, N.185, now re-engined with three Armstrong Siddeley Leopard III 700 h.p. radial motors, and designated Mark IV.

The same designer's Ripon IIC, S.1468, was also re-engined and re-evaluated with a 1,420 lb torpedo, reports stating that it was well received. Short's Gurnard, N.229, put in another appearance, this time as a single-float amphibian, and re-engined with a Rolls-Royce Kestrel IIS motor. After trials it remained at Felixstowe as a cooling system, radiator installation and engine flying test bed.

Another large civil flying boat was the Short Kent, G-ABFA, with its 113 foot wingspan, and accommodation for 15 passengers in luxurious style. Later named "Scipio" it went into service with Imperial Airways' Mediterranean fleet. Avros sent their two seat biplane trainer Type 621, G-ABGH, powered by an Armstrong Siddeley Lynx engine and trials proved satisfactory, the Air Ministry placing orders for a further one for trials and fourteen production aircraft to be known as Sea Tutors.

Saros had several monoplane amphibians in residence, a revised Cloud, G-ABHE, with an auxiliary aerofoil above the two motors, a Cloud prototype K.2681, numbered No. 12 for the Hendon Air Display, and the three-engined Windhover G-ABJP.

Originally known as the Southampton IV, the Scapa did not greatly resemble the original aircraft, but was capable of 141 m.p.h. After trials, S.1648 went out to Malta for further trials and then returned to Felixstowe where it lived for several years.

A Hawker Danetorp, No. 202, destined for the Royal Danish Naval Air Service rests on its beaching gear. This was an export version of the R.A.F's Horsley day bomber.

Hawker Siddeley Aviation

The diminutive Parnall Prawn, S. 1576, single seat fighter flying boat with its unique pivoting motor and airscrew. Top picture shows the motor and tiny four-bladed airscrew in the take-off and landing position, whilst bottom shows it in the normal flying position. *via Paul Leaman*

The Hawker contingent comprised the Nimrod floatplane, S.1578, with Ospreys Mark I, K.2777 and Mark II and the prototype, S.1678 all undergoing extended test flying.

After a partial rebuild at Rochester, the Singapore II, N.246, arrived back at the M.A.E.E. during the spring of 1931, resplendent with three fins and a rear gun position. In this guise she carried out extensive trials and then returned again to Rochester to have a large long-range fuel tank fitted in the hull. Back again at the M.A.E.E., during August, it set out under the command of Flight Lieutenant Davies for tropical trials at Aden, accompanied by the Saro Severn, N.240. Completing the journey of 6,500 miles, the Singapore II returned during September and then it was back to the makers for a new planing bottom and enclosed cockpit.

Another 2,800 mile cruise round the Baltic ports took place during 5th-24th September, when the Southampton III commanded by Wing Commander R. Leckie made the round trip.

Supermarines further developed the Southampton into the Mark IV, S.1122 being evaluated followed by the next, the Mark X, which was flown with a variety of different motors. This machine was an advance in design in that it had a stainless steel hull and inboard wing floats.

Eyes were raised to the skies during August, 1932 when the giant six-engined Short R.6/28 Sarafand, S.1589 flying boat, arrived for evaluation and service trials. This 70,000 lb monster handled well, but for the first few days was flown by its maker's test pilot, John Lankester Parker. Under his guidance, the M.A.E.E. pilots gradually took over and the Sarafand was a familar sight out on the moorings for several years. Unusual markings were displayed by a large single-engined floatplane when the Hawker Danetorp, No. 202, was tested for the Royal Danish Naval Air Service during November, 1932. Its blue and yellow flag emblem markings brought a touch of colour to the "Seafront" as also did the triangular markings of the Hawker Hart floatplane, No. 151, on trial for the Estonian Air Force. Local skies were filled with noise when the American-built Vought Corsair V-66E was tested, its ungeared radial motor announcing its presence when airborne. This aircraft had just previously been evaluated at Martlesham Heath as a dive bomber.

Another experiment was carried out in order to investigate the effect of aircraft "ditching" and the victim was the Blackburn M.1/30, K.3591, which had been transferred from the A. and A.E.E. for the purpose. After the various tests had been concluded the remains of the aircraft were sent back to the makers at Brough.

Diminutive in size, Parnall's fighter flying boat, the Prawn, S.1576, incorporated many novel features such as a 4' 3" four-bladed airscrew mounted on an adjustable shaft so as to clear the water spray. Not much is known of its flight capabilities since whilst at the M.A.E.E. it was never possible to get it airborne, the engine overheated and broke down and a complete lack of spares prevented repairs being carried out.

Hawkers were in the export market again when the Bristol Pegasus IM2 powered Hart floatplane, No. 1303, was tested for the Royal Swedish Air Force. Once again its three yellow crowns insignia made a bold and unusual sight both on the ground and in the air. Always worthy of an upward glance when airborne, the wingless Avro 671 Rota, autogyro, K.4296, was resident during 1935, during which time it had several exciting adventures whilst being test flown.

The second Blackburn Iris V, S.1264, which had been rebuilt at Brough, arrived at the M.A.E.E. on 2nd January, 1933, but was lost when it sank at its moorings during the following night. Perth, K.3580, from the same stable, basically a developed Iris V, came later in the year and was novel in that the armament which it could mount was a 37mm Coventry Ordnance Works cannon which fired 100, 1½ lb shells a minute from the front gun position.

To illustrate the work of the M.A.E.E., the following example of a series of tests conducted during 1934 shows the detailed work involved. The trials were to establish the static stability of six full scale twin float seaplanes, the Vickers Vildebeest, Fairey IIIF, Hawker Osprey, Hawker Nimrod, Avro Sea Tutor and the Armstrong Whitworth Atlas. Experiments were made to determine the longitudinal and lateral metacentric heights and capsizing moments of the seaplanes. Attempts were made in the first place to carry out these measurements in the sea, but as this was rarely smooth and the tests were interrupted by the wash produced by passing vessels, a tank was constructed to carry out the work. It had to be large enough to take the displacement of an aircraft weighing up to 10,000 lbs, and calculations showed that it needed to be 34 feet by 20 feet and 4 feet 9 inches deep. It was situated in the hangar beneath an overhead crane, this being necessary to lift the aircraft in and out of the tank.

Stability tests were carried out with the aircraft loaded to their normal weights which ranged from the Vildebeest's 8,350 lbs to the Sea Tutor's 2,760 lbs and for the first measurements, the centre of gravity was placed in the correct position. Further tests were then made and measurements taken with the centre of gravity at its forward and aft limits, prescribed for each type. By means of mechanical devices, pressures were then exerted on the aircraft to simulate displacement loads in both the lateral and longitudinal axes. Angle of heel were also able to be exerted and the pitch angle measured for each applied moment until the seaplane became unstable or until the lower wing tip touched the floor.

Reports were then made by pilots who had handled and flown the seaplanes under test, and no serious adverse reports were made as to the machine's stability. Tests were carried out in both calm water and the roughest

Being prepared for launching during 1932, the Supermarine Scapa S.1648 was a development of the long serving Southampton. *Mrs M. Tillyer*

Remembered by many for its thunderous engine note, the American Vought Corsair V66E, K.3561, was on evaluation trials during 1932. *Mrs M. Tillyer*

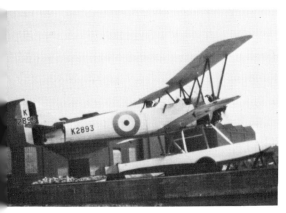

Two seat seaplane trainer, the Avro 626, Sea Tutor, K.2893. This aircraft was the seaplane development of the standard Avro Tutor trainer. *Mrs M. Tillyer*

109

Cruising serenely, the majestic Blackburn Perth 1, K.4011, final aircraft of the first production run shows her fine lines and the gun position aft of the biplane tailunit.

Hawker Siddeley Aviation

water in which it was expected the machines would be expected to operate. The conclusions of the tests was that the moment required to capsize the seaplanes when trimmed aft was in order, and from the opinion of the experienced pilots, the aircraft tested had adequate stability. The tests were conducted by three civilian Scientific Officers of the M.A.E.E., Messrs R. K. Cushing, A. S. Crough, D.I.C., A.C.G.I., and R. W. Angell.

Mr Roland Angell who worked at the M.A.E.E. from November 1927 until October 1936 recalls his days: "It was in November 1927 that I began working at Felixstowe as a civilian test assistant, mainly concerned with the day to day planning, management and observation tests on the flying boats during their development stage. I was responsible for conducting the flight tests of the Singapore I in its later evaluation days when it was fitted with more powerful Rolls Royce engines and for the flight testing of its successor, the Singapore II. Later I was involved in work on the best known member of the Short family, the famous Sunderland.

For many years I worked with others of the experimental staff at Felixstowe in two small buildings close to the beach, in front of the main hangars and the large stretch of concrete known as 'The Tarmac'. From our windows we could see all that went on both in the harbour and on the tarmac. The wind used to blow with almost hurricane force between the two main hangars and I remember seeing tricks played by this wind on both men and machines.

Many were the famous men who served at the Station, including the Schneider Trophy pilots, and many of us carry memories of these men. On one occasion to test their nerve, so they said, Atcherley and Waghorn borrowed

110

bicycles from our office and rode out in single file along a single plank gantry over the water. Imagine the amazement of us who were watching! We were considerably relieved when they returned safely and leaned the cycles up against the office wall.

I have vivid, and mixed, recollections of a long test flight in the Singapore I, from Felixstowe along the coast by way of Ramsgate, Dover, Portsmouth and Start Point to the Scilly Isles. The outward journey was relatively calm and uneventful and we landed at St Mary's at 12.30 p.m., moored the flying boat and then enjoyed a first class lunch at a hotel owned by an R.A.F. Squadron Leader who had been our passenger.

On the return journey however, one engine gave trouble over Calshot and we had to alight in rough water in the Solent, then taxi for a mile or so to Calshot. I was terribly seasick. In spite of my sickness I enjoyed the meal we had in the Officers' Mess — after waiting for the officers to finish their dinner! But the next morning when we left after an excellent breakfast of bacon and eggs, I was again very sick, and I continued to be so all the way back to Felixstowe. Never have I felt so bad!"

Long range delivery flights now became the order of the day and during 1935 Singapore, K.4581, left for Singapore with Squadron Leader Plenderleith, Pilot Officer Hobbs, Flight Sergeant Jackson and three airmen to join their new squadron.

Several pre-war M.A.E.E. members have recalled how the Singapore II made her final contribution to the cause of marine aviation. Stripped of all valuable equipment she was lifted by the 50-ton Titan crane, and by means of quick release shackles was dropped some sixteen times into the water. Starting at 2 feet the last drop was up at 14 feet, and although sections of the wing spars failed and some of the hull bulkheads buckled, the bottom of the hull remained intact. This was a tribute to the solid design which in its final stages

First of a long line to come of best known aircraft, the Supermarine Seagull, N-2 for the Royal Australian Air Force. Later the Seagull became the famous Walrus. *Vickers Limited*

The interim version Short Singapore II, N.246, frequent visitor to the M.A.E.E., and finally developed in the famous Singapore III, standard equipment of several pre-war R.A.F. squadrons.   *Mrs Campbell*

Short Empire flying boat, Canopus, G-ADHL, lifts from the water whilst on makers' trials at Rochester.   *Short Brothers*

First of the many, the prototype Short Sunderland rides at anchor during acceptance trials in pre-war natural metal colours.   *R. G. Pratt*

had been jointly developed by Short's Chief Designer, Mr Arthur Gouge, and Mr Garner, who was at that time the Principal Scientific Officer at Felixstowe.

What was to be one of the world's well known aircraft made its first appearance, the Supermarine Seagull V, N-1, later to be renamed the Walrus, known to the Navy as the Purser's Duck or Shagbat, and serialled K.4797. Nimrod II, K.2823, with a more powerful motor and the Osprey Mark III, K.3615, appeared in their stainless steel versions, this being the final development.

A new aircraft design always caused a stir and the modern looking Short R.24/31, K.3574, affectionately known as the "Knuckleduster" was no exception. An aviation magazine of 1934 commented that strange angles in the wings of aeroplanes were becoming the fashion with first the Handley-Page 42 with its downward sloping lower inboard wing. Short Brothers have reversed the trend with the upward inboard angle of the gull-winged boat, an arrangement which makes it look stranger still. It is an aircraft whose looks are quite foreign to the Medway (Shorts' works) and now we must wait and see what Felixstowe thinks of this craft.

First of the many Singapore III's, K. 3592, completed acceptance trials during July and differed only in minor aspects to N.246 and, by the end of the year, three had passed through the Station including K.4577, the first production aircraft. Saro's London, K.3560, also successfully passed trials and went into production as the London Mark II, K.5908, doing the production tests.

A neat little five-seat twin float seaplane, the Short Scion, G-ACOX, came for C. of A. certification and then served in the Far East, lasting in service in Australia until the 1950s. Its big brother, the four-engined Scion Senior, VT-AGU, was also evaluated and after purchase by the Irrawaddy Flotilla Company of Rangoon was shipped out to its new Far Eastern home.

Fairey's Seafox, K.4305, a double bay equal span biplane designed for Catapult work with the Royal Navy, went through the course, and later made a name for itself during the Second World War Battle of the River Plate.

On 15th September, 1936, a new exciting shape appeared over the M.A.E.E., the Short Empire flying boat, Caledonia, G-ADHM, a graceful four-engined high wing monoplane designed to ply the Empire routes. Caledonia was not fitted-out but carried extra fuel tanks with a capacity of 2,320 gallons in order to carry out North Atlantic survey flights. Certificate of Airworthiness trials were conducted by the M.A.E.E. pilots who proved the aircraft, and on one occasion Squadron Leader Martin made a take-off in overload conditions of 45,000 lbs. When she was scrapped during 1947, after being the last British Overseas Airways Corporation flying boat in Africa, she had amassed the magnificent total of 15,143 hours in the air.

Distinctive with its monoplane gull-wing, the Short R.24/31 Knuckleduster, K.3574 shows its armament and bomb load. The turrets on top of the wings are the radiators for the steam-cooled Rolls-Royce Goshawk motors. A Southampton and a Scapa are at anchor off the "Sea-Front".

H. F. King

At this stage, with the larger aircraft being tested, a new standard was laid down by the M.A.E.E., applicable to both service and civil machines. This required that all aircraft become airborne in a time limit of 60 seconds, in still air and smooth water conditions. With the increased wing loading of the new aircraft it is worth comparing types to get an idea of this feature. The Southampton in its hey-day had a wing loading of about 12 lbs per square foot, which means that each square foot of lifting surface carried a load of 12 lbs. The Empire boat increased its wing loading to 27 lbs per square foot, the Short Sunderland, to 54 lbs and, for the record, the modern fighters, now jets, along with each square foot of wing carrying approximately, in the case of the Phantom F4, 114 lbs and the Starfighter, 156 lbs.

A new sound was in the skies over the Estuary during September, 1937, when the Blackburn Iris V, S.1593 was tested with three diesel engines, the British built Napier Culverin Series I version of the German Junkers Jumo IVC., of 720 h.p. They were not considered a success, and a feature of the Iris when flying was the long black exhaust trails left in its wake. Also at this time the single float Hawker Osprey III, S.1700, met with a minor accident when alighting and was hurriedly taxied up onto the slipway to prevent it sinking. As S.1700 did not fly again it was despatched to the R.A.F. College at Cranwell as an instructional airframe.

Activity was stepped up after the 8th April, when the first of the grand ladies of the air arrived for trials, Short Sunderland, K.4774. Its clean lines and new look caused a great stir and the railings alongside the tarmac were lined with enthusiasts attempting to get a good look at the silver giant. No great roar came from the 4-1010 h.p. Bristol Pegasus XXII radial engines, more of a deep throated whisper, a most purposeful sound which came to be dreaded by many a U-Boat crew. On 9th May, L.2159, the second production aircraft arrived for service trials, followed shortly afterwards by L.2158 during June, this one being fitted out with more comprehensive equipment. A new procedure in British aircraft was the dumping of the fuel load in emergencies, and during June, L.2160 arrived to carry out these experiments. The all-up weights of the boats gradually increased and the Sunderland was now cleared to take-off at 48,700 lbs.

The most unusual aircraft of all arrived on 17th March, 1938, when the Short Mayo Composite components arrived separately, "Maia", G-ADHK, the lower unit being piloted by John Lankester Parker and Harald Piper brought the upper unit, "Mercury", G-ADHJ. "Maia" was a large four-engined high wing monoplane of now conventional lines, resembling a large Empire boat, powered by 4-Bristol Pegasus radial engines, it spanned 114 feet, and could be furnished for 18 passengers if need be, but in practice remained unequipped. "Mercury" was a conventional twin float high-wing monoplane but powered by four Napier Rapier air-cooled in-line motors which gave it a range of 6,100 miles in her record breaking trim. Normally, carrying 1,000 lbs of mail, the range was reduced to 3,900 miles.

The object of the combination was to enable a very heavily laden seaplane to be taken aloft by a "mother" aircraft, which, when it had launched its "passenger" returned to base and the upper unit continued on its way. This was similar to the aerial launch carried out over the Harbour during May, 1916, but differed in that the combination was a flying boat and a landplane. The Mayo Composite aircraft had been conceived by Major Mayo, a First World War pilot and inventor who had been stationed at Martlesham Heath at that period.

The great day was on 9th May, 1938, when two Short Brothers' pilots made the first full load separation. This was observed by two M.A.E.E. pilots.

An unusual Hawker Osprey Mark III, S.1700, fitted with a large single float and large wingtip stabilizers which finished up as an instructional airframe at R.A.F. Cranwell, Lincolnshire.
Hawker Siddeley Aviation

The Short Mayo Composite units on the tarmac giving a good idea of the size of the two aircraft. Full load separation trials were carried out at the M.A.E.E., and "Mercury" returned later as a seaplane trainer with a Dutch flying boat squadron. *via Paul Leaman*

Squadron Leaders Martin and Pickles flying alongside, and they then made the next separation whilst the Short pilots did the observing. The two components returned to Rochester separately on 19th May, 1938.

The Yugoslavian Government purchased a few Hawker Harts, and one of them, No. 1, was fitted with Armstrong Whitworth built floats, and evaluated successfully at the M.A.E.E. before going overseas.

Resembling the Sunderland, the twin-engined Saro Lerwick, L.7248, ran trials, but did not live up to its early promise and in spite of prolonged trials and modifications, had only a very limited service life. A neat two-seat light biplane which had previously been evaluated at the A. and A.E.E. showed up, the De Havilland Hornet Moth, P.6785, and this aircraft was still flying over the district in 1978, beautifully restored and kept in first-class trim by its proud owner, Doctor Helena Hamilton. Registered G-AHBL now, the author has flown over the Air Station in this veteran's nostalgic return after forty years.

On 2nd January, 1939, the ever-attentive Clacton R.N.L.I. lifeboat was launched to go to the aid of a Felixstowe flying boat down on the surface some miles off that town, when it reached the aircraft, the lifeboat found that it was not in trouble but merely at anchor! One wonders if they had fish for dinner in the Mess that night?

Following in the steps of the Fairey Swordfish, K.4190, and the Blackburn Shark, K.4295, both of which had entered service, the last of the biplane floatplanes, the Fairey Albecore, L.7075, was tested during the year, but was not greatly liked by the M.A.E.E. staff, the rest of the production order all being produced as landplanes. Designed for carrier work, this single bay,

116

folding wing biplane powered by a Bristol Taurus II radial motor was only capable of 150 m.p.h., but nevertheless did good work later in the Middle East operating from the Western Desert as a torpedo bomber.

A strange un-British sound echoed in the district during January, 1939, when the then unfamiliar looking, long-winged Consolidated 28-5, P.9630, arrived after a non-stop flight across the Atlantic Ocean. Purchased by the British Aircraft Purchasing Commission in America, this was the first of the later named Catalinas that were to give such yeoman service to the R.A.F. in their wartime patrol role.

With the outbreak of hostilities during September, 1939, the M.A.E.E. moved, lock, stock and barrel to its new home at Helensburgh on the River Clyde in Scotland, where marine aircraft testing reached new levels in order to cope with the influx of British and American purchased aircraft.

After an absence of six years, the M.A.E.E. returned to its old home during August, 1945, and one of the first aircraft to carry out trials was the Saro A.37 Shrimp, TK.580/G-AFZS, a two-seat flying scale model for a larger design which was never built. Powered by four 95 h.p. Pobjoy Niagaria III radial engines, the Shrimp had been built to try out a large flying boat design, and was used during the war as an experimental aircraft. Used to also air-test scaled down components, the Shrimp was a familar sight and sound around Felixstowe and was deceptive in its size until viewed at close quarters.

A feature of post-war Felixstowe was the number of ex-enemy marine aircraft being evaluated by the M.A.E.E., and the German counterpart of the Saro Shrimp was the also tiny FGP-227, flying scale model of the giant Blohm und Voss BV.238 transport flying boat. Powered by six 2-stroke motor cycle engines, it was a two-seater and so small that many seeing it for the first time

The Fairey Sea Fox, K.4305, suns itself whilst undergoing armament trials at the M.A.E.E. Designed for catapult operation from cruisers, aircraft of this type performed yeoman work during the Battle of the River Plate. *H. F. King*

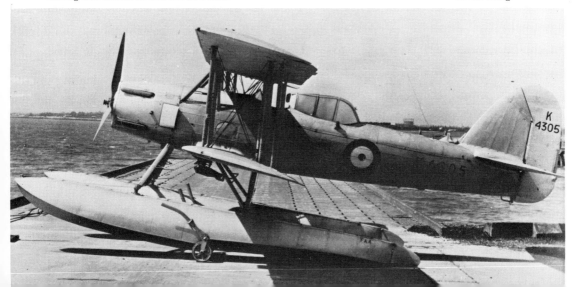

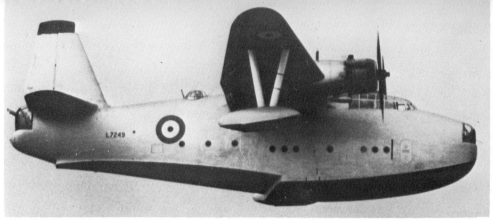

First production Saro Lerwick, L.7248.   *Westland Helicopters*

De Havilland Hornet Moth, P.6785 twin float seaplane at the M.A.E.E. The Hornet Moth was evaluated at Martlesham Heath during 1937, at the M.A.E.E. during 1938.

Dr Helena Hamilton

Consolidated 28-5, P.9630 at Felixstowe, January, 1939 after flying non-stop from Newfoundland. Later named Catalina, large numbers of these aircraft performed magnificent service in the Battle of the Atlantic.

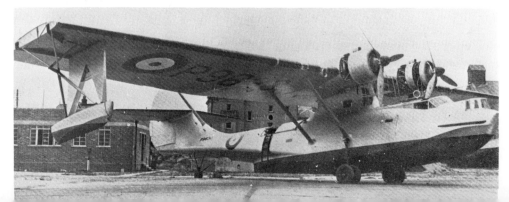

thought it incapable of flight. Mr Donald Smith of Ipswich recalls seeing the two "babies" in the same hangar at this time and it was interesting to compare the two. Built by Fluttachnische Fertigungsemeinschaft Prag, construction was started during 1942, but it was not ready until 1944. Built near Prague, it was eventually ready for transport by rail to Travemünde for flight testing, but "forced labour" workers somehow managed to "interfere" and let it slip when being loaded and it suffered considerable damage. When it did arrive for testing, its giant brother the BV.238 had already flown, so its usefulness was now limited. It was damaged on its first flight and then fuel problems caused cancellation of further trials. Forgotten by its makers, it was found by the Allies, shipped to Felixstowe and examined, but as far as can be ascertained, it never flew from there and was broken up during 1946.

Other captured aircraft were flown from the Continent to the M.A.E.E. and caused a stir among local enthusiasts. Included among the "visitors" were Blohm und Voss 138.Bs, VK.895, VM.743 and VN.887, Dornier, Do.24s VM.484, VN.865 and VN.870, Arado 196, VM.748 and VM.761 and several assorted Junkers, JU.52/53Ms and Dornier 18s. History came full circle with the arrival of the BV.138s as they were powered by three Junkers Jumo 205c diesel engines similar to those fitted to the pre-war Iris V.

Mr Parke of Felixstowe remembers the "visitors" when he was stationed at the M.A.E.E. "After the war several members of the M.A.E.E. were flown over to ex-Luftwaffe marine stations in Northern Germany to bring home captured aircraft to Felixstowe for evaluation. After familiarisation, the crews flew the boats home, but before departing Mr Parke was surprised to be given operating instructions in perfect English by one of the German ground crew. Asking the speaker where he had obtained his knowledge of the language, he replied that he had worked for a number of years pre-war at the Birmingham Small Arms Works in Birmingham."

The aircraft were tested for several months and Mr Parke recalls another incident: "One afternoon a severe gale blew up suddenly so he was instructed to move one of the Dornier Do.24s over to the Shotley side, which was the lee shore of the Harbour. With the flying boat's hull obeying the pull of the strong ebb tide, and the wind's effect on the aircraft's tailplane which caused it to weathercock, the aircraft continually tried to turn into the wind. This machine did not have wing tip floats but stub wings or sponsons, "Dornier-Stummel", as extensions of the planning hull. The tow proceeded slowly with the wing continually dipping under the influence of wind and tide, and eventually the hull started to take water and fill. The auxiliary power unit could not be started as it was flooded, denying the crew the chance of starting the main engines and the use of the bilge pump. Gradually the aircraft turned turtle, its crew scrambling into an accompanying launch in the nick of time. Some time later, the wreck was raised, the light alloy components of the engines almost

Short Sunderland Mark III, ML.765 later converted to Mark V, alongside the Felixstowe control tower in post-war days. This aircraft carried out extended trials in both the aerodynamic and hydrodynamic fields.   *E. Graystone*

eaten away by salt-water corrosion, but the three airscrews were in good shape."

Another observer arriving in Harwich Harbour on a leave-boat from the Continent noted 3 Junkers JU.52/3.Ms, 2 Blohm und Voss 138s and 1 Dornier Do.24, all painted overall black, moored off the Air Station.

Six years after the early Sunderlands had arrived for trials, they came again but this time in the form of the Mark V, and TX.293 was specially equipped with instruments for hydrodynamic experimental work which it carried out for several months. Two Mark IVs, MX.269 and MZ.271, both carried out extended experimental work during July, 1947. An engine fire which occurred in MX.269 finished its useful life and both the Mark IVs were scrapped at Felixstowe.

During October, 1945, the giant Short Shetland, DX.166, descended to the Harbour surface, its 160 foot wingspan being the largest that the M.A.E.E. had ever seen. Powered by four Bristol Centaurus radial engines, the 125,000 lb aircraft had a top speed of 263 m.p.h. and a range of 4,000 miles.

Misfortune stuck this aircraft early on 28th January, 1946, when it was moored off-shore. The duty crew started up the auxiliary power unit but as the ventilating vents were accidently left shut, the unit overheated and burst into flames. Unable to quell the fire, the crew abandoned ship, and the giant disappeared in a tremendous cloud of oily black smoke and flame beneath the surface of the Orwell. Trials had been satisfactory, and although the water characteristics were good, trouble was experienced with the wing floats and flying controls. Some years later, when dredging operations were taking place near the Felixstowe Dock Basin, one of the 2,500 h.p. Bristol engines was brought up complete with its huge four-bladed airscrew. When visiting R.A.F. Sutton Heath (Woodbridge) a few months later, Mr Donald Smith saw on a gigantic heap of wrecked aircraft near the runway, the lower hull of the

Shetland which had burned down to the water line. So ended the life of Britain's largest marine aircraft.

A great deal of research was carried out during the later half of 1946 into the water behaviour of flying boats, and the last Sunderland built, SZ.599, was engaged on these duties. Tests included alighting in choppy water to detect hull strains at weights of up to 80,000 lbs and the performance of wing floats and the rear fuselage. Two Short Seafords, NJ.200 and NJ.201, joined the test programme, but were not fitted with military equipment, operating only in the role of pure experimental aircraft.

During 1947, Sunderland SZ.599 was fitted with a faired main keel strip and a naturally vented after body. These devices were designed to break down water suction and improve take-off performance. Tests were not entirely satisfactory and further modifications were made, pieces put on and taken off, and all accurately recorded.

Unfortunately all this work was to no avail as the days of the flying boat were numbered and the valuable work merely became records. Another new venture to stand trial was the first jet fighter flying boat, the Saro SRA/I, TG.271. Designed as a single seat fighter for use in the Pacific, this sleek craft was novel in design and attained a top speed of 512 m.p.h., was armed with four-20 mm cannons and would have been a formidable weapon.

Tragedy struck this unique flying boat during 1949, when on the morning before the annual Battle of Britain Air Display, TG.271, piloted by Squadron

Largest ever for the R.A.F., the Short Shetland, DX.166, banks in graceful majesty, but alas its days were to be ended by the disastrous fire which destroyed it whilst at its moorings on 28th January, 1946. *Short Brothers*

Evaluated at the M.A.E.E. as a possible Air Sea Rescue aircraft, the Short Sealand amphibian enjoyed only limited success as a civil post-war aircraft. *Short Brothers*

The final development of the commercial flying boat, the Short Solent, many of which finished their days at Felixstowe awaiting the scrap-dealer's bid. *Short Brothers*

Leader Major took off to practice for the afternoon's event. Flying at speed offshore, the aircraft plunged into the sea and the pilot was killed, his body being washed up some time later.

A lady engaged in interesting work at the post-war M.A.E.E. was Mrs. Dawn Grace of Ipswich who was a Ministry of Supply Test Flight Observer. Starting during 1950 at the age of sixteen and half years, she progressed through the smaller routine jobs of calibrating speeds, cross-wind drifts and then to the more arduous tasks of flight test observations. With three other young lady colleagues, a variety of experimental work was carried out with the large post-war marine aircraft into many aspects of aerodynamic and hydro-dynamic behaviour. All was not plain sailing as many times the unexpected happened and Mrs Grace recalls that on the ominious date of Friday, 13th March, 1951, one engine of the test Sunderland she was in suddenly developed a serious engine oil leak after they were fully committed to taking-off. Many anxious moments were spent until the aircraft could be brought round over the harbour and alighted safely.

On another occasion, an engine malfunction caused a flying boat, which was just alighting, to turn violently. Mrs Grace, who was adjusting the Bell and Howell flight observation cine camera, had placed a pencil longwards in her mouth in order to use both hands, and the next thing she remembered was seeing a green wall of water through the cockpit forward windows. The pencil "bridled" her as she was hurled bodily against the side of the hull, but as the aircraft had alighted on the downward trough of the wave it lifted over the next crest and came to rest safely.

Some of the experiments demanded smooth water and still air conditions and so it was not unusual for the flight crews to be up and about at five a.m. in order to use the calm sea and air state. A great deal of flying was carried out in the early mornings with the Short Sunderland V, PP.162, and the Short Solent fitted with American built Pratt and Whitney radial motors. This later aircraft was worked up to a take-off weight of some 84,000 lbs or 37½ tons, considerably more than its initial design weight. Impact landings were also carried out and this necessitated the aircraft being put down very heavily on the water surface and then hurriedly brought ashore for hull damage inspection and assessment.

Mrs Grace and her colleagues remained with the M.A.E.E. until test flying ceased, when she carried on in the interesting work of the Blind Landing Experimental Unit at Martlesham Heath and finally at Farnborough.

As the interest in flying boats was on the wane, the M.A.E.E.'s work load decreased and the testing and trials of new marine aircraft almost became a thing of the past, and the work was mainly on testing new related systems.

Now a Ministry of Supply Unit, the M.A.E.E. was headed by a Civilian Superintendent, and under this cloak, worked on in the field of de-icing,

Too late for operational service, the unique Saro SRA.1 jet fighter flying boat served for a time at the M.A.E.E. before it crashed, but proved that this type of aircraft was a feasible proposition.
British Hovercraft Corporation

water stability, landing acceleration, boundary layer control and hull ventilation, and a number of established aircraft types were used for this work including the Sunderland, Seaford, Sea Otter and a few one-offs like the Supermarine Seagull A.S.R., all of which did a great deal of work and kept up an extremely good record of serviceability.

The wind of change blew over the banks of the Orwell when during June, 1948, for the first time the Operations Record Book was headed "R.A.F. Station, Felixstowe" instead of the more familiar Marine Aircraft Experimental Establishment. Even more gloomy was the recorded aircraft strength, one Sunderland, one Seaford, one Sea Otter, one Saro SRA/1.

Even the old-timers were disposed of, as now the tiny Saro Shrimp which had lived at the Station since its return from Scotland was broken up and sold for scrap. Short Seaford, NJ.201, had been progressively modified and during the years had collected a Solent type nose like the civil boats, as well as major modifications to the tail unit and wing floats. Re-named Solent, it was loaned to British Overseas Airways Corporation as a trainer, G-AGWU, and then during 1953 was sold to Aquila Airways as G-ANAJ and named "City of Funchal".

One of Short's last flying boats, the Sealand, G-AKLN, carried out trials at Felixstowe in the air-sea rescue role, being specially fitted with handrails on the hull, and dinghy packs under the wing. Felixstowe recommended better lateral control as the wing floats tended to dip in rough water and the aircraft had a starboard swing on calm water take-offs.

During March and April, 1951, the Short Solent IV, G-AKNS, "City of Liverpool" came to Felixstowe for stability trials at a weight of 84,000 lbs and for these trials the aircraft bore the R.A.F. serial, WM.759.

March 1956 was the dread month for it was then that the M.A.E.E. ceased to exist as a unit, the majority of the work being transferred to the Royal Aircraft Establishment, Farnborough in Hampshire. A small staff remained to carry on with experimental work which had been started on the design and development of scale models in plastic and wood for use as sub-sonic wind tunnel test pieces, and small metal models for supersonic wing tunnel tests.

Two years after the majority of the work had moved away, the Ministry of Supply Unit at Felixstowe ceased operations during March, 1958. The Superintendent in Charge at the time, Mr Spurr, began his retirement and so after forty-five years the name of Felixstowe and flying boats became history, a past era and the beginning of sentences "Do you remember at Felixstowe?".

A welcome sight to convoy seamen and shipwrecked mariners alike, the giant Short Sunderland, in many forms, served with several Air Forces in all parts of the world.   *Short Brothers*

CHAPTER FIVE

The Marines

IN ORDER to service and operate marine aircraft it was always necessary to maintain a marine section which embraced the necessary tenders, refuelling launches, rescue and fast fire launches.

Since the early days of the Air Station these servicing craft had been mainly ex-Royal Navy types of heavy construction and more suited for arduous sea duties than the speedy harbour work that was their role at Felixstowe.

The Marine Section had its own Officer in Charge, and a semi-permanent establishment of marine craft crews, as well as the unusual R.A.F. trade of "boat-builder". A member of this trade who served for many years at Felixstowe was Mr Symonds, who still lives within the sound of the Harbour, and possesses a wonderful photographic collection of the many and varied craft which served at the Air Station.

During 1923, the Marine Craft Experimental Unit was formed at Felixstowe and its purpose was to develop suitable boats for use with marine aircraft, and it carried out these duties until disbanded during 1934.

Several of the craft employed at Felixstowe were comparatively locally-built, being designed and constructed by Brooke Marine at Lowestoft. The first such craft were R.N.A.S. Nos. 972 and 973 which were delivered during November, 1977, whilst another batch of 35 foot Brooke launches, R.N.A.S. 1128, 1131 and 1133 were delivered during early 1918.

The next Brooke launches were again 35 foot designs, R.N.A.S. 147-148, and they arrived during November, 1928. The following year, two different craft appeared in the form of 24 foot Seacat Nos. R.A.F. 100 and 101, capable of 30 m.p.h. and used effectively by the High Speed Flight. It is recorded that they made the voyage from Lowestoft to Felixstowe in 95 minutes, and later ran from Felixstowe to Calshot in two days, without the slightest trouble.

Ex-Flight Sergeant Middleton, now living near Oxford, served in the Marine Section from 1924 until 1934 and remembers his days on the harbour waters with great clarity.

"The complement of marine craft at this time was one 50 foot 'Kelvin Cruiser' which was eventually replaced by a naval type diesel-engined pinnace and four 35 foot motor boats built by Brooke Marine at Lowestoft. The crew usually comprised a coxswain (a corporal), an engineer and two deck hands, and in service one boat patrolled the take-off and alighting areas, whilst a second remained at the slipway with engines running. Other duties involved towing flying boats and seaplanes to and from their moorings and the slipways.

One long tow was to the 'safe anchorage' up the River Orwell at Butterman's Bay near Pin Mill, when bad weather threatened. The wooded banks of the river provided a lee-shore for the flying boats against south-westerly gales, and the servicing crews stayed aboard the aircraft whilst they were anchored out. One of the facilities of the flying boat was that it was practically self-contained providing for its crew, sleeping and messing, and in many cases a small workshop for running repairs.

There was a floating dock permanently moored up-river off Fagborough beach but it was used only very rarely to repair below water damage to flying boats and marine craft. It was permanently manned by Flight Sergeants Thorne and Fell.

With the high water speeds of the High Speed Flight aircraft, the Brooke motor boats were wholly inadequate for rescue duties, and the high speed Chris-Craft boats of American design were introduced. They were similar to the ones used at seaside resorts for pleasure trips and their speed was appreciated by the pilots who after alighting, switched off their engines and the aircraft then just drifted with the wind and tide until taken in tow. The Chris-Craft boats were quickly on the scene in case of emergency, and tended the aircraft until the slower Brooke boat arrived. This then took the pilot off and picked up the tow. The American-designed boats were very unmanoeuverable at slow speeds when they also tended to wallow a great deal.

Another attempt to speed up the craft of the Marine Section came about when one of the Royal Navy's Motor Torpedo Boats (M.T.B.), was removed from its mothballed state of reserve in which it had been since the end of the First World War. A light wooden hull with two 12 cylinder Thorneycroft petrol engines which were started by compressed air, the craft was capable of 40

R.A.F. Launch No. 7, one of the ex-Naval craft used by the Marine Section of the R.A.F. for a number of years.   *S. D. Snell*

R.A.F. Launch No. 973, a 35ft Brooke fast craft, originally R.N.A.S. 973 delivered to Felixstowe, November, 1917.   *S. D. Snell*

knots. A crew including myself took over the boat at H.M.S. *Fishguard*, a shore based station at Gosport.

After the Schneider Trophy event we brought the M.T.B. back to Felixstowe for use with the High Speed Flight. Not long afterwards we were ordered to go to Donibristle in Scotland, for target towing duties with a squadron of torpedo bombers.

On the way north we hit very heavy weather and took a pounding in the Wash where we sprung a leak, but were able to limp to Bridlington and beach the craft in the harbour. For a fortnight we were billeted whilst repairs were carried out, and then the rest of the trip was cancelled and we were ordered back to Felixstowe. Very bad weather was encountered again on the way back, especially when we came abreast of Orfordness where the position became rapidly worse as we had to fight fires in both engines, which had been running very badly owing to foreign matter in the bottom of the nearly empty petrol tanks. We crawled into Felixstowe Dock with a sigh of relief, the coxswain on this occasion being Flight Lieutenant 'Laddie' Cliffe, a pilot from the M.A.E.E.

An unusual incident occurred when a Supermarine Southampton flying boat made a forced landing in the river near Orfordness and Motor Boat No. 150, a prototype of the modern A.S.R. launch, was despatched to Orford to attend to it. This involved quite a trip, including the hazardous entry to the River Ore at Shingle Street, and the boat could not return the same day, having to wait for the next daylight high tide. Overnight we were billeted out at the Jolly Sailors Inn in the village, and returned home safely the following day.

Another occurrence was when the rebuilt Blackburn Iris returned to Felixstowe and put the whole of the Station into a spin. Arriving safely, the large flying boat was taken to her moorings and put to bed for the night. To everyone's amazement the next morning only the top mainplane showed above the surface, the aircraft having sunk at her moorings overnight."

Another ex-"Marine-man" was Mr Hippersley of Chelmondiston who spent two spells at the M.A.E.E., and saw the gradual advance in design and performance of the boats. An ex-boy from Halton Apprentice School, he passed out as a Fitter, Marine, and serviced the earlier petrol-engined boats, and later, the more reliable diesels, many with names long since forgotten, Kelvin, Armstrong and Coventry.

As mentioned previously the Schneider Trophy events caused an additional work load at the M.A.E.E., and the Marine Section was busy attending to the various requirements of the High Speed Flight. Although the aircraft were usually launched from the slipways, high-speed launches and tenders were always at hand owing to the somewhat unstable nature of the high speed racing seaplanes.

As I write, a reminder of the small high speed racing aircraft's days at Felixstowe can been seen on the mud of the River Orwell near Ipswich Docks, in the shape of a flying boat towing lighter. Originally designed to carry flying boats across the North Sea on tow behind destroyers, as described in Chapter Two, the idea was conceived during the First World War and used from Felixstowe.

This particular craft was built at Cowes, Isle of Wight, and after various duties at Felixstowe was employed to service the Schneider Trophy aircraft when they were at the M.A.E.E.

Mr Robert Fox, the grandson of the boatbuilder who bought the lighter in a sale at Felixstowe during the early 30s says, "The engines of the seaplanes had castor oil lubrication and the oil had to be warmed before it was put into the engines, which were then started up. Likewise after the flight the oil was drained from the engine to prevent it thickening and gumming up the delicate machinery. This operation was carried out on the lighter which was fitted with

Brooke 35ft High Speed Launch, No. 151, roars along the "Sea Front" during 1928, powered by her 65 h.p. Brooke 6 cylinder motor.   *M. Tillyer*

Brooke 24ft Sea Cat, No. 101, powered by a 100 h.p. Brooke motor which gave it a speed of over 30 knots, leaves the Crane Pier during Empire Air Day, 1938.

via John Venmore-Rowland

compressed air bottles to enable it to be lowered into or raised up in the water in order to launch or retrieve the aircraft cradled in it. The specially developed hull enabled the lighter to be towed at speeds up to 30 knots when it was carrying the flying boats on their war errands.

The Ipswich example is in a bad state of disrepair but it is hoped that it will eventually be preserved for future viewing and as a memento of the First World War days and when speed in the air called for such support craft.

During 1945, No. 1103 Marine Craft Unit arrived at Felixstowe and was attached to the M.A.E.E., becoming a familiar sight and sound in the harbour and off the seafront as the boats roared about their business. A further development was the establishment of a Marine Training School. This latter unit stayed until 1948 when it moved to Pembroke Dock, South Wales.

The Station's craft assisted the Royal Navy in rescue work during the massive tidal surge of 31st January, 1953, whilst during April a fire float from the Station assisted the Fire Service at Parkeston Quay when the Danish North Sea ferry, *Kronsprins Fredric*, caught fire and capsized alongside the quay.

The following month, the rescue launches were in action again when the British Railways ferry *Duke of York* was in collision off Felixstowe. Their high speed was invaluable in taking blood plasma and medical staff to the crippled vessel and in bringing the injured ashore swiftly.

In a farewell demonstration on 20th May, 1938, H.S.L. 2688 of No. 1103 Marine Craft Unit and a Westland Whirlwind helicopter roared along Felixstowe seafront much closer inshore than usual to give the many spectators a close-up view of the operation. Later in the day, the launches left for their new station at Bridlington in Yorkshire.

One of the members of the Marine Section during the early 30s was 338171, Aircraftsman, First Class, Shaw T. E.; T. E. Lawrence, the Lawrence of Arabia. Shaw who during his previous service in the R.A.F. had been known as 352087 Aircraftsman John H. Ross, was posted to the Marine Craft Experimental Unit at Felixstowe during April 1932. Part of his assignment was to give advice, as well as test and report on suitable boats produced for the R.A.F. by British Power Boats Limited at their works at Hythe, Southampton. One of the conditions imposed on his posting was that he was to wear civilian clothes at all times when off the Station, and when he was visiting boatbuilding firms, in order to elude the ever-present publicity.

Shaw is reputed to have taken up the cause of the high speed rescue launch after witnessing a fatal flying boat crash when he was serving at R.A.F. Cattewater, now Mount Batten, Plymouth during 1931, and from that time he became obsessed with the development of what would be later called "Air-Sea Rescue Launches". Designs he put forward caused a stir in this sector of boat building, but it evidenced that his thinking bore fruit as the ex-Admiralty boats used by the R.A.F. at that time were replaced by the faster, lighter craft envisaged by his forward thinking.

Another aspect of his work was the testing and development of the R.A.F.'s then new armoured target launches, used as a moving target for live bombing by aircraft. In this connection it is reported that he would pilot the boat whilst the aircraft overhead bombed it, in order that he could make a first hand assessment of the results. The missiles used were of the light practice smoke bomb type.

Motor Launch, ex-R.N.A.S. No. 1359, alongside R.A.F. Seaplane Tender No. 1. Note the motorboat crew's "monkey-jacket" uniform, and the general spick and span appearance of the boat's equipment. *S. D. Snell*

This somewhat fragile looking collapsible dinghy was designed for stowage aboard aircraft to be used for ferrying duties.   *J. T. Hill*

An early inflatable rubber dinghy also used for ferrying purposes to and from moored aircraft. This type was named the "Airobote".   *J. T. Hill*

Many remember his personal speedboat which he brought to Felixstowe with him by its colour of light brown from which stemmed its curious name "The Biscuit". This craft, which Shaw treasured and used with great skill, had been given to him by an American gentleman, Major Colin Cooper.

An ex-companion recalls that after being away for a few days, Shaw arrived back at Felixstowe one day during 1932 in order to refuel an armoured target launch which he was taking from a South Coast boat yard round the coast to Bridlington, Yorkshire. During the evening he was observed walking along one of the jetties, hands behind his back, gaze fixed out across the silent waters of Harwich Harbour, his thoughts doubtless on the sands, not of the Orwell Estuary, but of the hot shifting wastes of the Middle East deserts.

Small and wiry, with soft blue eyes and a strong chin, he had a severe wound in his hip which prevented him taking any more than walking exercise.

One who knew him recalls that he arrived among their company in the routine manner and with no advance information, and no suspicion as to his identity. He declared that he was quite happy in the service, secure in his lowly rank from the charges that were made from time to time that he was acting for a mysterious agency in various parts of the world. He was absorbed in the day's routine which kept him healthily occupied and still left him with leisure for his first love of reading, writing and observing. This simple life was such as he would ordinarily have led outside the service had he been left alone to do so. He did not smoke or drink and ate very little. He had, in fact, monastic traits but could not have lived the restricted life, as he was a man of the open spaces.

It is difficult to work out studied appreciation of this fine character, who did the Royal Air Force such service; who left it with respect and with a legacy of his tribute, in his own cheerful conscientious record of duty. A man of intellect, great honours and pre-eminence who found a niche in the simplest grade.

Mr C. V. Pettitt of Cowlinge, Suffolk, recalls Shaw serving in the Motor Boat Section, going about his daily tasks of towing flying boats in to the slipway or refuelling them at their buoys. His work was always carried out to the letter of the law and no matter how long a task took, it was always executed in a first class manner. He was always regarded by his fellow airmen as a "lone wolf".

Mr L. F. Asbury of Colchester was in the same Barrack Room and remembers that he was not particularly approachable, keeping himself very much to himself. When he was in barracks he devoted his time to playing classical music on his gramophone. Most weekends he roared off on his Brough Superior motor-cycle on a Friday night and returned to Camp in the early hours of Monday morning.

Mr Good of Dovercourt also served with Shaw both at Felixstowe and in India and recalls that this genius of a man always refused promotion and that he absorbed the barrack room atmosphere, preferring it to the Officers' Mess where he was occasionally invited to attend Guest Nights. He thoroughly appreciated good music to the extent of very many classical records and as Mr Good was involved with the Station Orchestra at that time, he did have some talk with him on that subject.

Indications of the capabilities of this man occurred from time to time and one who knew him recalls: "One day on the firing range, when some of us had fired our annual pistol course and were departing, Shaw, who was acting as Range Orderly, quietly picked up a pistol when only two others were present and put six 'bulls' in the target!

He also made a point of volunteering for guards and pickets on any special occasion when the average airman wanted to be free, and I distinctly remember him on Christmas Day, absent from the feast in the Dining Hall, but very prominent as sentry at the Main Guard Room. Yet, in the same breath, this man could be equally at ease conversing with the Air Officer, Commanding."

Mr C. E. Hippersley of Chelmondiston served with Shaw both at Felixstowe and Bridlington and remembers him, not always as the recluse, but on the odd occasion, joining in with the boats' crews in an evening's entertainment.

Whilst at Felixstowe he had visitors of a secretive nature, and it is rumoured that Mr George Bernard Shaw was one of his regular visitors.

Shaw left the R.A.F. on 26th February, 1935, and ten weeks later, on the 13th May, whilst riding his motor cycle near his cottage in Dorset he was involved in an accident on a lonely country road. He died six days later without recovering consciousness, aged forty-seven.

Thus, the legendary Lawrence of Arabia, who had braved the burning deserts and for a while, the cruel moods of the grey North Sea, is remembered in a quiet Dorset churchyard at Moreton by this inscription:

TO THE DEAR MEMORY OF
T. E. LAWRENCE,
FELLOW OF ALL SOULS COLLEGE,
OXFORD.
BORN 16 AUGUST, 1888.
DIED 19 MAY, 1935.

The hour is coming, and now is
When the dead shall hear
The voice of the
SON OF GOD
And they that hear
Shall live.

DOMINUS ILLUMINATIC MEA.

The Second World War saw an outstanding example of co-operation between two of the Services, when the Royal Air Force and the Royal Navy combined their resources to carry out the vital operation of Air Sea Rescue. These two arms were assisted in their efforts by the Royal National Life-boat Institution, the Royal Observer Corps, Trinity House and the civil maritime

Left: Squadron Leader W. H. Jinman, M.B.E., Commanding Officer of the Marine Section and M.T. Officer, 1931-1937, and right: the wading clothing worn by aircraft handling parties when launching and retrieving aircraft off the slipways.

Right hand illustration J. T. Hill

fleets. To show the importance of the tasks performed, the rescue services saved 5,700 Allied airmen from the sea around the British Isles in the period February, 1941 to May, 1945.

As mentioned previously, the R.A.F. had been developing its high speed craft proven for this role, and were using designs by the established firms of Thorneycrofts, Vospers, British Power Boats and Walton Thames, joined later by those of Fairmiles.

Measuring between 60 feet and 70 feet in length, the H.S.Ls had rakish lines and were lightly constructed using the latest methods of laminated plywood as used in aircraft construction. They were also akin to their airborne colleagues in that they used, in the main, liquid cooled aero engines ranging from the pre-war Napier Lion to the modern Packard built Rolls Royce Merlins.

The gentlemen's agreement that the opposing rescue boats would operate umolested came to an end during August, 1941, when Luftwaffe aircraft carried out attacks on A.S.R. craft. The early type defensive gun turrets, of aircraft design, usually two in number and mounting a 0.303 inch machine gun, were replaced by harder hitting twin Browning guns in each turret. The last of the Vosper A.S.R. launches, a 72 foot design, carried three such turrets, two forward alongside the bridge and another one aft.

With their dark blue or black hulls and bright orange decks, large white number and R.A.F. roundel on the forward hull, the craft of No. 26 A.S.R. (Marine Craft) Squadron made a brave sight, roaring across the North Sea. With up-lifted prow and signal flags streaming back from their short masts, the hull was almost hidden behind the pulsating white bow wave of spray whilst astern lifted the arc of wake thrown up by the fast revving twin screws. The roar of the boats at speed was most impressive, but most welcome to men down in the sea, no matter from which side they came.

In order to cover the scene of the action, the A.S.R. boats from Felixstowe and other East Coast bases maintained standing patrols far out in the North Sea. This put them under the bomber streams which were on their way to and from their European targets, and thus they were in a far better position to effect rescues. These patrols were in constant danger of attack by Luftwaffe aircraft and on several occasions they were attacked and casualties inflicted on their crews.

With the arrival of the American Eighth Air Force in the United Kingdom, based as it was in the Eastern Counties many more calls were made on the A.S.R. services. As the fleets of day bombers passed out towards Occupied Europe, the boats took up their positions, and when the smoking and failing bombers returned, many to drop into the sea, the boats' engines roared out as they raced to pick up the survivors.

Three differing types of R.A.F. marine craft in Felixstowe Dock are from left to right: Refuelling Launch, High Speed Fire and Rescue Launch, and High Speed Tender Launch.

After 1943 it became a twenty-four hour vigil with the U.S.A.A.F. by day and the R.A.F. by night requiring the assistance of their watching and waiting colleagues afloat.

A notable rescue was made by an A.S.R. launch from Felixstowe during June, 1942. Defying the repeated attacks by five German "E" Boats it carried out its task and successfully picked up the complete crew of a bomber from their rubber dinghy in the mouth of the River Maas. This action was the basis for the post war film "The Sea Shall Not Have Them", made at Felixstowe during 1954.

The A.S.R. launches which operated from Felixstowe during the war were responsible for saving 484 lives for the loss of one launch. Two officers, one senior N.C.O., and five other ranks were killed in action.

In the post-war days, as related elsewhere, the A.S.R. launches carried out valuable work, both military and civil, and when the helicopters arrived to carry out this work the launches worked in co-operation with them, in most cases supporting the airmen or seamen if badly injured until they could be picked up by their airborne companions. They operated, as far as possible, with the Royal National Life-boat Institution's lifeboats.

During the summer months when the air and sea rescue units were exercising off the seafront, they were always a centre of attention, and many a hand was waved to the helicopter crews as they flew low along the beach on their daily patrols. Many visitors will recall the airmen, wearing their bright yellow lifejackets, sitting in the open door hatches as the Whirlwind passed slowly along the shoreline.

These aircraft of No. 22 Squadron, "B" Flight, took up residence during May 1956, when they transferred from Martlesham Heath and they became a very familiar sight in the district.

Two Norwegian seamen suffering from severe burns were picked up by a helicopter, 38 miles off Orfordness, Suffolk, on 11th November, 1956. Their vessel was the *San Miguel*, and the men were hurt when fire broke out in the engine room, but was eventually got under control.

On Monday, 19th May, 1958, a report in the local newspaper stated: "The winchman was killed when an R.A.F. A.S.R. helicopter crashed into the sea off Felixstowe. He was named as Sergeant D. W. Frampton of Manor Park, Essex, whilst the pilot, Flight Lieutenant K. Alderson of Felixstowe suffered a broken leg and spine injuries. A third member of the crew, the navigator, was not injured."

When the A.S.R. launches of No. 1103 Marine Craft Unit left during May, 1959, the Whirlwinds stayed on, but now had to carry the whole operation through by themselves or in co-operation with the R.N.L.I.

On 21st August, 1960, a Whirlwind rescued two men whose yacht had capsized off shore. The two Ipswich men were spotted clinging to the side of their upturned boat by a look-out at the Coastguard Station. Within ten minutes of the call going out, the helicopter had landed the men at the Air Station where they were given hot baths and a tot of rum.

The dreaded day approached for the cessation of activities from Felixstowe and this came on 29th May, 1961, when the Whirlwinds of "B" Flight made their last sortie from the Air Station and departed for Tangmere, Sussex, their new home.

CHAPTER SIX

High Speed Flight

ONE of the most coveted trophies in the history of aviation was the Schneider Trophy, given by the French armament manufacturer and aircraft enthusiast, M. Jacques Schneider, to the French Aero Club and valued at the time, 1912, at 25,000 francs. This spectacular trophy crafted in gold, silver and bronze was the premier award in an international speed race for marine aircraft. The award also carried a considerable amount of prize money.

To be held annually, the contest's winner would retain the trophy until the next event, but the first contestant to win the event on three consecutive occasions would then keep the trophy for all time. Limitations were that the contest would take place over open water, that the aircraft were seaworthy, and the contestants from any one country were restricted to three in number. Seaworthiness trials took place before the trials proper and comprised three take-offs and landings, two taxi-ing tests of half a mile at a speed of not less than twelve knots, followed by mooring trials with the aircraft riding at a buoy for six hours to ensure that the landings had not produced leaks in the hulls or floats. No major components such as engines, propellers, wings, etc., were allowed to be changed although parts of these could be replaced.

The first race was organised by the French and flown during April, 1913 at Monaco, the winner being the home team, the only other contestant being a French-built Nieuport seaplane flown by Mr C. T. Weymann of the United States of America.

As the French were now the holders, the 1914 event was held at Monaco again, but this time the trophy was brought home to Great Britain by Mr Howard Pixton who flew his Sopwith seaplane over the 28 lap course of 150 nautical miles at an average speed of 86.8 m.p.h.

War intervened for the next four years, and then Great Britain as the holder staged the 1919 event. To be flown over a 220 nautical mile course, the competitors took-off in a heavy mist and the only one to find his way almost round the course, and finish, was Janello of Italy. The race was declared null and void, but Italy was awarded the venue for the next contest, which was held at Venice the following year and won by the host country at a speed of 107.2 m.p.h. They won again during 1921 at an average speed of 111 m.p.h., but this time there were no challengers, so the Italians had merely to fly the course.

Italy, still the host country, and looking for the all-important third win, moved the venue to Naples for the 1922 series, and put in a team of seaplanes against the privately sponsored British entry, a Supermarine Sea Lion flying

R.A.F. High Speed Launch 2561 slips out of the Dock Basin.   *F. V. Powell*

boat with a Napier Lion engine. Flown by Captain Biard, this somewhat ungainly biplane managed to attain an average speed of 145.7 m.p.h. and bring the Trophy back to Great Britain again.

Cowes, Isle of Wight, was the meeting place for the 1923 series, when Captain Biard was to do battle again in his further modified Sea Lion III, but both Great Britain and France had to give second best to the U.S.A., the race being won by the American Navy Curtiss R-3 seaplanes.

Technical progress had enabled a top speed of 177.3 m.p.h. to be reached, and the fastest pilot was Lieutenant Rittenhouse of the United States Navy, the team being wholly financed, prepared and manned by the U.S. Government.

In preparation for the 1924 event, to be held in America, in which the Royal Air Force were to participate, two specially built racing seaplanes, the Gloster IIs, were being readied. The first one, serialled J.7504, was taken by road to Felixstowe on 12th September, 1924, where it was erected and prepared for test flights. One week later, piloted by Captain Hubert Broad, the first flight took place, but once airborne, the pilot found the seaplane excessively tail heavy. Making one or two gentle circuits, he brought the racer in as slowly as possible to alight, but as soon as it touched the surface of the water, it porpoised and a float collapsed under the stress. The Gloster II sank rapidly, but the pilot managed to struggle out of the small cockpit and was rescued, shaken but unhurt.

The second Gloster II racer was never flown as a seaplane but was later involved in a tragic 200 m.p.h. landing crash at Cranwell, Lincolnshire.

With Great Britain's entry non-existent, and the Italians forced to withdraw, the Americans sportingly called off the 1924 series, and decided to hold the event over until the following year. This series, held at Baltimore was won by the hosts, Lieutenant James Doolittle* of the U.S. Navy attaining a speed of 232.5 m.p.h. in his Curtiss R3C-2 seaplane. This was ironical, for if the United States had only flown over the course the previous year, they would now be the all-time holders of the trophy.

The Royal Air Force entry for the 1925 event was another Gloster built highly streamlined racing biplane seaplane, the Gloster III. Serialled N.194, it arrived at Felixstowe and began taxi-ing trials on 16th August, 1925, the first flight being made on the 29th August, piloted once again by Captain Broad. Powered by a 700 h.p. Napier Lion, the 20 foot wingspan biplane was of wooden construction with metal floats, and in order to provide adequate cooling for the motor coolant, considerable areas of the airframe carried radiator surfaces.

The first flight passed off without event, but certain modifications were carried out in order to improve the directional stability, the modified aircraft being re-designated Gloster IIIA.

---

*Lieutenant James Doolittle some twenty years later led the first air attack on Japanese mainland in Mitchells from the carrier U.S.S. *Wasp*.

The second Gloster IIIA aircraft, N.195, was also flown at Felixstowe by Mr Bert Hinkler, appointed by Gloster to test it, and then with N.194 was crated and shipped to Baltimore for the race, where N.194 finished second at a speed of 199 m.p.h., 33 m.p.h. slower than the winner. Ill luck had dogged the British team, as Captain Biard had crashed into the sea in the Supermarine S.4., N.197, whilst Bert Hinkler, in N.195, had been forced to retire during the taxi-ing trials when his aircraft's float struts collapsed.

On their return to England, both Gloster racers were modified and returned to Felixstowe for trials and development flying and were used eventually as high speed trainers by the 1927 team. In their modified IIIB form they were capable of 252 m.p.h., had an alighting speed of 80 m.p.h., and were outstanding for their clean lines and small dimensions.

The National Physical Laboratory at Teddington conducted tests on a scale model of the Supermarine S.5 in preparation for the 1926 event, but these were abandoned and Great Britain could muster neither men nor machines for the the eighth series. The Italians sent a strong force to the United States, comprising Macchi M.39 monoplane racers fitted with 800 h.p. Fiat engines, and these outpaced the American Curtiss seaplanes, winning the event at a speed of 246.4 m.p.h., and the Trophy once again went back to Italy.

The Air Ministry now took up the challenge of the Schneider Trophy seriously, and on 1st October, 1926, the High Speed Flight was formed at

Gloster III Schneider Trophy racing biplane at the M.A.E.E., with a paddle steamer at the Dock Pier and a view of Harwich Church across the river.   *J. T. Hill*

Known as "The Curious Ada", the Short Bristow Crusader Schneider racer was unusual in having an air-cooled radial motor which caused considerable panic on many occasions whilst being flown at the M.A.E.E.   *Short Brothers*

Felixstowe, commanded by Wing Commander Maycock and Squadron Leader Leslie J. Slatter, the purpose of the Flight being to provide a source of experimental high speed seaplane pilots. Overall responsibility was in the hands of Air Vice Marshal F. R. Scarlett, and the members of the Flight were Flight Lieutenant O. E. Worsley from the M.A.E.E., Flight Lieutenant S. N. Webster and Flying Officer H. M. Scholefield from the A. and A.E.E., Martlesham Heath, whilst Flight Lieutenant Kinkead joined shortly afterwards.

One of the objectives of the High Speed Flight was to investigate ways and means of improving British aircraft speed which, at this time, was lacking when compared with foreign types.

High speed development work was carried out at the M.A.E.E. using the Gloster racer, N.195, further modified and reclassified Gloster IIIB and now sporting additional radiator surfaces and larger tailplanes areas. Its sister, N.194, was used to test propellers of various designs and to gather data on propeller tip speeds. Wing Commander A. L. Orlebar, who had now assumed command of the High Speed Flight, flew N.195 and described her as "a nice little thing, but a bit fierce".

The first of the British contenders for the 1927 Contest arrived at Felixstowe late in April, this being the Short Bristow Crusader, N.226, which became known to all and sundry at the M.A.E.E. as the "Curious Ada". A twin float low-wing monoplane, it was unusual in that it was powered by a nine-cylinder Bristol Mercury air-cooled radial motor of 800 h.p. First flown by a civilian, Mr Bert Hinkler, it buckled a float whilst alighting and had to be hastily run up onto the slipway to prevent it sinking. The first R.A.F. pilot to fly the Crusader was Flight Lieutenant Webster and he was followed by Flying Officer Scholefield, both of whom discovered erratic behaviour with the not fully developed power unit.

This caused many anxious moments for all concerned, as it was unpredictable in every way, and many fast touch-downs had to be made when the motor cut out. Flying Officer Scholefield experienced one particularly nerve-racking occasion, when during July he was flying eastwards along Felixstowe seafront and the motor "played up" suddenly. With the beach on one side, the pier in front, and choppy open sea on the other hand he had no alternative but to put down straight ahead, and this he did successfully. A few days later, after it was alleged that all the troubles had been sorted out, another engine malfunction manifested itself, but by careful nursing, the pilot managed to get the Crusader back onto the surface of the River Orwell. It was later discovered that unsuitable sparking plugs caused the motor to give reduced power, and although a second power unit was fitted, this was still only capable of reduced power.

During mid-July, the High Speed Flight moved from Felixstowe to Calshot, in Hampshire, and it was there that they received their other aircraft, the three Supermarine S.5s, N.219, N.220 and N.221, and the two Gloster IVs, N.223 and N.224, all of which were Napier Lion powered. The Supermarine aircraft were delivered to Calshot in order to be close to the maker's works at Woolston, near Southampton, and in any case were only ready shortly before the event.

The "Curious Ada" had remained at Felixstowe when the High Speed Flight left for Calshot, and the Press had been invited to the M.A.E.E. during

Fairey Flycatcher alights off the Air Station. This type of aircraft was used as a high speed trainer by the High Speed Flight in order to give the pilots the necessary high speed training.   *M. Tillyer*

143

Fairey Firefly III, S.1592 was used as a high speed trainer by pilots of the High Speed Flight.
Westland Aircraft

early August to see it in action. Flying Officer Scholefield came back to Felixstowe to fly it, but must have been relieved when he arrived to see the choppy water which would make flying impossible. The gentlemen of the Press had to be content with a quick but noisy engine run-up, and a close look round. Later in the month, the Crusader was crated and despatched to Venice, where it was to be the reserve machine.

On the 1st September, Flying Officer Scholefield made a full load trial after the Crusader had been reassembled, but, soon after take-off, the aircraft rolled over and plunged into the water at over 150 m.p.h. The pilot, who had been thrown out, was picked up badly bruised but without broken bones. Investigations showed that the aileron control wires had been wrongly assembled, thus giving the aircraft reverse control characteristics to those desired by the pilot. For the record, the Bristol Mercury motor was later fully developed and powered a number of successful British aircraft.

Misfortune also struck one of the Gloster machines, N.223: when being flown by Flight Lieutenant Kinkead on 26th September, at a speed of around 275 m.p.h., the motor faltered and vibrated. Cautiously slowing up, the pilot brought the IV.B down safely and examination revealed that the propeller shaft was cracked three-quarters of the way through it. The decision to abandon the flight had saved Flight Lieutenant Kinkead's life.

Nevertheless it was a good day for Great Britain as Flight Lieutenant Webster in the Supermarine S.5, N.220, won the event at an average speed of

144

281.65 m.p.h., bringing the Trophy back to the British Isles. Flight Lieutenant Worsley in the other S.5, N.219, was second at 273 m.p.h., the difference between N.219 and N.220 being that the former had a direct drive Lion motor as opposed to the latter's geared engine.

The Operations Record Book for 1927 very coldly records:

"Schneider Cup Team returned to Unit". No mention was made that they had won the Trophy, merely the fact that they had returned!

Squadron Leader Coombes recalls, "The High Speed Flight days were full of incidents and recollections. Squadron Leader Slatter was not the most popular of C.Os and wasn't on the best of terms with his pilots. Originally there were six pilots. Webster, Worsley, Kinkead, Scholefield, Rex Stocken and Johnny Chick. Earlier on, Stocken had made a practice flight in the Gloster and after alighting he was supposed to keep the engine running until the motor boat had fixed the towing line. He stopped his engine as the boat approached and the wind turned him over—the floats' lack of buoyancy aft causing this. Slatter promptly sacked him from the Team, and a little later he sacked Chick for some alleged act of insubordination—quite trivial, I'm sure. He never flew any of the high speed seaplanes; Orlebar insisted on being the first to fly each new plane. Mr Bert Hinkler was engaged to make the first flight of the Crusader and he arrived at Felixstowe in his famous bowler hat. He took the aircraft off, flew it around very cautiously and landed badly. He was obviously relieved to get out of the aircraft and the Flight Lieutenant Webster took it up and threw it around in vertical banks—such a contrast which showed how good the service test pilots were. I was the Technical Officer for the Fiight and accompanied it to Venice. Flying Officer Moon was the Service Engineering Officer and he fitted up an aeroplane case as a

The graceful Gloster IVA biplane Schneider racer, Napier Lion powered, and one of the fastest biplanes ever built. Served at Felixstowe for a considerable period as a high speed trainer when its racing days were finished.

travelling workshop, loading it with much heavy equipment. When the crane lifted it from the jetty at the M.A.E.E. to load it onto the ship taking it to Venice, the bottom, weighed down by the contents, remained on the jetty, as the side and top soared aloft.

At Venice, when the Crusader was assembled, there were no markings on the aileron cables and they were connected up wrongly. The fact that the ailerons were working the wrong way was not detected by the ground engineers or the pilot and Scholefield took off in perfectly calm conditions, Just after becoming airborne, he corrected a bump and, of course, wrongly, so that the aircraft rolled over and crashed in the water. The cockpit was a very tight fit and Scholefield was lucky to escape — he lost his shoes. He was badly shaken and was out of the race.

The Italians sent a floating crane which lowered a grapnel and pulled up the main electric power cable between Venice and the Lido! Luckily it wasn't damaged and a diver went down and put the slings on the sunken aircraft.

The day before the race all the competing aircraft had to be moored out for twelve hours to demonstrate seaworthiness. A great storm blew up, but fortunately all the aircraft survived, but conditions remained so bad that the race was postponed for 24 hours."

A decision was taken at the end of 1927 to hold the Trophy Competition every other year, so the next series would be held in England during 1929.

During this year a new High Speed Flight was formed at Felixstowe on 1st February, commanded by Squadron Leader A. H. Orlebar, A.F.C., and other members of the Unit were Flight Lieutenants D. D.'A. A. Greig, D.F.C., A.F.C., G. H. Stainforth, and Flying Officers R. L. R. Atcherley and H. R. D. Waghorn. The Engineering Officer was Flying Officer T. H. Moon, who had been with the 1927 Team and only he and a nucleus of airmen remained from this Team. Of the former members, Flight Lieutenant S. N. Webster had been posted to other duties, whilst Flight Lieutenant H. M. Kinkead had been killed flying the Supermarine S.5, N.221, whilst making an attempt on the World's Air Speed Record.

Awaiting their aircraft for the 1929 contest the team practised at Felixstowe with the Gloster IVs, N.222, N.223 and N.224, and a Fairey Flycatcher, S.1288, seaplane. Much apprehension was caused at the M.A.E.E. when Atcherley on his first flight in the Gloster IV rolled and looped the essentially "straight and level" racer. The aircraft did not suffer in any way, the manoeuvres being carried out perfectly, but the "powers that be" frowned at the happening and strict orders were issued forbidding all such stunts.

The full complement of the Flight was complete on 1st February, 1929, and all the pilots put in as much flying as possible on the high speed trainers. Ground crew numbered about thirty, as stated previously, with a core of the "old hands" and the number made up with known "good" men.

Members of the High Speed Flight. Left to right: F/Lt Hope, Lt Brinton, F/Lt Long, F/Lt Stainforth, S/Ldr Orlebar, F/Lt Boothman, F/O Snaith and F/Lt Dry. *Vickers Limited*

The Schneider Trophy returned to Felixstowe on the occasion of the Closing Down ceremony.

An aged motor boat allocated to the Flight proved very troublesome in service, so two Lowestoft-built Brooke motor boats were made available, one for the use of the medical crew in case of trouble and the other for towing the aircraft and their lighters.

Wing Commander Orlebar described flying the aircraft thus; "Very much like single-seat fighters, but they sink a lot on the alighting approach and must be kept in the air until touch down which is at a quite high rate of knots. The approach to the surface must be as level as possible."

Training started on the two-seat Vickers Vendace, N.208, borrowed from the M.A.E.E., and this was followed by the single seat Fairey Flycatcher and the Avro Avocet, N.209 and N.210, also borrowed from the same source.

The competition aircraft, built solely for racing, responded to the slightest changes made in their rigging and as the engines were in the same category they needed plug changes every third flight and a complete examination every two hours, followed by an engine change every 12½ hours flying time. Everything had to be at the peak of perfection as the Rivers Orwell and Stour did not offer a great deal of room for a hasty landing, the harbour with its shipping being the only real landing place into the wind in any direction.

Another hazard at this time were large floes of ice floating off the Air Station, carried down by the rivers, and this in March! These caused a great deal of discomfort to the waders whose job it was to work in the water up to their waists in order to launch and land the aircraft. Wash from large vessels also caused a halt to flying as this had to be allowed to subside before the frail aircraft could taxi.

During March, the Gloster IV.A, N.222, and IV.B, N.223, were returned to their makers for modifications to their tail units, and on their return to the Flight were used as "hacks" by the team.

The Flight left Felixstowe for Calshot on 9th April, 1929, the equipment by train, the Gloster IV, N.223, by road and "Waggon" (Waghorn) and "Batchy" (Atcherley) flew the Flycatcher and Avocet to their new home. Three civilian technicians from Farnborough joined the Flight before they left, Messrs Clarke, Hardy and Wright, and they were responsible for the special instruments carried by the aircraft.

The 1929 Contest took place off Ryde, Isle of Wight, and for the first time Rolls-Royce motors were used, these being a special racing design for the new Supermarine S.6 seaplanes, N.247 and N.248. Evolved from the Buzzard, the "R", as the new motor was named, was capable of 1,900 horse power at 2,900 r.p.m., and this for a weight of 1,530 lbs, a truly remarkable achievement. Mated to R. J. Mitchell's elegant airframe it was the smallest possible combination of engine and airframe, presenting the minimum frontal area. Incorporated in the airframe were radiators to dissipate the terrific engine temperature of 50,000 B.T.Us per minute and virtually the whole of the airframe including the floats were used for this purpose.

As a stable mate the S.6s had the gold-painted Gloster VI, N.249, this time a monoplane with beautiful lines and of mixed wood and metal construction. Unfortunately its Napier Lion VII D motor was not performing as well as desired and in spite of endless work by the ground crews it was forced to retire from the event.

The other contestants, the Italians, requested, but were refused, extra time to sort out their machine problems, but nevertheless put up a good show in their new Macchi M.67s, capable of 350 m.p.h. The United States Navy refused Lieutenant Al Williams permission to race in the Mercury monoplane, so it was left to Great Britain and Italy.

Despite the strong opposition, Flying Officer Waghorn won the 1929 Contest in S.6., N.247, covering the 50 kilometre course seven times at an average speed of 328.63 m.p.h., with Flying Officer Atcherley second in the other S.6., N.248, at 325 m.p.h. He was later disqualified for missing a marker after losing his goggles, but a few days later, S.6, N.248 was flown by Flight Lieutenant Stainforth to a new world airspeed record of 336.31 m.p.h., only to have it broken by Squadron Leader Orlebar at a speed of 355.8 m.p.h. in the same aircraft.

Back at Felixstowe in preparation for the 1931 event, the Flight was hampered by the lack of engines for the aircraft. The 1929 winner, S.6A, N.247, had been packed off on a grand exhibition tour, and N.248 was awaiting a new engine which arrived during April. New pilots were also posted to the Flight, Flight Lieutenants Long and Boothman to replace Waghorn and D'Arcy Greig.

Supermarine S.6, N.247 aboard its launching lighter, where the castor oil for the engine was heated and put in and then removed when the racer returned to the lighter.

Practice flying took place when the weather allowed and a speed course was laid out from Landguard Point to Felixstowe New Pier, which gave good approaches to it, and no shipping to interfere with their high-speed runs.

Squadron Leader Orlebar had a frightening experience during August 1930, with the Gloster VI, N.249, when, after launching from the slipway, the motor failed to pick up and as the idling speed was greater than that of the rescue boat, Orlebar switched-off in order that it could catch up. In the meantime, N.249 was being carried by a strong tide onto one of the several piers. The handling crew, led by Boothman, dashed along the water front to give assistance, Orlebar having climbed out of the cockpit and slid as far aft as possible along the rear fuselage in order to fend the rear of the aircraft off from the pier, but smart work by the attendant boat crew placed their craft between the aircraft and the pier and so saved a casualty.

Flight Lieutenant Boothman also had a nasty few moments in the same aircraft a little later, when a rudder control turnbuckle became unlocked and he could only move it to one side. By careful use of the ailerons he got the racer back on the water without damage, but the machine was taken out of service shortly afterwards.

Two up and one to go, but the Air Ministry were still very reluctant to fund money for the third and, hopefully, final attempt, which Great Britain had a very good chance of winning. The 1929 machines had made almost faultless performances and the High Speed Flight Team had the experience to man them. Still no word came from the higher circles and eventually a public outcry stemmed from publicity regarding this indecision.

At the eleventh hour, the richest lady in Great Britain, Lady (Lucy) Houston financed the 1931 Team for the event and the £100,000 needed for the airframes and engines became available.

Supermarine and Rolls-Royce applied all their expertise to the project and modified versions of the "R" engine and the S.6 airframe were proceeded with. The S.6.B was even more covered with radiator cooling surfaces in order to dissipate the even greater heat from the more powerful motor, and as an example of the ingenuity of design, even the tail-fin became the integral oil tank.

The Gloster IV.A, N.222 and IV.B, N.223 were used once again as high speed trainers and experimental aircraft, but on 19th December, 1930, N.223 broke in half when alighting in fog, but the pilot, Flight Lieutenant Boothman, was not injured. The weather had been foggy, but cleared and Boothman took N.223 up; however, soon after take-off the fog clamped down again and he decided to come down as quickly as possible. Being apparently deceived by the hazy horizon he decreased his flying speed to a dangerous degree and landed very heavily, the racer breaking its back on impact. Going down with the wreckage, Boothman managed to get clear and, on surfacing,

The final victor, Supermarine S.6.B, S.1595, the type which during the 1931 Schneider Trophy Event won the Trophy for Great Britain for all time.   *Vickers Limited*

clung to one of the floats until rescued. With shoes filled with mud he could prove that he had really been to the bottom of the river.

The 1931 Team comprised: Squadron Leader A. H. Orlebar, A.F.C.; Flight Lieutenants E. J. L. Hope, A.F.C.; F. W. Long; J. N. Boothman; G. H. Stainforth; Lieutenant R. L. Brinton, Fleet Air Arm; Flying Officers L. S. Snaith; Leech; Flight Lieutenant W. F. Dry, Engineering Officer; Flying Officer Castaldini, Marine Officer; Flying Officer M. F. Tomkins, Stores Officer; Mr Ransome, A.I.D. Inspector, Supermarines; Mr Lovesey, Rolls Royce Representative; Mr Cushing, Test Assistant.

The Flight were grieved when the news was received that their former colleague, "Waggon" (Waghorn) had been killed in an experimental Hawker Horsley at Farnborough. He was respected and loved by all the previous Flight members. After a short stay with the Flight, Lieutenant Brinton and Flying Officer Leech were posted, but Brinton returned before the event and was killed in N.247 at Calshot.

The majority of the practice flying was carried out in the Fairey Firefly, S.1592, the Fairey Fleetwing, N.235, and an Armstrong Whitworth Atlas, J.9998, all biplane twin float single-engined floatplanes borrowed from the M.A.E.E.

On 14th May, 1931, the High Speed Flight which had been formed at Felixstowe once again for the 1931 event, left for Calshot for advanced training. Their aircraft comprised two S.5s, N.220 and N.221, two Gloster VIs, N.249 and N.250, and a Gloster IV, N.224, joined later by the two S.6.As, N.247 and N.248.

During July the two new S.6.Bs, S.1595 and S.1596, were received and the chances appeared very good.

The Italians and the French were the other contestants, but the former's Macchi aircraft were too far advanced in design to be ready in time for the event, and they withdrew. The French team also "called off" and so it merely left Great Britain to over-fly the course. This was carried out on 13th September, 1931, firstly by Flight Lieutenant Boothman in S.6.B, S.1595, who averaged 340.8 m.p.h. which won the Trophy permanently for Great Britain. Later in the day Flight Lieutenant Stainforth set off in the other S.6.B, S.1596, to have a crack at the World Airspeed Record, and this he did splendidly with a speed of 379.05 m.p.h. over a 3 kilometre course.

On 29th September, Flight Lieutenant Stainforth took up the special engined S.6.B, S.1595, and broke his own record with an average speed of 407.5 m.p.h., although on one run he had achieved 415.2 m.p.h.

This famous machine with its 2,530 h.p. Rolls-Royce "R" engine can be seen in the Science Museum, London, as part of the National Aeronautical Collection.

The Gloster machines did good work in the background and the VI, N.250, carried out experimental work at the M.A.E.E., but the motor troubles which had plagued it throughout its life still persisted and latterly it was rarely flown, and then only at reduced throttle settings. Giving a limited period 1,320 h.p., the Napier Lion VII.D made the VI capable of 351 m.p.h., but unfortunately the ingenious airframe was frustrated by the unreliable sprint motor.

Before leaving these highly developed aircraft it is interesting to note the fuel used in the sprint engines consisted of 74.78 per cent petrol, 25 per cent benzole and 0.22 per cent dope, and the formula was arrived at after a great deal of experimental work. The benzole and dope content also created problems with the sparking plugs, causing them to carbon-up, and after only a short period of idling the engines would misfire badly when opened up to full power.

CHAPTER SEVEN

The Little Ships

DURING the summer of 1940, the Continental ports from Bordeaux to the far north had fallen to the enemy, and a desperate struggle ensued for control of the narrow seas formed by the southern North Sea and the Straits of Dover. Over the next four years, the motor torpedo boats, motor gunboats and motor launches battled to disrupt the German coastal shipping and at the same time protect the Allied coastwise convoys. Operating mostly at night their opponents were enemy shipping and their escorts, and the marauding "E-Boats" which sped across the dark waters to harass our own convoys.

The Royal Navy had operated motor launches and coastal motor boats during the First World War, these being mainly of American design and build which had arrived in the United Kingdom during 1916.

To augment this force, the Admiralty gave the famous shipbuilders, Thorneycrofts, an order for twelve 40 foot motor torpedo boats, which were to be powered by three 600 h.p. Napier Lion water cooled aero type engines, and delivery was to be effected during 1937. Vospers also designed a 40 foot boat, and this type went into service powered in its developed form by three 1,250 horse power converted aero engines. The German Navy had developed the diesel engine to a fine pitch and both the "E" and "R" boats were powered by these high speed units.

To describe the vessels' duties, the Royal Navy used their motor torpedo boats, (M.T.Bs) to attack enemy shipping, motor gunboats, (M.G.Bs) for attacking enemy light craft and the motor launches, (M.Ls) for patrol and general duties. On the other side, the "Schnellboot" (Fast Boat) or "E" Boat was the equivalent of the M.T.B., whilst the "Raumboot" (Sweeping Boat) or "R" Boat was engaged in mine-sweeping and patrol duties.

January, 1940 saw the Dock Basin at Felixstowe the first operational M.T.B. base, residence of the 1st Flotilla, under the command of Lieutenant Commander C. M. Donner, R.N. Operating the 60 foot British Power Boat type craft built during 1937, they had hastily returned from the Mediterranean, through the French canals, before hostilities had commenced. Their depot ship, H.M.S. *Vulcan*, converted trawler, had come home the long way round across the Bay of Biscay and up the English Channel eventually to berth in Felixstowe Dock Basin.

The Pier Hotel, between the Dock Basin and the Air Station, was requisitioned as offices and also used as the Officers' Mess. Arrangements were

Motor gun boats from H.M.S. *Beehive* operating in the English Channel prior to "D" Day.

F. V. Powell

made with the Royal Air Force regarding the seaplane base, which had no major war role, to take over one of the hangars for the maintenance and repair of the boats; some of the no longer used married quarters to house the boats' crews and for use by medical staff and other facilities. Some of the junior officers were accommodated in the R.A.F. Officers' Quarters.

The Cliff Hotel on the cliff top in the nearby town was requisitioned for accommodating officers downstairs and W.R.N.S. (Womens Royal Naval Service) upstairs. Although there was a guarded barbed wire barricade on the stairs between the two quarters, no one ever thought to interfere with the access provided by the outside fire escape!

Coastal Forces bases were named after stinging insects, this originating from the First World War when the coastal motor boats were known as "Mosquito Craft" because of their ability to dash in, sting the enemy and roar out again before they could be swatted. Thus Felixstowe became H.M.S. *Beehive*, with H.M.S. *Midge* at Lowestoft and H.M.S. *Mantis* at Great Yarmouth.

The Royal Navy shared with the Royal Air Force the task of Air Sea Rescue and a quite extraordinary mixture of fast or fairly fast craft were used for this important duty. As the R.A.F. developed the A.S.R. launch and more came into service, the Navy dropped their part in this role, although records show a number of incidents where M.T.Bs from Felixstowe saved the lives of airmen ditched in the North Sea.

During March, 1940, the 1st Flotilla was joined by the 4th Flotilla with the Vosper craft and the 10th Flotilla which still operated an assortment of mainly experimental Thorneycroft craft. At this stage their duties ranged from local rescue work to general patrol duties. A Felixstowe boat, M.T.B. 24 under the command of Sub-Lieutenant R. Parkinson, R.N., had the distinction of being the first Coastal Forces unit to shoot down an enemy aircraft, a Heinkel 115 floatplane.

Lieutenant Commander Ian Trelawny, D.S.O., R.N.V.R., remembers the M.T.Bs with their two torpedoes and very few small guns:

"Vulnerable, being built of thin wood and fuelled with petrol, their tanks held 4,500 gallons of high octane spirit. The crews were very young, and for most of the young officers, one of these boats was their first command.

Finding the enemy was difficult as the M.T.Bs were not fitted with radar until later on in the war, and even then with a rather primitive type. Instead of the revolving scanner, the craft had a fixed detector attached to their low masts and the whole boat had to be turned in order to detect another vessel. Before radar was fitted, hydrophones were used, and in order to operate them the boat had to be made silent, even the ventilating fans being switched off. During these periods, the worst place in the boat was the engine room where the temperature rose rapidly until it was almost unbearable. The heat, accompanied by the terrific engine noise when the powerful motors were running, made these quarters a real hell afloat.

The boats of the 1st Flotilla had no proper bridges and the captain was normally the only person, except the gunners, above the deckline. In winter it

A motor torpedo boat at speed with her bow lifted high and pennants streaming roars across the North Sea on a mission from Felixstowe. *F. V. Powell*

Motor torpedo boat crew pose for the photographer on the fore deck of their craft during May, 1945.

F. V. Powell

was not unusual for the cold to stiffen the above deck's crew so that on returning to port they had to be lifted from the boat by a dockside crane.

The weather was the greatest bugbear for the *Beehive* boats, as it so quickly ranged from the perfect when all boats could go to sea, to that when it was too rough to go to sea, whatever happened, and shore leave was called, although this was restricted to the town of Felixstowe. Never were we allowed out of the town, not even as far as Ipswich. As the performance and design of the boats improved the impossible weather conditions became a rarity!"

After the fall of the Low Countries, the Felixstowe craft were engaged in evacuating refugees, and also participating in the Dunkirk withdrawal, making many runs to that stricken port in order to ferry back their cargoes of servicemen to South Coast Ports.

During March, 1941, a new formation arrived at the Basin, this being the 6th Motor Gunboat Flotilla, consisting of British Power Boat-designed craft armed with Lewis and Oerlikon guns. Some also mounted an aircraft type gun turret with four Browning 0.303 inch machine guns. Commanded by Lieutenant P. Howes, R.N., the Flotilla's assignment was to counter the enemy light craft which were making forays against our coastal convoys along the East Anglian coast, the area becoming known as "E-Boat Alley". The M.G.Bs made after-dark dashes to take up positions off the Dutch coast, where many actions were fought to the bitter end against the enemy boats.

The pre-war equipment of the M.A.E.E. was put to good use by the Royal

156

Navy when it discovered that the ex-Armoury contained a stock of old but serviceable guns, and these were "requisitioned" to re-arm the boats which had suffered armament losses.

Roaring boats leaving the Harbour became a familiar sound to the residents still living within earshot of *Beehive*, departing after dark with their fluorescent, foaming wake and up-lifted prows. Returning at dawn often limping and battle scarred, the odd occasion occurred when a Nazi flag, streaming back in the morning breeze beneath the White Ensign, signalled a good night's work.

The ladies of the service, the W.R.N.S, are also remembered by Lieutenant Commander Trelawny, "Whenever we came home from sea, there were always the Wrens to welcome us. They were the mainstay of the establishment. Wonderful cooks, they provided most excellent and substantial meals, but we did not always love them so much at sea, at night. Provided with thermos flasks of hot soup, coffee and sandwiches, it was obviously sometimes difficult to find fillings for the latter. However tasty prunes would be as a sweet after a good dinner they were not as tasty when taken in a salt water-soaked sandwich in a rough sea.

Wrens looked after our guns and ammunition and torpedoes and they were superb. One of the nastiest jobs was cleaning salt-coated ammunition in the gun belts. When a boat came in, all the ammunition was immediately taken ashore and a complete new outfit of clean, dry rounds put on board.

A torpedo is hoisted aboard during the Second World War, whilst the Torpedo Officer in Charge, Lieutenant P. J. M. O'Dell (near stanchion) supervises the operation. *F. V. Powell*

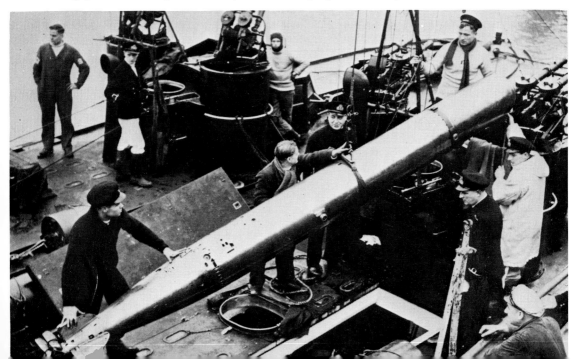

Motor gun boats in the Dock Basin show the sparse nature of the above deck shelter on these craft. The bridge is situated between the two gun positions and when at speed in a wild North Sea, conditions above deck on these craft were indescribable.   *F. V. Powell*

Wrens manned the teleprinters and telephone switchboards, and messengers flitted about the Base on bicycles. One such being, on her first morning of that duty, was so intent on saluting properly a fierce pipe-smoking Chief Officer, W.R.N.S., that she fell off the machine at her feet, still saluting!

The Communications Centre, the S.D.O., was in the cellars under the Pier Hotel and was sometimes flooded, particularly at night. At its entrance, in the forecourt, was the tail end of a lanyard which had to be pulled to fire off a special rocket in the event of invasion, this being the Wrens' job, as they would receive the signal. One poor girl, going off duty in the blackout, slipped on the slippery steps and saved herself from falling by grabbing the lanyard. The rocket soared up in a shower of sparks and burst overhead, and as a consequence all the armed forces and civilian services in Felixstowe rushed to their invasion stations.

These ladies also drove the tractors used for hauling the boats between the hangar and the 50-ton crane on the Crane Pier, which was used for lifting them in and out of the water. M.T.B.232 was in collision with an R.A.F. van whilst being towed by a Wren and the official "Report of Collision or Grounding" went through the proper channels up to the Commander-in-Chief and made interesting reading.

Beehive had the honour of providing the crew for the Admiral's Barge, and these young ladies were considered to be the absolute cream of the W.R.N.S. Extremely smart, most efficient and very attractive, they were the

158

only Wrens allowed to wear trousers, these being ordinary sailor's issue, which gave them a somewhat plump, cheeky appearance."

Lieutenant Commander R. P. Hichens arrived back at Felixstowe during the autumn of 1942 after spending some months in the West Country. H.M.S. *Beehive* was now under command of Commander T. Kerr, O.B.E., R.N., overall command being from the Headquarters of the C. in C., The Nore, at Chatham, Kent. Under the enthusiastic leadership of Lieutenant Commander Hichens, new methods of attack were devised and during the following months many violent actions took place off the Dutch coast between Felixstowe-based boats and German shipping with its E-Boat escorts. Many deeds of valour were enacted on those darkened waters and Lieutenant Commander, later Sir, Peter Scott's fine book, *The Battle of the Narrow Seas*, published by White Lion Limited, describes in great detail those hectic and dangerous hours.

The Base suffered a great loss on the night of 12/13th April, 1943, when Lieutenant Commander Hichens was killed, not in a spectacular action of which he was a past-master, but in a routine patrol. Embarked for this operation in the boat of Lieutenant D. C. Sidebottom, the M.G.Bs were escorting M.Ls which were mine-laying, when a small force of enemy light craft were encountered. Shots were exchanged, and a stray cannon shell from enemy return fire struck the bridge of the M.G.B. and Lieutenant Commander Hitchens was killed instantly. Lieutenant Sidebottom was seriously injured, together with Midshipman D. Okey, R.N.V.R., who was First Lieutenant. An R.A.F. officer observing on this operation, Wing Commander T. H. E.

German E-Boat crew line up as their surrendered craft slowly enters the Dock Basin. Note the low profile of their craft, squat bridge position and black panther emblem.   *F. V. Powell*

Edwards, R.A.F.V.R., was also injured, but under the direction of Lieutenant Sidebottom, took control of the boat and cleared it away from the action until relieved by Lieutenant S. J. J. Edwards, who had been controlling the guns. Lieutenant Commander Hichens was the only fatality of this affray, and after carrying out fourteen actions and one hundred and forty-eight operations, being awarded the D.S.O., and Bar, D.S.C. and two Bars and three times Mentioned in Despatches, this was a tragic end to a wonderful leader. He was buried at Felixstowe and his battle ensign hangs in St John's Church, Felixstowe, above a brass plaque worded thus:

THE ENSIGN ABOVE WAS FLOWN IN H.M.M.G.B. 77 COM-MANDED BY THE LATE LT/CMDR R. B. HICHENS, D.S.O., R.N.V.R. KILLED IN ACTION 13TH APRIL, 1943, AND WAS DEPOSITED IN THIS CHURCH IN HIS MEMORY BY H.M.S. BEEHIVE, AUGUST 1ST, 1943.

Commander of the 11th M.T.B. Flotilla was now Lieutenant Ian C. Trelawny, D.S.C., R.N.V.R., who was to be, in later years, a great name in connection with Felixstowe Dock, and the Senior Officer was Lieutenant P. G. C. Dickens. As if to avenge Hichens, Lieutenant Trelawny led an attack on an enemy convoy off the Hook of Holland on the 19th April, 1943, and two of the enemy ships were sunk and the attackers returned home to Suffolk without casualties.

"The engines of the earlier boats were rather unreliable," said Lieutenant Commander Trelawny, "and the boats often returned to harbour with only one engine still working. Similarly they got a lot of holes in them, put there by the enemy. M.T.B. 356 arrived at *Beehive* one evening, shining new from the builders. That night she had to go out to attend to a German convoy and the next morning had to have thirteen patches, some very large, on her hull.

The Hull Repair and Engine Maintenance Departments were always working at full stretch, parts which couldn't be obtained had to be made, yet it was very seldom that a boat was not back in the water, ready for operations, by the time that it was needed.

Going in to the attack in an M.T.B. was quite hair-raising, if you had time to think about it. A seemingly solid stream of bullets and shells of all sizes, many of them fiery tracers and incendiaries were directed at you; you could actually hear the things buzzing over your head and all around you, yet the number of casualties was not really high. When they did occur, each was a tragedy, because the men, or rather boys, of Coastal Forces were a close knit community, in which everyone knew everyone and liked everyone and relied upon everyone. It was always a friend whom you accompanied to that dreary cemetery and whom you mourned so sincerely."

Just as every civilian has his bomb story, so the number of near misses experienced by Coastal Forces crew members were the subject of many stories.

Lieutenant Commander I. C. Trelawny, D.S.C., R.N.V.R. displays a German ensign at a reunion in the Little Ships Hotel, Felixstowe Dock, where an ex-member of H.M.S. *Beehive*, Mr F. V. Powell, is mine host.   *F. V. Powell*

A man, standing by a ventilator cowl, watched it being systematically disintegrated by gunfire from an E-Boat, while remaining unscathed himself.

A very large shell hitting the water and ricocheting through an engineroom hatch of only 2 feet in diameter without touching the sides and going out through the bottom without exploding.

A shell hitting a torpedo-sight whilst the captain was using it to aim his missiles, yet not injuring him.

The fire on a sinking M.T.B. being extinguished by the explosion of one of its own depth-charges and the boat getting home under its own power.

More frequent than any — a shell passing straight through the boat from one side to the other, without touching anyone or anything on board.

The comic events were recorded as well although they may appear a bit macabre by peace-time standards.

A non-combatant specialist used to go to sea as one of the boats for some mysterious reason. On one occasion there was a furious exchange of fire between his boat and one of the enemy. Bullets and tracer flew in all directions, yet when it was all over there was only one casualty on the British boat, the captain. When they extracted the bullet from his backside, as he lay swearing on his stomach, they found it was from a British service revolver, carried without authority, by the "boffin".

A badly damaged M.T.B., limping home from a battle off the Dutch coast, all electrics and wireless gone, was attacked by a British destroyer on patrol off the Suffolk coast. Grabbing the Aldis signal lamp the M.T.B.'s captain flashed a message "Excuse me, are you firing at us?"

Felixstowe boats were involved in a large encounter on the night of 1st October, 1944, when five M.T.Bs of the 11th Flotilla set off under the command of Lieutenant F. W. Bourne, D.S.C., R.N.V.R. Their rendezvous was off the Dutch coast at Ijmuiden, and watching and listening, they waited for the first signs of the enemy, not an easy task as low clouds and rain squalls lowered the visibility. About midnight the enemy hove into sight, a small convoy of merchantmen, and the M.T.Bs moved into position, torpedoes were fired and a hit observed on one of the merchantmen. The convoy escort replied with great vigour, the M.T.Bs being raked with cannon and machine gun fire, and one of their number, M.T.B. 347, burning furiously, slid beneath the waves after being abandoned by its crew.

Another Felixstowe boat was badly damaged after firing her torpedoes, and she withdrew with engine room on fire and several casualties sustained, shortly afterwards joining her companion on the seabed. The remaining three boats set course for home with some nine of their crew members killed or missing. On the credit side, two enemy merchantmen had been torpedoed and two of the escorting trawlers and a tug had been damaged. For the naval historians, the craft involved were M.T.Bs 349, 350 and 351, with M.T.Bs 347 and 348 being lost in action.

The last round-up occurred on 13th May, 1945, a few days after Germany's unconditional surrender, when two E-Boats, flying large white flags, left Rotterdam and set course for Felixstowe. On board was Admiral Braüning and he was bringing to the Commander-in-Chief, the Nore, the charts bearing the location of all the enemy sown minefields. Fifty miles off Felixstowe, at the South Falls Buoy, they were met by a small fleet of ten M.T.Bs, bearing the majority of the Service Officers of East Coast-based Flotillas, Lieutenant-Commanders Wright and Marshall, Lieutenants Clayton, MacDonald, Magnus and Dixon and the Senior Officer, Lieutenant Commander Hodder. Lieutenant Commander Peter Scott was aboard the latter's boat for his last experience of Coastal Forces.

Making 20 knots, the E-Boats were escorted on either flank by the M.T.Bs and on entering harbour, the German crews were fell-in on deck to be watched by a large assembly of spectators, as they entered the Basin. Long and sleek, with a leaping black panther painted on their sides, the enemy craft which no doubt on previous occasions had been close to *Beehive* were now right inside it. These two greyhounds were later followed by a number of their companions and they made an impressive sight, berthed in the spot from which their adversaries had set out to do battle with them.

German Commanding Officer having surrendered his craft, steps from the Dock Basin Pontoon onto a W.R.N.S. manned harbour launch for the crossing to Harwich.

F. V. Powell

The German Admiral, met by Commander McCowen, was taken over to Harwich in a launch, once again manned by the W.R.N.S. boat-crew, to complete the handing over arrangements.

Other German Navy vessels arrived shortly afterwards, the most interesting being an example of an unmanned, radio controlled craft, which would have been filled with high explosive and set to run among British or Allied vessels, as the need arose. It is not clear if these ingenious craft were ever used but they would have proved extremely destructive if they had been.

So ended the stay of the Little Ships, their work completed, and their crews awaiting demobilisation, but in the tidal creeks that abound along the Suffolk and Essex coastline, can yet be seen hulls and hulks, some still spritely and well kept, others only visible at low tide, reminders of the days when their purpose was to keep the sea lanes around this coast open. The Pier Hotel has been renamed the "Little Ships" and the landlord, Mr "Sandy" Powell, himself a coxswain operating from *Beehive*, has a splendid collection of mementoes and photographs in his "Beehive Bar Room".

The Dock Basin full of craft, including German E-Boats. A busy scene after the arrival of the surrendered enemy Light Naval Forces craft.   *F. V. Powell*

CHAPTER EIGHT

Tails and Spinners

OVER the years very many men, both service and civilian, served at the Air Station on the windswept shores of the Orwell, and many still recall events and incidents which highlight their memories.

Mr R. C. Rowbotham of Ipswich can still visualise the site when only the Pier Hotel (Little Ships) and a few bathing machines graced the scene, and the wooden jetty with its adjacent railway tracks jutted out into the swift flowing tidal waters of the river. Great Eastern Railway trains ran to the Pier Station after passing through Beach Station, and steamers belonging to the same company plied between Felixstowe and Ipswich from the Dock Pier. The Dock Basin and its few warehouses attracted small coastal vessels, whilst all the business of commercial shipping and naval activity took place across the Orwell at Harwich and Shotley, linked by a ferry service from Felixstowe.

After the first two hangars, or sheds as they were called, had been erected, Mr Rowbotham remembers seeing the first seaplanes arrive. These only ventured out on calm or moderate days as they were launched from the beach, and their fragile construction did not lend itself to rough treatment.

Felixstowe's two "R" officers, Risk and Rathbone, were both ex-Marines and made their Headquarters further inland at the Melrose Hotel (North Sea Hotel) and later at a house in Bacton Road, near to the two centres.

Service ranks were peculiar at this time, being a mixture of Army and Navy tradition, and Mr R. D. Milward of Heacham says: "I qualified as an Aerial Gunlayer' on the Curtiss boats, being in actual fact an air gunner operating a Lewis Gun." Air crews of this period all remember the erratic functioning of the flying boat's fuel systems, the vibration causing fractured petrol pipes necessitating many descents to the surface in order to carry out temporary repairs. One gentleman recalls having to get down very quickly in the middle of the North Sea in order to lash-up an interplane strut which had been severed by one of the aircraft's gunners in his enthusiasm to get his shots into an enemy seaplane.

An ex-R.N.A.S. pilot, Mr Earl L. MacLeod of Sardis, Canada vividly remembers his Felixstowe days:

"I was posted to Felixstowe Air Station at the end of May, 1918, to pilot flying boats and these were mainly two types operating, Small Americas and F.2As. The Small Americas were being used for practice flying only, with Lieutenant Carnegie and Captain Aplin as instructors, whilst Lieutenant

A Supermarine Southampton twin-engined flying boat rides at her moorings off the "Sea-Front".
Mrs Campbell

Norman Fraser was instructing on the F.2As. This type of aircraft was modified and known as the F.3, several being sent to Canada after the War for use at newly established Canadian Air Board bases. We received one at Jericho Beach Air Station where I was serving as an 'Air Pilot Navigator' and we assembled it and flew it on many diversified civilian operations. The F.3 proved in a startling way the great value of aircraft for peace-time service, in forestry operations, and with the Customs Department in combating drug and liquor traffic.

Back again to Felixstowe and whilst I was there I was sent on the 25th June, 1918, to Cowes, Isle of Wight, as second pilot, to pick up an F.2A at the factory, and ferry it back to Felixstowe. The first pilot was Captain 'Dinty' Moore, many years later the well-known proprietor of Moore's Restaurant in Winnipeg. There were two incidents, from my point of view, the first being when an engine cut out over the English Channel about fifteen miles off Eastbourne. Moore damaged a wing tip float whilst making a landing in rough water and I had to stand out near the lower wing tip to maintain stability, waves breaking over me throughout the long taxi-ing to the lee of Eastbourne's pleasure pier. A crowd had gathered and we were warmly welcomed with a hundred cups of hot tea proffered. The proprietor of the luxury hotel near the Pier loaned me a suit of his own clothes whilst my uniform was being cleaned and pressed.

We were guests of the town whilst repairs to our aircraft were being completed. 'Dinty' Moore's future father-in-law, a Paymaster Captain in the Royal Navy, visited us several times during our stay.

After leaving Eastbourne we alighted at Dover Harbour where we refuelled at its small seaplane base with its single hangar. To carry out this operation we had to taxi onto a trolley on the slipway and then be towed across the main waterfront public street to the hangar!

The second incident was a 'might have been' thing. Just after passing the Thames Estuary on continuing our flight from Dover, both 'Dinty' and myself

166

observed three seaplanes that we could not identify, anchored not far from the shore. When we alighted at Felixstowe we learned that an air fight had been in progress and the planes that we had seen were high performance German monoplane fighter seaplanes that had, apparently, been laying in wait for our regular three-plane morning patrol from Felixstowe to come that way, as this was their usual route.

We were grateful that the Germans had disdained our lone plane, passing overhead in the wrong direction, because we, of course, carried no armament of any kind on our ferrying flight.

On the 4th July, 1918, I flew as second pilot with Captain J. Lindsey Gordon, later Chief of Staff, Royal Canadian Air Force, leading a formation of F.2As in search of three other F.2As that were overdue from a routine patrol. As navigator, the job of the second pilot, I flew a haphazard search course across the North Sea, keeping continuous track of our position at all times.

We were fortunate to sight one of the missing machines, fifteen miles south of the North Hinder Light, the other two having been forced down in Dutch territorial waters, where they were interned 'for the duration'. We could see gunfire holes in upper wing of the aircraft we spotted, and wireless calls directed a destroyer to proceed to the rescue of the crew, of whom the engineer had been killed, and Lieutenant Syd Anderson, acting as an air gunner on this operation, had been wounded. The latter was a longtime friend in Vancouver.

The pilot of one of the boats forced down was Gerald 'Gerry' Hodgson, and he and I had known one another in Vancouver during 1916. We had attempted to construct an aircraft with which to qualify for our 'wings', at our own expense, but as far as I know it never did fly. Gerry got his wings in California, whilst I gained mine at Vendome, France.

After being interned he wrote to me at Felixstowe requesting me to forward to him in Holland his Gieves* R.N.A.S. Tin Trunk containing his personal belongings. This I did, withholding at his request, a pistol which he felt might not get through. I returned this pistol to him about two years later in Vancouver. This was all part of his colourful career, as when a high school lad he had played Rugby Football in a team representing Vancouver against the famous New Zealand 'All-Blacks'.

After the Armistice he took a law course in London, and returning to British Columbia, was admitted to the Bar there by a Special Act of the Provincial Legislature.

I also flew several times at Felixstowe with another Flight Commander, Captain Cecil Clayton of Victoria, B.C., later a well-known commercial pilot in Canada.

After Armistice Day, we continued for a while to do patrolling as there was a possibility that a U-Boat, away from communications, might still be a

*Gieves Ltd., famous naval outfitters.

danger, and also to search for enemy mines that might still be adrift. At this time personnel were very much at a loose end, and I was appointed Education Officer, and I tried to organise useful lectures and courses, but I am afraid with somewhat indifferent success, as everybody wanted only to get home."

During his stay at the M.A.E.E., Squadron Leader Coombes encountered several interesting episodes, and the Annual Contractors' Dinner always provided incidents. After the formal proceedings at this event there was usually a great deal of horseplay in the Officers' Mess and a favourite sport was to roll up the distinguished guests in the carpet, despite broken glass and cigarette butts.

On one such evening, Mr (later Sir Richard) Fairey was rolled up and strongly resented it. Mr A. J. A. Wallace-Barr, the Managing Director of Cellon Dope Ltd, was also rolled up, but in contrast to Fairey's wrathful letter to the C.O. Barr wrote that as his evening suit had been ruined by the condition of the carpet, he was sending the Mess a new vacuum cleaner!

One Adjutant was relieved of his duties as a test pilot because of his erratic methods of testing. Once a barographic chart climb to height showed a sudden dip to low altitude — he had seen a girls' school and dropped down for a closer look! When given a set of best climbing speeds, his records showed very different ones, and he would explain that he had found much better ones. The Senior Technical Officer was Flight Lieutenant Brooke and he invariably forgot to take up a notebook, and wrote his observations down on a match box or any scrap of paper he could find in the aircraft. He filed everything in one office drawer working on the theory that one was bound to find it in the end. A later Technical Officer was Flight Lieutenant Nicholas Comper who left the M.A.E.E. to start making the small Comper Swift single seat civil aircraft which he had partly designed whilst at Felixstowe.

The names of many famous visitors come to mind and I recall Mr Mitchell of Supermarines, the Spitfire designer, Mr Folland who designed the famous Gnat, and Sir Arthur Gouge of Short Brothers, whilst a Pilot Officer

A Napier Lion engined Fairey IIIF, Mark 3 S.1532 taxies on smooth water after being launched during 1934.   *Mrs Campbell*

who came to the M.A.E.E. from Cranwell was later knighted, C. E. Chilton, as well as the Schneider Trophy pilots, Boothman and Atcherley and of course, Sir Frank Whittle.

Mr J. T. "Tolly" Hill was posted to the M.A.E.E. during 1928 and during the next six years saw many changes and events to recall:

"Having always been a keen musician I was promptly organised into the Station Voluntary Band, all spare-time musicians. This band which boasted over 50 members was considered to be one of the best in the Service during the period 1928-1934. For special occasions it was amalgamated with the Martlesham Heath Band, but under the baton of the Felixstowe conductor, Sergeant Chester.

In great demand for functions both Service and civil, one of the regular duties was the Church Parades at St John's Church, and on one occasion when the organ failed, the Band provided the music for the service at very short notice. The Vicar was Canon Cocks, whose son later became the Church of England Chaplain-in-Chief to the R.A.F."

Flight-Sergeant Middleton of Oxford was a clarinettist in the Voluntary Band and recalls the Band being under the baton of a sergeant who was on loan from the R.A.F. Central Band, Uxbridge. Leading Aircraftsman Jacobs, a photographer, was the soloist, and it was widely acclaimed, expecially when giving sacred concerts in the Spa Pavilion.

During the Annual Martlesham Heath Sports Day, the Band Race was won by Flight Sergeant Middleton, the prize, a hair-brush which he still possesses. He carried the big drum for the event, and was given a half-way down the course handicap!

The Station personnel arranged a pantomime each Christmas with an all-male cast, and this was usually staged at the Playhouse Cinema, in Hamilton Road. The 1929 production "So This is Pantomime" was a great success in spite of the Fairie Queen being played by a nineteen stone aircraftsman nicknamed "Tiny". On another occasion, an even larger Corporal Smith stole the show in this role.

Another regular Yuletide event was the Christmas Day Football Match, played with a Rugger ball, and all members of the Station in residence participated. Everyone donated a small sum, the proceeds being used to buy the licence for the Station's mongrel dog, "Paddy".

When duties or otherwise confined the love-sick airmen to the premises all was not lost to those "in the know", as the tall fence which ran alongside the Dock Road had one peculiarity. By counting from a certain post, one could locate the railing which had been "doctored" by having its bottom rivet removed and, therefore, a gentle push would open the gates to paradise. Also alongside this fence was a small tea-hut, and a similar technical arrangement allowed the exchange of money for tea and cakes.

The giant Short Sarafand, S.1589, rides at anchor whilst a paddle steamer bound for Ipswich passes by in the stream.   *I. Scrivener*

Pleasure always stands out in the memory and an event stands dear to the recollections of Mr Pettitt of Cowlinge who recounts: "One day my flying boat was flown to Calshot to see the large German twelve-engined flying boat, the Dornier Do.X. Our passengers included Squadron Leader Orlebar, Flight Lieutenant Boothman and other members of the High Speed Flight and a very pleasant time was had by all. During this time I also flew with another extremely interesting character, Mr (later Sir) Alan Cobham, who was at the M.A.E.E. carrying out trials on the large three-engined Short Valetta seaplane, prior to his survey flights in Africa. I was the rigger and had the job of sitting on the toe of the float with a boathook when mooring up to a buoy. The floats were about forty feet long — and I still can't swim!

During very rough weather when severe gales were imminent we would leave our anchorage off the Air Station and fly up the River Orwell to Pin Mill, and moor up not far from the waterside public house, the Butt and Oyster. We could then conveniently row ashore in our rubber dinghy to get some refreshment and maybe some eggs to cook when we returned to the aircraft. My Commanding Officer at this time was Group Captain G. R. Bromet, D.S.O., O.B.E., later Sir Geoffrey Bromet and Governor of the Isle of Man."

Mr George Hill of Ipswich was posted to Felixstowe during September, 1934, and was attached to the Airframe Repair Section, and his memories of the following four years cover a wide scene:

"Looking skywards one day to locate the source of a queer flapping noise, I was amazed to see the one and only Cierva. S.30 autogyro seaplane flapping around all over the place. The rotor blades had become unbalanced due to some minor damage, but the pilot, after a great struggle, managed to get this unusual aircraft down safely. On another occasion, an Avro Sea Tutor, on trials, rammed a mooring buoy whilst taxi-ing and had to make a very hasty run for the beach before the floats became waterlogged.

170

When the large six-engined Short Sarafand, S.1589, suffered an engine fire, one of the lower mainplanes was badly damaged, necessitating a replacement. This duly arrived from the makers at Rochester, Kent, loaded on a large barge, which was berthed alongside the Crane Pier. The Station fire siren was then sounded, all ranks mustered and marched to the pier. There they gathered around the large wing, and all lifting together, positioned it for attaching to the flying boat. A portion of the damaged stainless steel wing spar was 'converted' by an enterprising Senior N.C.O. into a very fine fire fender!

One afternoon, whilst forming up for the work parade, a trickle of water began to run along the parade ground gutter. Gradually gaining volume the whole site was eventually covered, this being another of the East Coast tidal floods which occurred from time to time. The Old Station at the Landguard end was always the most effected by virtue of its low-lying position.

During the 1937 summer season, the Station tug-of-war team won the No. 1 Division Championship and medals were struck and presented to all the members of the team. Nearby Martlesham Heath were the winners of No. 2 Division. The Felixstowe Team appeared in the pre-war R.A.F. propaganda film "The Lion has Wings", their appearance emphasising the spirit of sport and the leisure side of the service. When appearing at country fetes the team usually received a fee of a free tea and five shillings, but this became a stumbling block for them. When entered for an A.A.A. Competition, they were barred as having been paid for their fete appearances, they were therefore professionals!"

The Station had a very good hockey team which won the R.A.F. Junior, (under 200 men) Station Hockey Championship for two consecutive years. Some members later played for the Suffolk County Hockey Team, and several recall the Catchpole and Cordy brothers who played for the local Felixstowe Town Hockey Club.

Volunteers were called for to attend the Silver Jubilee Royal Review being staged at R.A.F. Mildenhall on 6th July, 1935, but when only two airmen stepped forward, the majority of the Station personnel were detailed for the duty. Living in a large tented camp near the Main Road at Mildenhall, the hot fine weather made an ice-cream vendor on his three-wheeled machine a frequent visitor, where a steady trade ensued. It is reported that as a result of his enhanced sales he received appropriate promotion within his company.

In 1935, on the first Empire Air Day, almost at the far end of the line-up of aircraft on display stood a rather dilapidated Fairey IIIF seaplane. Not many visitors had ventured this far from the more popular exhibits, and the "forgotten plane" stood alone until two lads appeared and looked interested. At this stage, its guardian was forced to leave his charge for a few minutes, and on his return found one of the lads kicking holes in the wing fabric in order to gain access to the cockpit, whilst the other was attempting to crank the motor!

Guards were posted around the Station, the major duty being that at the main gate, and the others at various places along the "Seafront", that side of the Station which faced the river, and here they patrolled to and fro. Naval time keeping was the order of the day, bells being struck every half-hour. Throughout the hours of darkness, once every hour the guard had to walk along one of the jetties and shine a searchlight on the aircraft riding at their buoys. They were then counted and noted as being all present and correct, or otherwise. All guards carried rifles and bayonets, and the favourite place of refuge in inclement weather was the incinerator near the Station Sick Bay.

A civilian airframe fitter went to the Stores to draw some anti-corrosive painting material, but was inadvertently issued with castor oil paste, with which he proceeded liberally to coat the inside of a flying boat hull. The resultant fumes from this mixture played havoc with him and several other airmen working on the aircraft who were "closeted" for some hours afterwards.

Whilst strolling along the "Seafront" one Sunday afternoon, being restricted to the confines of the Station as a result of three days "Jankers" for riding a bicycle without lights, Mr Hill was mustered into a party to salvage a Miles Magister two seat training aircraft from Martlesham Heath which had spun into the sea near Felixstowe Golf Links. Several people had witnessed the pilot descending by parachute and at first it was thought that a passing paddle steamer had rescued him, but this was not so. Ten days later, whilst on guard on the Crane Pier, a local shrimping boat came alongside with a parachute trailing astern. The boatman called out to the guard, and on examining the parachute they both discovered that the Magister's pilot was still attached to it. He was taken from the water, and after the necessary formalities was buried with full military honours.

The giant Dornier Do.X, 12-engined flying boat which the Felixstowe officers inspected at Calshot.

Mr Pettitt

When Bawdsey with its radio-location work came into being, the W/T staff from Felixstowe went there each day, dressed in civilian clothes, so security minded were the administrators of this new project.

The "Dooley" Public House was a favourite haunt of the personnel when money was available, but on other occasions the "Wet Bay Gang" had to do with the N.A.A.F.I. When leaving the Dooley at the end of what was Walton Avenue, often in high spirits, course was set for home, and no matter what stood in the way, be it marsh, dyke, garden or whatsoever, the straight line was maintained. While returning from hostelries in the town, the model yacht pond on the town's seafront was often traversed whilst these exercises were being carried out."

A few extracts from the Station's quarterly *Felixstowe Foghorn* make interesting reading:

> Twinkle-twinkle little star,
> I don't wonder what you are,
> Just a kite from "Two-o-nine"
> Putting in some overtime.

May, 1935.   Mr Babb won the prize of twenty shillings for his design for a M.A.E.E. tie, approved by the Commanding Officer. Dark blue ground with a light blue thin stripe running diagonally from top right to bottom left, two inches apart.

For charter. Three engined house boat, comfortably appointed, all conveniences, able to move short distances under its own power. Apply. "Doctor", No. 1 Hangar. Sea Front.

Interviewer. "Have you the firmness of character that enables a person to get on and do his duty in the face of ingratitude, criticism and heartless ridicule?"

Applicant.   "I ought to have. I was cook in the Airmen's Mess at Felixstowe."

Another ex-Felixstowe resident recalls that during a holiday weekend the majority of the Station personnel had departed on leave, but he and a few more were confined to Camp because a member of their billet had been stricken with an infectious disease. On the Sunday afternoon, at a loss for something to do, they wandered down to the seafront and were there inspired by the A.M.W.D. rowing boat which looked "just the job" for a row. Proceeding upriver to Fagbury Beach, all went well, and after a rest, they returned safe and sound to their departure point, for tea. Heartened by their previous voyage, they then set out after tea for a greater expedition, and rowing westwards, crossed the Harbour to Harwich where they tied up their craft and adjourned to a waterside place of refreshment.

After a while, a local boatman entered the premises and enquired of our lads if they were the custodians of an A.M.W.D. boat, and if they were, to go and have a look at it. The receding tide had left the craft, held by its painter, at an unusual sky-pointing angle, with only the stern near the water. Beating a hasty retreat, our gallant band embarked, rowing strongly back through the gathering gloom, missing several vessels on their way and duly arrived back on the other shore. A case of where angels fear to tread!

Mr Grace, who was the Air Traffic Controller at Felixstowe, and Mrs Grace, Flight Test Observer, recalled their wedding night which was being spent on the Station. Being responsible for air safety, Mr Grace received a telephone call in the early hours of the morning, stating that flying boats were being diverted to Felixstowe and it was imperative that the illuminated floating flare-path be laid out so that the aircraft could alight.

Somewhat reluctantly, the "bridegroom" and the boats' crews set out into a very rough Harwich Harbour to lay down the flare-path, the positioning of which was hazardous owing to the prevailing elements. Having carried out this operation, they awaited the arrival of the aircraft, but the expected "visitors" made their home base on the South Coast, and so the "happy band of pilgrims" picked up the flare-path and returned to the sheets.

A captured German Brandenburg single engined fighter seaplane with R.A.F. markings. These aircraft were the main opponents of the War Flight patrol aircraft operating from Ostend and Zeebrugge. Note the unusual rear fuselage designed to give the gunner a clear field of fire over the stern.   *Mrs Pomeroy*

CHAPTER NINE

War Load

A LTHOUGH Felixstowe did not carry out armament research to the same extent as its sister station at Martlesham Heath, nevertheless certain work was carried out on armaments fitted to marine aircraft.

In the main, the weapons employed were basically free-mounted machine guns for defensive purposes, and marine bombs and airborne torpedoes.

From the very earliest days, floatplanes protected themselves with a primitive machine gun, usually a standard field weapon stripped down for lightness and utilising the air-flow for cooling instead of the usual water jacket. They also endeavoured to inflict damage on the enemy with bombs of fairly light calibre, grenades and darts. The torpedo was always a must, and as soon as aircraft were capable of doing so, they carried this destructive engine of warfare.

Records show that the first offensive missiles were the 20lb T.N.T. bombs and four of these would constitute the war load. Although over the months these bombs grew in size and weight to some 50 lbs, their impact was not greatly destructive and they were usually on racks beneath the lower mainplane. The design of these racks caused considerable concern as in many cases the attacking aircraft positioned itself ideally for the action only to be frustrated when the bombs failed to release onto their target. Release was effected by cable in the early aircraft but this was considerably affected by frost and rain, and eventually electrical actuation became the order of the day.

Torpedo design did not alter to a great extent as the 18 inch Mark VIII of 1918 weighed in at 1,423 lbs, whilst the Mark X was slightly lighter at 1,000 lbs.

Short 184 seaplane, No. 8349, was engaged for several weeks at Felixstowe during 1916 carrying out dropping experiments with 14 inch torpedoes. It is interesting to note that this aircraft was almost of local construction being made by Mann Egerton at Norwich. Also during 1916, the first Felixstowe-built Porte Baby, No. 9800, carried out trials with a 14 inch aerial torpedo carried under each lower mainplane. During this period this aircraft also carried a Davis 6-pounder quick firing gun on a temporary mounting in the front gun position.

An early weapon specially devised for combating the Zeppelin was the Hales Grenade, designed to be dropped by aircraft onto the enemy airship

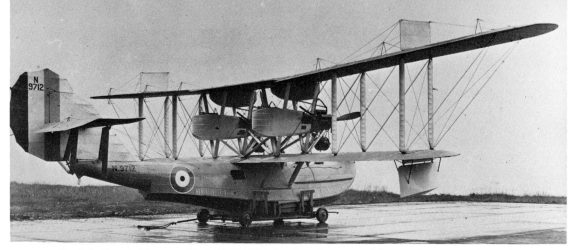

English Electric Kingston Mark II, N.9712 showing the gun positions at the rear of the engine nacelles.
Harald Penrose

where it was intended to explode and ignite the highly inflammable hydrogen lifting gas. Some two hundred had been produced for the Royal Naval Air Service and during the first week in August, 1914, they were distributed to the most important stations. Felixstowe received twelve and after they were exhausted it was assumed that anything else available would have to be used. It is recorded that 6 inch shells were fitted with fins and striking pins as substitute bombs. Luckily the occasion for their use never arose so their effectiveness was never assessed.

The provision for carrying bombs remained practically the same during the between war years, the large biplane flying boats being equipped with racks beneath their lower wings. Winching gear was incorporated in the installation in order to lift the bombs from the craft carrying them up to the racks overhead. When the Short Sunderland appeared it caused a considerable stir with its novel bomb rack equipment, which comprised racks under the mainplane which under normal conditions remained in the roof of the hull, but when the aircraft went into action, doors in the upper hull opened and the racks with their load ran outboard on underwing rails to position the missiles for dropping. The later Saro Lerwick employed the same system, but this aircraft did not remain in operational service long enough to drop its bombs in anger.

One of the first seaplanes to carry a machine gun, a Maxim 0.45 inch, was the Short S.41, No. 10, the first naval aircraft to do so, and it was flown quite extensively by Commander Samson at Harwich before the outbreak of First World War.

The usual installation was a free mounted Lewis gun mounted in the rear cockpit of the early war floatplanes and generally provided with three drums

176

of ammunition each containing 47 rounds. In some cases double drums of 97 rounds were used. Towards the middle of the war, the floatplanes appeared with one or two fixed Vickers machine guns with 600 rounds of 0.303 inch belt fed ammunition, the guns being synchronised to fire through the airscrew disc by means of interrupter gear. The Vickers guns also appeared as a free mounted weapon for use by the observer/gunner, but not to the same extent as land-based aircraft.

As the floatplane gradually gave way to the flying boat around 1916, the number of machine guns carried by aircraft increased, and one of the defensive features of the flying boat was that they generally incorporated a gun position in the bow and another aft of the mainplanes. These guns were most important on operational flying boats and the lack of them showed up on the Felixstowe-built Porte Baby types, as these were only armed with two guns. As a consequence they were only allowed to patrol where there was no possibility of an encounter with marauding German fighter seaplanes.

In the light of operational experience, the Felixstowe boats were modified to carry additional guns in a position above the cockpit roof, sometimes referred to as the main hatch, and in two additional positions on the hull top aft of the mainplanes to give more protection over the stern.

The hull outline of the Felixstowe F.2A flying boat was a vast improvement on the earlier H.12 in that the tailplane was positioned higher and thus allowed better sightings from the rear hull gun positions. Sliding hatches on the hull top allowed a wide field of fire and altogether the F.2A mounted six Lewis guns, two in the forward position, one on the cockpit roof, one aft of the wing on the hull top, and one in each of the hull hatch positions. These guns

The torpedo was carried by marine aircraft on crutches under the fuselage between the float struts and dropped from a low altitude towards its target.   *H. F. King*

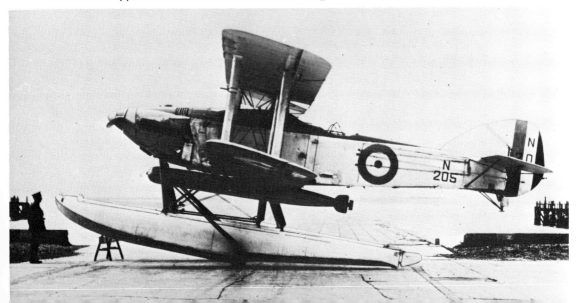

Torpedoes were often transported on cradles built onto the upper deck of flying boat hulls as shown on this Supermarine Scapa, S.1648.

were fitted with Norman Vane Sights which allowed the gunners to range for the aircraft's speed and the velocity of the bullet.

Armaments varied as recorded by Mr R. D. Milward of Heacham, stationed at Felixstowe during 1915: "I qualified as an 'Aerial Gun-Layer' being one of the second group of volunteers to do so. The Curtiss boats in which we flew carried twin guns in the box position, another pair on a Scarff Ring Mounting over the main hatch forward of the twin propellers, and a single Vickers gun each side of the aft hatch. These boats were very well armed for their day and were a very formidable machine to attack. For shooting-up submarines and surface vessels they could bring several guns to bear on the target at any one time."

A description issued for the standard F.2A stated: "A gunner is positioned in the bow with ammunition boxes and trays. Abaft this is the cockpit for two pilots with upholstered seats which can be used as lifebuoys if required. Behind this position is the wireless cabin and the engineer's position is just aft of this. Above this situation is the main hatch gunner's position, and just behind the mainplanes is the third gun position which gives a good field of fire aft."

Attempts to increase the firepower was made by double-yoking the Lewis guns mounting and they proved very successful on operations.

Other attempts were made to provide the gunners with a better field of fire by reducing obstacles like the tail unit and interplane struts which restricted their sighting. These experiments ranged from the staggered rear positions to those at the rear of the engine nacelles, and most unusual of all,

178

those on the upper wing trailing edge of the experimental F.2A, and the second prototype English Electric Cork flying boat. There was a certain amount of risk for the gunners in the later installation as they gained their positions in flight by climbing up steps on the wing interplane struts.

After the war the English Electric Kingston also appeared with extended mid-wing engine nacelles with a gunner's position at the rear of each. It must have been an extremely uncomfortable situation for the occupants of these positions in direct line with the slipstream from the airscrews.

The large biplane flying boats of the between war years were usually equipped with several free mounted Lewis guns. An unusual installation tried out experimentally on the Blackburn Iris S.1593 at the M.A.E.E. was a large 37 mm Coventry Ordnance Works quick-firing cannon. This was a one only fitting, although the experiments continued for some time. Blackburn's next flying boat design, the Perth, also appeared with this bowmounted weapon, whilst the bomb load had also increased to four 500 lb or eight 250 lb bombs.

A not too often mentioned armament carried by early R.N.A.S. aircraft was the American designed 6-pounder Davis recoil-less gun which was installed initially in the front cockpit of the Porte Baby.

An innovation which stayed for a number of years appeared when the Blackburn Iris Mark II arrived back at Felixstowe after its rebuild. It incorporated a gun position behind the tail unit, the central rudder of the triple ruddered biplane tail being deleted to accommodate it. As the later types of patrol flying boats appeared they were designed with a gun position aft of the tail unit, culminating through the Sunderland and Lerwick to the last of them all, the Shetland.

Conventional armament employed by Fairey Seal, K.3577, consisting of a fixed forward machine gun firing through the airscrew arc and a free mounted machine gun in the rear cockpit.

H. F. King

A Blackburn Shark displays her bomb load on underwing racks whilst resting on the M.A.E.E. slipway. The projections at the lower wing tips are Holt flare holders used for alighting at night.

H. F. King

Mr H. F. K. King, M.B.E., an armament expert stationed at Felixstowe, recalls a nerve wracking experience in the tail gun position of the Blackburn Perth in pre-war days. Carrying out armament trials off Felixstowe he was almost strangled in his lonely outpost not by the surrounding equipment, but by the whipping slipstream of three Rolls-Royce Buzzard motors tearing at his old school scarf!

Many aircraft manufacturers designed gun mountings for standard armaments to be incorporated in their aircraft and one such design was the Fairey High Speed Mounting which enabled a free mounted machine gun in the rear cockpit of an aircraft to be deployed or stowed in much less time than hitherto. Westlands also patented their own designs for standard machine gun mountings as well as the C.O.W. Gun. Aircraft designers had always to take into consideration the placement of armaments and their feeding and access in the event of jamming or other malfunction. Another consideration was the disposal of spent cartridge cases so that they did not damage the aircraft structure when ejected from their chutes.

As aircraft speeds increased so did the problems associated with aiming free mounted machine guns in the battering slipstream. Many ingenious devices came into being in order to try and cope with this problem, mainly in the form of compensating sights to allow for slipstream and drift. The problem was eventually solved with the advent of the totally enclosed multi-gun turret, but this did not appear until the last days of the flying boat, only the Sunderland and Lerwick being so equipped. The American designed and built Consolidated Catalina which was used in considerable numbers by the R.A.F. during the Second World War, although of modern design, still used free mounted machine guns in enclosed cupolas.

When the Sunderland arrived during 1937 it boasted a Nash and Thompson FN.13 four gun turret in the stern, and a F.11 in the bow with a

180

single Vickers gas-operated gun. Pillar-mounted Vickers guns were positioned in the upper hull aft of the mainplane, firing from hatches, but these were later replaced by the F.7, power-operated two gun turret. The armament eventually totalled 18 machine guns, giving just cause for the Luftwaffe to nickname the Sunderland the "Hedgehog". Flying low over the surface of the water, it was indeed a formidable opponent for any attacking aircraft. The not too successful Saro Lerwick also mounted three Frazer-Nash power turrets, four guns astern, two amidships and one in the bow.

An interesting feature of the later flying boat bow gun position was the sliding Scarff Ring Mounting, necessitated by the need for a clear area to work in when picking-up or slipping moorings. When this operation was being carried out the gun ring was slid aft, and the front turret of the Sunderland and the Lerwick also incorporated this feature.

It is interesting to note that the Scarff Ring Mounting which had been invented by Warrant Officer F. W. Scarff during 1916 was in action 23 years later when a Saro London flying boat engaged German aircraft in action.

An unusual feature of flying boats front armament was the sliding Scarff gun mounting ring which slid aft, as seen here, in order that the crew member could pick up or release moorings. Saro Severn N.240.   *H. F. King*

CHAPTER TEN

From A Muddy Creek

JUST over a century ago a somewhat eccentric gentleman named Colonel
George Tomline resided at Orwell Park, a large mansion situated in park-
land on the banks of the Orwell midway between Felixstowe and Ipswich.
Foremost among his many ideas were those to commercialize the Landguard
area of Felixstowe which lay on the eastern shores of Harwich Harbour. So
fervent were his claims to the locality, having acquired the manorial rights
from the Duke of Hamilton, that he demanded transit charges for all goods
destined for Landguard Fort that were carried over his land. On one occasion
he stopped the Fort's water supply when the Government failed to conform to
his wishes. In furtherance of his ambition he stood as member elect for the
Harwich constituency but failed to achieve sufficient support at the poll.

Tomline's next project was the construction of a railway line from the
Great Eastern Railway's station at Westerfield, north of Ipswich, to the shores
of the River Orwell near Horseshoe Creek, Felixstowe. Named the Felixstowe
Railway and Pier Company the first passenger train ran to Felixstowe on 1st
May 1877 and freight trains followed a month later. The line met with a mixed
reception although during the first six months of 1878 it carried some 52,927
passengers.

Colonel Tomline, a farsighted engineer, decided to construct a large
dock, believed to have been a graving or dry dock, and entered by a lock in a
tidal basin at the mouth of Horseshoe Creek. An Act of 1876 gave authority for
the scheme and in the summer of that year navvies, in spite of the Great
Eastern's grand scheme across the river at Harwich, were set to work digging
out the creek entrance. The wages of the day are interesting being five and a
half old pence (under 2½p) per hour. A further Act in 1879 changed the name
of the Company to The Felixstowe Railway and Dock Company and later the
same year yet another Act made if The Felixstowe Dock and Railway Company
— the same name that it has today.

Work on the dock was interrupted when the contractors engaged went
bankrupt, but the dock was opened for trade and the first commerical vessel
entered in 1886. Flanked on either side by wooden piers, the 147 foot wide
dock entrance gave access to a six acre tidal basin on the south side of which
were warehouses and railway tracks. This new installation only attracted small
coastal vessels in an area where the sole previous trading activities had been

Aerial view of the Port of Felixstowe. Foreground to Background: Container Terminal,
T.F.S./Townsend Thoresen Terminal, Dock Basin, Oil Jetty and Tank Farm of Felixstowe
Tank Developments Limited. Northern development with Ro/Ro Berths 3 and 4 and general
cargo quay.   *The Felixstowe Dock and Railway Company*

barge traffic which beached at high water for loading and unloading local produce and collecting shingle.

The Colonel also built the Pier Hotel and the Manor Hotel: these names have now been changed to The Little Ships and Manor House — the latter, near the Amusement Park and endangered by sea erosion is now a Country Club. On the face of The Little Ships can be seen two crests, the left one, lions' paws, being that of the Pretymans of Bacton and the right, the dove, the Tomlines of Rigby.

In 1887 the Colonel died and the Great Eastern acquired the thirteen mile long track of his railway and its stock which consisted of nineteen passenger coaches and fifteen goods wagons. In 1898 the G.E.R. added the Town Station to the 1877 Beach and Pier Stations. After the Colonel's death his nephew, Canon Fredrick Pretyman, became the main shareholder and his son, Captain E. G. Pretyman, was elected Chairman of the Company, a post he held for the next forty years.

Up to 1904 trade and progress were slow but things improved when, on the completion of a new quay on the north side of the basin, E. Marriage and Son Limited erected their East Anglian Flour Mill and also leased a large grain warehouse built by the Dock Company. On the south side the Company's newly erected Maltings were, at that time, the largest in country and these two concerns generated considerable trade for local vessels.

Many of these works had been inspired by Captain Pretyman's wife, Lady Beatrice Pretyman, who was very interested in and concerned with the welfare of the Company's employees. During 1894 the Captain had been instrumental in the building of a new parish church in the rapidly growing town of Felixstowe. This was St John's Church in Orwell Road which was to be connected in so many ways, in later years, with the Dock and Air Station.

Among the first exports from the Dock was malt for South America and it is of interest to note that this was shipped in metal cisterns, made in Ipswich and destined for export to the same port as the malt.

During 1907 the basin saw some coastal motor boats and destroyers residing there whilst the battleship *Blenheim*, acting as their base ship, was moored just off the dock entrance. The threat of war was taken very seriously at that time and King Edward VII's yacht, which had been based at Felixstowe, was requisitioned by the Royal Navy. Large oil fuel tanks, still in existence in 1978, were also erected for bunkering Naval vessels and this operation was carried out at the north entrance pier which had been converted into a refuelling jetty. Another interesting function was the provision of water for vessels carried in the Company's waterboats which were filled from their own wells.

Activity was intense on the outbreak of hostilities in 1914 and throughout the war with the dock as a base for destroyers, coastal motor boats, minesweepers and boom defence vessels. Commercial activity almost ceased and with the peace did not resume at its pre-war level. One of the more prosperous concerns was that of a shipbreaker whose activities were mainly based on clearing up the debris of war.

This downward trend continued and the economic depression of 1929 created even greater difficulties, traffic was basically grain carrying barges and sections of the basin began to show evidence of disrepair. The timber trade had been lost to other ports and increased tariffs on imported stone resulted in the disappearance of this traffic, which up to that time, had been at a steady rate owing to the road building programmes being carried out in East Anglia.

The Royal Navy's Boom Defence Depot returned to the basin in 1938 and established itself at the east end of the dock but war again in 1939 saw immediate activity when units of the Royal Navy once again arrived and the basin became a Naval Establishment, H.M.S. *Beehive*. Every building was requisitioned, filled with stores and guarded day and night, whilst later a 200 foot long jetty was constructed down the centre of the basin.

The south end showing a slipway and jetties remaining in 1966. The three old hangars were part of the old station and housed the High Speed Flight.

The Felixstowe Dock and Railway Company

After the intense activities of the war years peace saw the departure of the Royal Navy and the Dock in a sorry state as its dredging equipment had been requisitioned by the Ministry of War Transport and had all been lost. No dredging had been carried out since 1939 and the basin had silted up from its previous 23 feet of water at low tide to a now semi-useless 12 feet. Now only the smallest vessels could enter the dock and the war time jetty down the centre restricted all movement in the basin. Once again salvage firms carried out their business of clearing up the wreckage of war but the Dock Company's warehouses were still full of military stores and thus not available for commercial operations.

On the death of Captain E. G. Pretyman during 1931 his son, Mr G. M. T. Pretyman, inherited his father's shares and in 1951 he sold the majority of them to a well-known East Anglian corn merchant, Mr Gordon Parker, C.B.E., M.M. Under the leadership of the new Chairman a small and enthusiastic group of men, including Lieutenant Commander Ian Trelawny, O.B.E., D.S.C., who had been a Flotilla Commander at H.M.S. *Beehive* in the Second World War, started the immense task of restoring the dock to commercial activities.

The erection of new warehouse facilities went on apace and storage of such things as copra, ground nuts, maize, palm kernels, sugar and wheat was undertaken. De-requisitioned oil tanks became available for linseed, ground nut and palm oils.

Of course there were setbacks and the January 1953 floods, which almost wiped out the new work that had been carried out, will certainly be remembered. Undaunted the gallant band retrieved all that could be salvaged and commenced to rebuild. Dockside steam cranes, red with rust, were stripped down, refurbished and put into service on the dockside rail tracks and for some years these formed the means of loading and unloading vessels alongside the quays. One of these veterans is still working on the preserved Stour Valley Railway in Essex but before their departure a local film enthusiast, Mr Michael Woodward of Ipswich, made an impressive film of these machines of yesteryear at work.

In 1955, with the dredging of the basin and entrance channel restoring the low water depth to 22 feet, and the removal of the war time jetty, trade gained momentum and the beaver-like efforts of the devoted group of workers began to gain their due rewards. A Government contract for the storage and handling of explosives and military stores greatly assisted the traffic flow and during 1957 some 10,000 tons of these items were shipped. One interesting aspect of this operation was that in view of the dangerous nature of the cargoes, diesel cranes were hired for loading purposes. Grain, chemical fertilizers, industrial solvents, timber and other cargoes, previously handled by the dock, arrived in increasing quantities whilst an oil fuel depot was leased to

In 1964 the Titan crane, a slipway and piers were still out in front of the hangars. They were in use by the Dock Company. At the river end of the old dock basin can be seen the Harwich Ferry ready to make the crossing to Harwich which can be seen in the background.

The Felixstowe Dock and Railway Company

Jet Petroleum Limited. To many the arrival of another new cargo during 1959, the year following the appointment by H.M. Customs and Excise of the Port's first Landing Officer, brought wishful thinking when loads of Danish lager beer arrived for storage and dispersal in a newly erected warehouse for this trade.

One of the first shipping companies to use the Dock was James Fisher and Son Limited who commenced a heavy lift service to Rotterdam using the former 50-ton R.A.F. Titan crane for loading and unloading, whilst the General Steam Navigation Company Limited and the Great Yarmouth Shipping Company Limited established a regular weekly service to Harlingen, Holland.

In 1960 the Ministry of Labour, having appointed someone to have a look at Felixstowe, received a report subsequently which stated, "The security of men employed on dock work in this Port is as much as that of the average industrial worker," and went on to say that the appointee had come to the conclusion, without any hesitation, "That Felixstowe is not a Port which ought to be brought into the Scheme." The Scheme referred to was the National Dock Labour Scheme opposed by the Company's management and its tenants and, on this occasion, with the vigorous support of the employees. By 1960 the management had established a policy of keeping employees acquainted with progress and future developments and everyone was taking a deep and personal interest in the project. The Company introduced its own pension scheme and all members were covered by free life assurance in addition to the normal Employers' Liability Insurance, the Stevedores' Indemnity policies and the like. Meetings of the Dock Workers Committee and of heads of departments, foremen and chargehands were inaugurated on a more formal basis and new canteen facilities, a first aid room, locker room and other amenities were provided.

During 1961 the port's improvements in shipping turnround time, a factor of great importance, and the efforts made to seek new trade led to the inauguration of three regular cargo liner services between Felixstowe and east and west coast ports of Sweden. The cargo-handling was such that Felixstowe became the most efficient port in Europe, taking the title from the Swedish port of Umea, and study groups of shipowners and agents, exporters' clubs and others concerned with shipping and cargo-handling began to visit the port to study its handling methods. Felixstowe was the only British port and one of

In 1967 work had begun on the completion of the Container Quay. Crane, slipway and piers had now disappeared. *The Felixstowe Dock and Railway Company*

only six British companies to take part in the important first Europort Exhibition.

Tanker vessels up to 5,000 tons deadweight for some time had been berthing and discharging cargoes through pipelines terminating on the North Pier. This facility was additional to the pipeline terminal provided on the North Quay for imported solvents. The berthing of tankers on the North Entrance Pier reduced the width of the entrance and interfered with the safe passage of vessels. Regular cargo service vessels were occasionally delayed because of a ban, for safety reasons, on entry whilst hazardous chemicals of low flash point were being discharged. It thus became necessary, because of this and an expansion of trade, to construct an oil jetty and jetty head. The largest tanker able to negotiate the entrance to Harwich Harbour was one of 15,000 tons deadweight and it was found possible to obtain enough depth of water for a ship of this size to lie afloat at the terminal at all states of the tide. An increase to this size tanker would result in substantially lower freight charges for importers of hydrocarbon oils making the port even more attractive.

Dry cargo handled by the port had increased by over 25 per cent per annum over the last few years and there was every indication that it would continued to increase in the same proportion at least. Calculations showed that in 1965 the amount would rise to some 50,000 tons more than the maximum capacity. It was not possible to increase the number of berths in the existing Dock Basin nor to enlarge the Basin. A new dry cargo quay and approach was proposed, the quay to be 700 feet in length and with depth at low water of at least 30 feet to accommodate larger vessels. This led to consideration of new trade such as newsprint from Canada and general cargo services with Commonwealth ports. Assuming that increased traffic could be maintained the new dry cargo quay would be working to capacity by the middle of 1968. There were increasing demands for warehousing, offices, marshalling yards to cope with the increasing tonnages being consigned by rail, the provision of a Roll on/Roll off (Ro/Ro) service and the necessary parking space for the heavy goods vehicles. In addition the Dock Company were having to look to improve services and amenities for the growing complex and these included a new fire station for the port's own fire brigade and accommodation for the port's vehicles and mobile plant.

In 1964 an oil jetty was constructed extending 1,100 feet into Harwich Harbour where vessels could discharge their cargoes of petroleum products, chemicals and liquified gas. The Harwich Harbour Conservancy Board proceeded to deepen the channel into and through Harwich Harbour and this increased, at the end of 1968, the deadweight tonnage of vessels able to use the oil jetty.

189

Townsend Thoresen's *European Gateway* at No. 1 ro-ro berth. In 1982 this vessel was involved in a collision in the Harwich approaches and sank clear of the shipping channel. After lying on her side for some months she was raised and towed away to be rebuilt, later to serve in the Middle East under a new owner.   *The Felixstowe Dock and Railway Company*

The Transport Ferry Service terminal (No. 1 Ro/Ro Berth) was completed early in 1965 for bow and stern loading vessels up to 450 feet long. The terminal consisted of a floating pontoon which connected with the marshalling area by two steel girder bridges.

In 1966 a derrick crane was erected in the Dock Basin to handle containers to and from the United States via Continental ports. In July a serious fire badly damaged the Maltings but in November work began on the Container Terminal. The first part of the quay was available for use by the end of June, 1967 and a Paceco Vickers was worked on 1st July and by March 1968 the whole facility was completed. This comprised 1,300 feet of quay with two container berths, two Portainer cranes, a Ro/Ro Berth and had involved the reclamation of 13 acres of land. It was at this time that what was probably the old Air Station's most remembered feature disappeared. The construction of the Container Terminal involved the demolition of the old 50-ton Titan hammer-head crane and the pier which had served both the R.A.F. and the Dock Company for so long and so efficiently.

Due to the growth of container requirements and the expansion of Ro/Ro traffic the Company sought and obtained by a new Act of Parliament in 1968 to extend the Container Terminal and provide new facilities to the north of the port for future development.

190

Trelawny House, a six storey office building, was completed in 1969 and work was started on an outside warehousing complex adjacent to the port capable of expanding with the growth of the port.

In 1970, through the National Ports Council to the Ministry of Transport permission was sought to extend the Container Terminal by 700 feet in length and to reclaim a further three acres of land for the building of a Freightliner Terminal and the development of a further fourteen acres of open storage behind the Terminal. The northern development consisted of the reclamation of 60 acres to be enclosed by a quay wall with a frontage of some 1,600 feet to the north of the Dock Basin to provide for future Ro/Ro terminals and general cargo berths together with marshalling and open storage areas, transit sheds and warehouses.

In 1971 the port agreed to purchase some 60 acres of land from the Ministry of Defence which were essential to provide the areas necessary for the efficient servicing of the container trade both then and in the future. Early in 1972 work commenced on the extension of the Container Terminal and in mid-year work commenced on the northern development. Work on the 60 acres ex-Ministry of Defence land was nearing completion and on 28th November the Freightliner Terminal opened. On 24th April, 1973 the 700 foot extension to the Container Terminal with a third Portainer crane was opened. A few days later, 7th May, the spur road linking the A45 at Trimley

An aerial view of the port showing the Dooley and Walton Container Terminals, added in 1981, at the top of the picture. The Landguard Container Terminal is in the foreground, with the old dock basin in the middle distance. This view can be compared with that on page 182, taken in the mid-Seventies.   *The Felixstowe Dock and Railway Company*

direct to the Dock road and bypassing Felixstowe, approved in 1967, was officially opened. The Car Terminal providing storage for 1,500 export vehicles on a six acre site was completed. On 19th November, 1973 No. 3 Ro/Ro Berth on the northern development opened.

April, 1974 saw the completion of an upper deck loading ramp, No. 1 Ro/Ro Berth, which was built on top of the existing pontoon enabling units to be driven on and off the upper decks of vessels. In July the first general cargo vessels were worked on the northern development whilst in October the twice daily passenger sails to Zeebrugge, the first regular such service from the Port, was started by Townsend Thoresen's m.v. *Viking II.*

1975 saw the No. 4 Ro/Ro Berth open, the building of the Tor Line and Townsend Thoresen Passenger Terminals and the first Tor Line passenger service to Gothenburg started. In September the Company celebrated its centenary marked by the official opening of the northern development by Lord Walpole. The Company, the Felixstowe Dock and Railway Company, reached an agreement with the British Transport Docks Board for the sale of the Company. In February 1976 European Ferries Limited made a counter bid for the Company and after a long and protracted passage through the House of Commons and the House of Lords the bill enacted by the British Transport Docks Board was defeated in the House of Lords on 22nd October, 1976 and the Company remained in the hand of European Ferries Limited.

As Felixstowe was added to the European Ferries Group's other port interests, at Larne, in Northern Ireland, Cairnryan in Scotland and at Harwich, an immediate investment of £670,000 for new equipment was made, and as by 1977 the whole complex was working near to capacity the Company invested in further mechanical equipment as part of the expansion and renewal programme to take capital expenditure past the £1 million mark. In November 1977 a near £2 million investment in the Port of Felixstowe was the first stage of a project planned to increase lift-on, lift-off container handling by 40% and provide the most modern handling equipment. It will be the first port in the U.K. to utilise Paceco Transtainer gantry cranes for container handling and the first in Europe to change from straddle carrier operation. The Transtainer moves independently on rubber-tyred wheels as opposed to rails; the wheels turn through 90 degrees, the machine has a 74 foot span and a lifting height of 40 foot. It is capable of carrying 35 tons beneath a telescopic spreader and it can stack eight foot wide containers three high with the ability to lift the fourth over the top.

Felixstowe has emerged as the largest and most successful container port in the United Kingdom as shipping companies recognise the unique geographical position of Felixstowe's modern dock facilities. The port has been able to provide access to many of the major trade routes linking the United Kingdom with North and Central America, North, East and West Africa,

Pakistan, India, Sri Lanka, the Middle East and Far East, and, of course, Europe.

More than £50 million has been invested in Felixstowe since 1976 and another phase of major expansion is expected to begin during 1985, when it is planned that the port limits will be extended further upstream towards Ipswich and what was once marsh will become riverside quays.

A feature of this growth port has been the excellent labour relations among the 1,500 people who daily carry out their tasks on the facility area of more than 400 acres. In recent years the influence of Felixstowe has spread far beyond the shores of the United Kingdom as the Port Consultancy Service completed port development feasibility studies in Tanjung Priok, Indonesia, and in Bahrain and Auckland during 1983, and in 1984 a similar contract was won in Kuwait. If this was not enough, Felixstowe is now managing a new port in the United Arab Emirates, Fujairah, a port in a prime position on the Indian Ocean coast for trans-shipment trading.

Regrettably an ex-Felixstowe serving R.A.F. officer and later Chairman of the Dock Company, Mr. K. W. Wickenden, F.C.A., was killed during 1984 when his private aircraft crashed while on a test flight; he was sadly missed by all who knew him.

At the time of writing only one hangar remains, rising majestically above the sea of containers. Doubtless many arriving at and departing from the port will look out on to this reminder of days past and not know its true history. Hopefully they will spare a few minutes to search out its history and learn some of the achievements of this hallowed Felixstowe site.

Townsend Thoresen's *Viking Viscount.* This luxury Super Viking Class Car/Passenger ship operates on the Felixstowe to Zeebrugge ferry service. Built at Aalborg, Denmark and launched in 1975, she carries 1,200 passengers and 255 cars at a service speed of 21 knots.

The Felixstowe Dock and Railway Company

Appendix I

Station Commanders

Captain C. E. Risk, R.M.	1913-1914
Lieutenant C. E. H. Rathbone, R.N.	1914-1915
Commander J. C. Porte, R.N.	1915-1918
Wing Commander C. E. Risk, R.A.F.	1918-1919
Wing Commander I. T. Courtney, R.A.F.	1919-1922
Flying Officer F. Wilton, D.C.M., R.A.F.	1922-1924
Wing Commander C. E. H. Rathbone, R.A.F.	1924-1925
Wing Commander R. B. Maycock, O.B.E., R.A.F.	1925-1928
Group Captain G. R. Bromet, D.S.O., O.B.E., R.A.F.	1928-1931
Group Captain A. J. Milay, O.B.E., R.A.F.	1931-1936
Group Captain N. J. P. Burling, D.S.C., D.F.C., A.F.C., R.A.F.	1936-1939
Wing Commander D. G. Fleming, R.A.F.	1939-1940
Wing Commander W. B. Hellard, R.A.F.	1940-1942
Wing Commander N. Keeble, R.A.F.	1942-1943
Wing Commander L. G. Martin, D.F.C., R.A.F.	1943-1945
Group Captain W. G. Abrams, R.A.F.	1945-1946
Group Captain W. P. Welch, D.F.C., R.A.F.	1946-1948
Group Captain C. A. Watt, R.A.F.	1948-1949
Wing Commander D. H. Thomas, D.S.O., D.F.M., R.A.F.	1949-1951
Wing Command C. V. Winn, D.S.O., O.B.E., D.F.C., R.A.F.	1951-1953
Wing Commander J. A. Chorlton, O.B.E., R.A.F.	1953-1954
Wing Commander W. O. Jones, R.A.F.	1954-1956
Wing Commander R. P. Burton, M.B.E., R.A.F.	1956-1957
Wing Commander J. T. O'Sullivan, O.B.E., R.A.F.	1957-1960
Wing Commander C. F. Price, R.A.F.	1960-1961
Wing Commander C. H. Baker, R.A.F.	1961-1962

Appendix II

Aircraft Associated with Felixstowe. 1912-1961

Type	Serial No. /Registration	Notes
1912		
Bleriot Monoplane	—	M. Henri Selmet's aircraft.
Short S.41.	No. 10	Samson's aircraft.
1913		
Borel Seaplane	—	French built. 80 h.p. Gnome.
Farman, Henry	No. 139	French built seaplane.
Farman, Maurice	No. 115	French built. 100 h.p. Renault.
Farman, Maurice	—	French built. 130 h.p. Salmson.
Sopwith Bat Boat No. 1	No. 38	First British flying boat.
Sopwith Seaplane	—	Green-engined civil aircraft.
1914		
Curtiss H.4. Small America	Nos. 950-951. 1230-1231. 3546	American built flying boats.
F.B.A. Flying boat		British built flying boat.
Farman, Henry	No. 139. 142	French designed seaplanes.
Farman, Maurice	No. 115	French built. 100 h.p. Renault.
Farman, Maurice	—	French built. 130 h.p. Salmson.
Short Type 74	No. 79	British built seaplane.
Short No. 19	—	British built seaplane.
Sopwith Bat Boat No. 1	No. 38	British flying boat. 100 h.p. Green.
1915		
Admiralty AD.1000 Seaplane	No. 1358	Twin fuselaged British seaplane.
Curtiss H.4. Small America	Nos. 950. 1230-1231. 3545-3546 3549. 3580. 3592	American built flying boats.
F.B.A. Flying Boat	—	British flying boat.
Norman Thompson. NT.2B	—	British flying boat.
Norman Thompson. NT.4 and NT.4A	—	British flying boat.
Porte/Felixstowe H.4 ex-Curtiss	Nos. 1230-1231	Modified American built flying boat.
Short Type 184	—	British twin float seaplane.
Sopwith Schneider	—	Small racing seaplane Scout.
Sopwith Baby	—	Single seat Scout seaplane.
Wight Twin Seaplane	Nos. 1450-1451	Large British seaplane bomber.
Wight Admiralty Seaplane. 840	No. 838	Large British seaplane bomber.
Wight Trainer	No. 8322	British 2-seat training seaplane.

1916

Admiralty AD.1000 Seaplane	No. 1358	Unsuccessful bomber seaplane.
Bristol Scout C.	No. 3028	Used in air launch experiment.
Curtiss H.4 Small America	Nos. 3545-3546 3569. 3580.	Operational flying boats.
Curtiss H.12 Large America	No. 8650	American built flying boat, later F.2.
Curtiss Wannamaker Model T	No. 3073	Massive American built flying boat.
Felixstowe Porte F.1	No. 3580	Felixstowe modified Curtiss boat.
Mann Egerton Type B	No. 9085	Norwich built seaplane.
Norman Thompson NT.2B	—	British training flying boat.
Porte Baby	No. 9800-9811	Twelve Felixstowe built flying boats.
Short Type 184	No. 8349	Seaplane for torpedo trials.
Sopwith Baby	No. 8164	Single seat seaplane Scout.
Wight Admiralty Type 840	No. 838	Large bomber seaplane. Trials.
Wight Baby	No. 9097	Experimental Scout seaplane.

1917

Admiralty A.D.	N.1522	Supermarine flying boat for trial.
Curtiss H.4 Small America	No. 3545-6 3580	Ex-operational flying boats for training.
Curtiss H.12 Large America	Nos. 8650. 8659 8660-1. 8663 8666. 8676-7 8683. 8689. 8691	Operational flying boats with War Flight
Curtiss Wannamaker Model T	No. 3073	Large experimental U.S.A. flying boat.
Fairey Hamble Baby	—	Single seat seaplane Scout.
Felixstowe F.2A	N.4302. N.4533 N.4545	Operational flying boats.
Felixstowe F.2C.	N.65	Experimental modified flying boat.
Felixstowe F.3	N.64	Experimental Felixstowe flying boat.
Norman Thompson NT.2B	—	Training flying boat.
Norman Thompson NT.4A	—	British built flying boat.
Phoenix Cork Mk. 1	N.86	Large British built flying boats for
Mk. II	N.87	operational trials.
Short Type 184	No. 8349	Seaplane for torpedo trials.
Short Type 320	N.1498	Operational biplane seaplane.

1918

Curtiss H.4 Small America	Nos. 3545-6 3580	Ex-operational flyings boats for training.
Curtiss H.16	N.4060	American built operational flying boat.
Fairey IIIC	N.2255	Twin float 2-seat seaplane.
Fairey Hamble Baby		Single seat Scout seaplane.
Felixstowe F.2A	N.4302. N.4533 N.4545	Operational flying boats.
Felixstowe/Curtiss H.12	Nos. 8683. 8689	Modified operational flying boats.
Felixstowe F.3	N.4230	Operational flying boat.
Felixstowe F.5	N.90	Felixstowe built prototype flying boat.

Felixstowe Fury	N.123	Felixstowe built triplane flying boats.
Norman Thompson NT.2B	—	Flying boat trainer.
Norman Thompson NT.4A	—	Flying boat used as trainer.
Short Type 184	—	Standard seaplane design as hack.
Short Type 320	—	Standard seaplane as trials aircraft.
Sopwith Camel. 2F1	N.6812	Culley's aircraft for lighter operations.

1919

Fairey Titania	N.129	Four engined prototype flying boat.
Fairey IIIC	N.2255 later G-EAPV	Trials aircraft.
Felixstowe F2As	Several on strength	Standard aircraft ex-operations.
Felixstowe F.3	No. 4041. N.4044	Standard aircraft on trials.
Felixstowe F.5s	Various Short built aircraft	As above.
Felixstowe Fury	N.123	Experimental triplane flying boat.
Short Type 184	Various	Resident aircraft on trials.
Short Type 184	—	Trials for Estonian Air Force.
Supermarine Baby	N.59	Trials aircraft with 200 h.p. Hispano.

1920

Fairey Titania	N.129	Extended evaluation trials.
Fairey III	G-EALQ	Air Ministry Competition aircraft.
Fairey Pintail Mk. I	N.133	Experimental aircraft from Grain.
Felixstowe F.5	N.4838. N.4044 N.178	Experimental trials aircraft.
Phoenix Cork Mk. I	N.86	Experimental flying boat for trials.
Mk. II	N.87	Modified version of above.
Short Type 184	Various	Wartime aircraft in storage.
Supermarine Seagull Mk. I	G-EAVE	Air Ministry Competition aircraft.
Vickers Viking III	G-EAUK	Air Ministry Competition aircraft.

1921

Fairey Titania	N.129	Further evaluation trials.
Fairey Pintail. Mk. I	N.133	Prototype 2-seat seaplane.
Mk. II	N.134	Modified version of above.
Mk. III	N.135	Further modified version.
Felixstowe F.5	N.177	Short "Tin Five" metal hull.
	N.178	Saunders ventilated hull.
Parnall Puffin	N.136. N.138	Two prototype seaplanes.
Phoenix Cork	N.86. N.87	Prototypes on extended trials.
Short Type 184	Various	Stored aircraft.
Vickers Viking III	N.147	G-EAUK purchased by Air Ministry.

1922

Fairey Titania.	N.129	Resident trials aircraft.

Parnall Puffin	N.136	Extended evaluation trials.
Phoenix Cork	N.86. N.87	Prototypes on armament trials.
Short F.5	N.4839	Standard production aircraft.
Short Cromarty	N.120	Modified F.5 for trials.
Supermarine Seal.	N.146	Modified Seagull for evaluation.
Supermarine Seagull II	N.158	Seagull with extra tankage.
Vickers Valentia	N.126	Prototype twin engined flying boat.
Vickers Viking V	N.156	Production amphibian for trials.

1923

English Electric Kingston I	N.9709	Prototype twin engines flying boat.
Fairey Atlanta	N.119	Prototype flying boat trials.
De Havilland 50	—	Experimental aircraft.
Supermarine Seagull II	N.158	Further evaluation trials.
Supermarine Sea Lion III	N.170	Ex-Schneider Trophy aircraft for trials.

1924

Avro Bison 1A	N.9594	Amphibian for evaluation.
De Havilland 18	G-EAWW	Ditching trials aircraft.
Dornier Dolphin III	N.176	German built flying boat for evaluation.
English Electric Ayr	N.148	Unusual flying boat for evaluation.
Fairey Titania	N.129	Continuing evaluation trials.
Fairey Flycatcher	N.9678. Various	Production aircraft for trials.
Fairey IIID	N.9777	Experimental trials machine.
Felixstowe F.5	N.178	Hull experiments.
Gloster I. ex-Bamel	J.7234	Ex-G-EAXZ racing biplane.
Gloster II	J.7504	Specially built racing seaplane.
Parnall Plover	N.9610	Prototype single seat seaplane.
Supermarine Swan	G-EBJY ex N.175	Twin-engined flying boat for civil trials.
Supermarine Seagull III	—	Modified aircraft for evaluation.
Supermarine Scarab	—	Prototype machine. Trials.
Supermarine Sea Lion II	N.170 ex-G-EBAH	Ex-civil amphibian for trials.
Vickers Vanellus	N.169	Rebuilt Viking VII for evaluation.

1925

English Electric Ayr	N.148	Hydrodynamic trials.
English Electric Kingston I	N.9709	Armament trials.
English Electric Kingston II	N.9712	Engine and armament trials
Fairey IIID	N.9464	Production machine for tests.
Fairey Flycatcher	N.9953	Amphibian version for trials.
Fairey Flycatcher	N.9913	Production machine trials.
Fairey Fremantle	N.173 ex-G-EBLZ	Long range biplane seaplane.
Fairey Titania	N.129	Resident experimental aircraft.
Gloster I	J.7234	Experimental racing seaplane.
Gloster III/A	N.194. N.195	Schneider Trophy seaplanes.

Hawker Hedgehog	N.187 ex-G-EBJN	Ex-civil aircraft for trials.
Parnall Peto	N.181	Extended service trials.
Rohrbach/Beardmore Inverness	N.183	Experimental German built flying boat.
Short F.5	N.177	"Tin Five". Hull experiments.
Short Cockle	G-EBKA; later N.193	Diminutive single seat flying boat.
Supermarine Southampton	N.9896	Service trials.
Supermarine Southampton I	N.218	Prototype twin engined flying boat.
Vickers Vixen II	G-EBIP	Civil seaplane for evaluation.

1926

Beardmore Inverness	N.184	Metal structure experimental flying boat.
Beardmore Inverness	N.193	Extended aerodynamic trials.
Blackburn Blackburn Mk. I	N.9833	Prototype seaplane trials.
Blackburn Blackburn	N.9828	Amphibian version of above.
Blackburn Iris	N.185	Prototype 3-engined flying boat.
Blackburn Ripon II	N.204	Seaplane prototype for trials.
Blackburn Sprat	N.207	Prototype seaplane trainer.
English Electric Ayr	N.148	Hydrodynamic testing vehicle.
English Electric Kingston	N.9712	Aerodynamic trials.
English Electric Kingston	N.9713	Resident experimental large flying boat.
Fairey IIID	N.9464	Production trials aircraft.
Fairey Titania	N.129	Resident large experimental flying boat
Fairey IIID	N.9632. N.9490	General 'hack' aircraft.
Gloster I	J.7234	Experimental high speed seaplane.
Gloster IIIB	N.194. N.195	Schneider Trophy aircraft.
Handley-Page Harrow	N.205	Biplane torpedo bomber seaplane.
Parnall Perch	N.217	Seaplane trainer prototype.
Parnall Peto	N.181. N.182	Small seaplane for submarine use.
Saunders Valkyrie	N.186	Operating and maintenance trials.
Short Cockle	N.193. ex-G-EBKA	Civil flying boat bought by A.M.
Short Singapore I	N.179	Prototype large military flying boat.
Short F.5 Modified	N.177	Extended metal hull trials.
Supermarine Southampton	S.1037. S.1038	Production aircraft for evaluation.
Vickers Vendace I	N.208	Seaplane trainer prototype.

1927

Blackburn RB I Iris	N.185	Large 3-engined patrol flying boat.
RB IA Iris	N.185	Modified version of above.
Mk. II Iris	N.185	Further developed version.
Blackburn Ripon	N.204	Seaplane version performance trials.
English Electric Kingston	N.9713	Large flying boat performance tests.
Fairey IIID	N.9633. N.9484	General 'hack' aircraft.
Fairey IIIF	N.198	Prototype seaplane for trials.
Fairey Titania	N.129	Still used for experimental work.

Gloster I	J.7234	Experimental racing seaplane.
Gloster IIIB	N.194. N.195	High speed experimental seaplanes.
Gloster IV	N.222. N.223	Schneider Trophy racing seaplanes.
Parnall Perch	N.217	Performance trials.
Parnall Peto	N.181. N.182	Submarine borne seaplanes for trials.
Saunders Valkyrie	N.186	Large wooden patrol flying boat.
Short Cockle	N.193	Used for experimental work.
Short Mussel 1.	G-EBMJ	2-seat civil monoplane seaplane.
Short Singapore 1	N.179	Prototype on development trials.
Short Sturgeon	N.199	Biplane floatplane for evaluation.
Short Bristow Crusader	N.226	Schneider Trophy racing seaplane.
Supermarine Southampton	S.1039. S.1059	Service performance trials.
Supermarine Southampton	S.1149-S.1152	Four aircraft for Far East Flight.

1928

Avro Avocet	N.209. N.210	High speed seaplane trials.
Avro Buffalo II	N.239	Private venture seaplane trials.
Beardmore Inverness	N.184	Further metal hull trials.
Blackburn Bluebird II	G-EBSW	Small civil seaplane performance trials.
Blackburn Iris	N.185	Trials for Mark IV version.
Gloster IV	N.222. N.223	High performance seaplane trials.
Gloster Goring	J.8674	General purpose seaplane trials.
Handley Page Harrow	N.205	General purpose seaplane trials.
Hawker Hawfinch	J.8776	Seaplane fighter performance trials.
Parnall Peto	N.182	Continued performance trials.
Short Calcutta	G-EBVH. G-EBVG	Large civil flying boat trials.
Short Sturgeon	N.199. N.200	General purpose seaplane trials.
Supermarine Seagull III	G-EBXH	Civil amphibian performance tests.
Supermarine Seamew	N.212	Amphibian performance trials.
Supermarine Solent	G-AAAB	Civil flying boat trials.
Supermarine Southampton	N.9826. S.1248. S.1059	Service aircraft for trials.
Supermarine Southampton	N.9896	Engaged on fishery patrol duties
Vickers Vireo	N.211	Fighter seaplane performance tests.

1929

Avro Avocet	N.209. N.210	Seaplanes used for high speed training.
Armstrong Whitworth Atlas I	J.8799. J.9998	Evaluated as twin float seaplanes.
Blackburn Iris Mk. II	N.185	Rebuilt aircraft for trials.
Blackburn Iris Mk. III	N.238	Further aircraft for evaluation.
Blackburn Ripon IIA	S.1268. S.1468	Production aircraft trials.
De Havilland Gipsy Moth	G-AADV	Evaluation as twin float seaplane.
Fairey IIIF	S.1336	Performance trials.
Fairey Firefly III	S.1592	Used as high speed seaplane trainer.
Fairey Flycatcher	S.1288	Used as high speed seaplane trainer.
Gloster IV	N.222. N.223	Schneider Trophy aircraft.
Hawker Hoopoe	N.237	Trials of single seat floatplane.
Hawker Horsley	S.1247	Torpedo seaplane performance trials.

200

Parnall Plover	N.9610	Extended tests on twin float seaplane.
Short Calcutta	G-ADDN	C. of A. trials of large civil flying boat.
Short Mussel II	G-AAFZ	Civil seaplane for C. of A. trials.
Short Singapore I	N.179	Rebuilt aircraft for evaluation.
Supermarine Air Yacht	G-AASE	Civil flying boat for trials.
Supermarine Southampton	N.9896	Fishery patrol duties aircraft.
Supermarine Southampton III	S.1059	Developed aircraft evaluation.
Vickers Vildebeeste	N.230	Single engined torpedo seaplane.
Westland Wapiti	J.9597	Evaluated as twin float seaplane.

1930

Armstrong Whitworth Atlas	J.9998	Continued evaluation trials.
Blackburn Bluebird	G-EBSW	Light civil biplane for C. of A. trials.
Blackburn Iris III	N.238	Engine and armament trials.
Blackburn Sydney	N.241	Three-engined monoplane flying boat.
De Havilland Gipsy Moth	K.2235	Trials as single float seaplane.
De Havilland Puss Moth	G-AAVB	Long range civil lightplane trials.
Fairey IIIF	N.198	Seaplane performance tests.
Fairey Firefly	S.1592	High speed seaplane trainer.
Fairey Flycatcher	S.1288	High speed seaplane trainer.
Fairey Fleetwing	N.235	High speed seaplane trainer.
Gloster IV	N.222. N.223	Schneider Trophy machines.
Gloster VI	N.249. N.250	Schneider Trophy machines.
Saro Cloud	G-ABCJ	C. of A. trials for civil amphibian.
Saro Severn	N.240	Evaluation of 3-engined flying boat.
Short Gurnard I	N.228	Prototype trials of single-seat floatplane.
Short Rangoon	S.1433-1435	Squadron aircraft for trials.
Short Singapore	N.179	Hydrodynamic performance trials.
Short Singapore II	N.246	Developed Mk. I aircraft for trials.
Short Valetta	G-AAJY	Large three-engined seaplane trials.
Short Kawanishi KF.I	M-2	Flying boat for Japanese Navy.
Sikorsky S.39.A	G-ABFN	American amphibian for trials.
Simmonds Spartan	G-AMMG	Civil lightplane for C. of A. trials.
Spartan Arrow	G-ABBE	Light civil seaplane. C. of A. trials.
Supermarine S.6A	N.248. N.247	Schneider Trophy aircraft.
Supermarine Southampton	N.251	General performance tests.
Supermarine Southampton Mk. IV	S.1122	Developed aircraft for evaluation.
Supermarine Southampton Mk. X	N.252	Further developed aircraft trials.
Vickers Vildebeeste	G-ADGE	Evaluated for Spanish Air Force.

1931

Avro 621	K.2893 ex-G-ABGH	2-seat seaplane trainer for trials.
Blackburn IV	G-AAUT	Civil lightplane seaplane trials.
Blackburn Iris Mk. IV	N.185	Further development aircraft.
Blackburn Ripon III	S.1272	Prototype developed aircraft.

Blackburn Sydney	N.241	Extended performance trials.
De Havilland Gipsy Moth	K.2235	Hydrodynamic trials for lightplane.
De Havilland DH.60T Tiger Moth	K.2588	2-seat seaplane trainer evaluation.
Fairey Firefly	S.1592	High speed trainer aircraft.
Hawker Hart	J.9052	Used as Osprey trials aircraft.
Hawker Nimrod	S.1578	Production aircraft performance trials.
Saro Cloud	K.2681 G-ABHG	Performance trials.
Saro Severn	N.240	Armament and performance trials.
Saro Windhover	G-ABJP	Certificate of Airworthiness trials.
Short Gurnard II	N.229	Evaluation tests.
Short Kent	G-ABFA	Evaluation as civil flying boat.
Short Singapore II	N.246	Successive developments on prototype.
Short Valetta	G-AAJY	Performance for long distance flight.
Sikorsky S.38B	G-ABYS	Civil performance trials.
Supermarine S.6	N.247	Schneider Trophy aircraft.
Supermarine Air Yacht	G-AASE	Performance trials for civil flying boat.
Supermarine Southampton III	Various	Squadron aircraft for No. 209 Squadron.
Supermarine Southampton X	N.252	Trials on developed aircraft.

1932

Avro Sea Tutor	K.2893	Service performance trials.
Blackburn Iris IV	N.185	Further development of prototype.
Blackburn Iris V	S.1263	Performance trials.
Blackburn Sydney	N.241	Armament and engine trials.
Bristol Fighter Mk. IV	G-ABYA	Tanker aircraft for endurance record flight.
Fairey Seal	K.3577	Service performance trials.
Hawker Danetorp	No. 202	Trials for Royal Danish Naval Service.
Hawker Hart	No. 151	Trials for Estonian Air Force.
Hawker Nimrod	S. 1578. S.1577	Performance trials, production aircraft.
Hawker Osprey I	S.1678. K.2777	Evaluation as service floatplane.
Hawker Osprey II	—	Performance of developed aircraft.
Parnall Prawn	S.1576	Trials for fighter flying boat.
Saro Severn	N.240	Resident for large flying boat trials.
Saro Windhover	G-ABJP "City of Portsmouth"	Flying boat used in endurance flight.
Short Rangoon	K.2134. K.2809	Performance trials for squadron aircraft.
Short Sarafand	S.1589	Trials of large 6-engined flying boat.
Short Singapore IIC	N.246	Final development of this flying boat.
Supermarine Scapa	S.1648	Prototype performance trials.
Supermarine Southampton	S.1229	Production aircraft trials.
Vought Corsair V.66.E	K.3561	American catapult aircraft for trials.

1933

Blackburn Iris IV	N.185	Prototype in residence for general use.
Blackburn Iris V	S.1264	Performance trials.
Blackburn Perth	K.3580	Development of Iris as patrol flying boat.
Blackburn Ripon	S.1272	Floatplane torpedo bomber trials.
Blackburn Sydney	N.241	Prototype used a general service aircraft.
De Havilland Queen Bee I	K.3584	Radio controlled target aircraft.
Hawker Nimrod II	K.2823	Stainless steel production aircraft trials.
Hawker Osprey III	K.3615. K.3635	Production aircraft performance trials.
Saro Cloud	K.2681	Training amphibian trials.
Short Sarafand	S.1589	Continued performance trials.
Short Singapore IIC	N.246	Prototype in residence as 'hack'.
Supermarine Scapa	S.1648	Prototype performance trials.
Supermarine Seagull V	N-1. Later Walrus. K.4797	Prototype amphibian for Royal Australian Air Force.

1934

Avro Sea Tutor	K.3372	Production aircraft performance.
Blackburn M.1/30.A	K.3591	Used for ditching trials.
Blackburn Perth	K.3581. K.4011	Armament and performance trials.
Blackburn Sydney	N.241	General 'hack' aircraft.
Hawker Hart	No. 1303	Trials for Royal Swedish Air Force.
Parnall Prawn	S.1576	Continued trials on fighter flying boat.
Saro Cloud	K.2894	Trainer amphibian performance tests.
Saro London Mk. I	K.3560	Prototype twin engined flying boat.
Saro London Mk. II	K.3560	Developed prototype performance test.
Saro London Mk. II	K.5258	Production aircraft trials.
Short Rangoon	K.3678	Service trials.
Short R.24/31	K.3574	Prototype monoplane flying boat trials.
Short Scion I	G-ACOX	Civil floatplane performance trials.
Short Singapore IIC	N.246	Prototype as general service aircraft.
Short Singapore III	K.3592-3. K.4577. K.4581	Production aircraft for service trials.
Supermarine Scapa I	S.1648	Prototype for production trials.
Supermarine Walrus I	K.5772. K.4797	Amphibian for F.A.A. catapult duties.

1935

Avro Rota I	K.4296	Autogyro floatplane for trials.
Avro Sea Tutor	K.3372	Flotation and buoyancy trials.
Blackburn Perth	K.3581. K.4011	Armament and performance trials.

Blackburn Perth I	K.3582	No. 209 Squadron aircraft.
Blackburn Shark I	K.4295	Prototype trials on F.A.A. seaplane.
Blackburn Shark II	K.5607	Production aircraft performance.
Fairey Seal	K.3577	General purpose floatplane trials.
Fairey Swordfish	K.4190	F.A.A. catapult floatplane trials.
Hawker Osprey III	S.1700	Single float seaplane trials.
Parnall Prawn	S.1576	Extended trials due to engine trouble.
Saro Cloud	K.2894	General service aircraft.
Saro London	K.3560. K.5908	Armament and performance trials.
Short R.24/31	K.3574	Continued prototype performance.
Short Sarafand	S.1589	Service and development trials.
Short Scion Senior	VT-AGU	Civil evaluation for overseas duty.
Short Singapore IIC	N.246	General service aircraft.
Short Singapore III	K.4577	Production aircraft trials.
Supermarine Scapa	S.1648	Prototype on extended trials.
Supermarine Seagull V	A.2-1	Trials for R.A.A.F.
Supermarine Southampton II	K.2888. K.2889	Trials aircraft
Supermarine Stranraer	K.3973	Prototype performance trials.
Vought Corsair V.66.E	K.3561	Trials on American catapult aircraft.

1936

Airspeed Queen Wasp	K.8888	Radio controlled target aircraft.
Avro Sea Tutor	K.3475	General trials aircraft.
Blackburn Perth	K.3581. K.4011	Armament and performance trials.
Fairey Sea Fox	K.4305	Prototype catapult aircraft trials.
Fairey Swordfish	K.4190	F.A.A. floatplane trials.
Hawker Osprey III	S.1700	Single float seaplane trials.
Hawker Osprey III	S.1699. S.1701	Production aircraft service trials.
Short Empire	G-ADHM "Caledonia"	Civil airliner performance trials.
Short R.24/31	K.3574	Armament and service trials.
Short Sarafand	S.1589	General flying test bed.
Short Singapore IIC	N.246	Test bed for systems testing.
Short Singapore III	K.4577	Aircraft for development testing.
Supermarine Southampton	S.1149	Extended trials.

1937

Blackburn Iris V	S.1593	Resident general service aircraft.
De Havilland Hornet Moth	P.6785	Light floatplane for evaluation.
Hawker Hind	No. 1	Evaluation for Yugoslav Air Force.
Hawker Osprey III	S.1700	Single float seaplane development.
Hawker Osprey III	S.1699. S.1701	Production aircraft service trials.
Short R.24/31	K.3574	General flying test bed.

1938

Blackburn Iris V	S.1593	Test bed for armament trials.
De Havilland Hornet Moth	P.6785	Light floatplane performance trials.
Saro Lerwick	L.7248	Prototype large flying boat trials.

204

Saro London	K.3560	Prototype aircraft trials.
	K.5257	Mark II type trials.
Short Mayo Composite	G-ADHK. "Maia"	Lower component of composite pair.
Short Mayo Composite	G-ADHJ "Mercury"	Upper component of composite pair.
Short R.24/31	K.3574	General flying test bed.
Short Singapore III	K.8567	Production aircraft trials.
Short Sunderland	K.4774	Prototype flying boat trials.
Short Sunderland	L.2158-60	Production aircraft for service trials.
Supermarine Stranraer	K.7291	Squadron trials aircraft.

1939

Consolidated Catalina	P.9630	First American aircraft for trials.
Fairey Albacore	L.7075	F.A.A. torpedo bomber trials.
Saro Lerwick	K.7248	Prototype trials.
	K.7249	Prototype trials.
	K.7251	Prototype trials.
	K.7252	Prototype trials.
Short "C" Class	G-AFCU	Civil flying boat trials.
Short Singapore III	K.6922	Squadron trials.
Short Sunderland I	L.2158	Production aircraft trials.
	L.5807	Production aircraft trials.
	N.9021	Production aircraft trials.
Supermarine Stranraer	K.7290	Production aircraft trials.
	K.7295	Production aircraft trials.

During the above years many established aircraft types resided at the air station and were used as general service and test bed machines, involved with aerodynamic, hydrodynamic, engine and armament trials.

1940

Consolidated Catalina	Various	Aircraft for modifications.
Fokker T.VIII.W	R.I-R.II. Later AV.985-965.	Dutch aircraft which fled during German occupation.
Short Mayo Upper Component	G-ADHJ	Used as trainer seaplane.
Short Sunderland	Various	Aircraft for modifications.
Supermarine Walrus	Various	Limited Air Sea Rescue duties.

1941

Consolidated Catalina	Various	Aircraft visiting Maintenance Unit.
Short Mayo Composite	G-ADHJ	Upper Unit for seaplane training.
Short Sunderland	Various	Aircraft visiting Maintenance Unit.
Supermarine Walrus	Various	Air Sea Rescue duties.

1942

Consolidated Catalina	Various	Aircraft for modifications.
Fokker T.VIII.W	R.25	Used for Special Duties. (Dutch)

Short Sunderland	Various	Visitors to Maintenance Unit.
Supermarine Walrus	Various	Air Sea Rescue Duties.

1943

Consolidated Catalina IB FB.222	Various	Aircraft visiting Maintenance Unit.
Short Sunderland	Various	Aircraft visiting Maintenance Unit.
Supermarine Walrus	Various	Air Sea Rescue Duties.

1944

Consolidated Catalina IVA	JX.268. Various	Visitors to Maintenance Unit.
Short Sunderland	Various	Visitors for radar fitting at M.U.
Supermarine Walrus	Various	Air Sea Rescue Duties.

1945

Arado 196. (Ex-Luftwaffe)	VM.748. VM.761	German aircraft for evaluation.
Blohm und Voss BV.138B. (Ex-Luftwaffe)	VK.895. VM.743. VN.887	German aircraft for evaluation.
Consolidated Catalina	Various	Production aircraft for modification.
Dornier Do.18 (Ex-Luftwaffe)	—	German aircraft for evaluation.
Dornier Do.24T. (Ex-Luftwaffe)	VM.483. VN.865. VN.870	German aircraft for evaluation.
F.G.P.227. (Ex-Luftwaffe)	—	German flying scale model flying boat.
Junkers Ju.52/53M. (Ex-Luftwaffe)	—	German aircraft for evaluation.
Saro Shrimp	TK.580	Flying scale model flying boat.
Short Seaford	MZ.269	Developed Sunderland IV trials.
Short Shetland	DX.166	Large prototype flying boat trials.
Short Sunderland IV	MZ.269. MZ.271	Production aircraft for development.
Short Sunderland V	TX.293	Hydrodynamic trials aircraft.
Supermarine Sea Otter	—	A.S.R. and general trials aircraft.
Supermarine Walrus	Various	A.S.R. duties.

1946

All German Ex-Luftwaffe aircraft as detailed in previous year.

Saro Shrimp	TK.580	Flying scale model flying boat.
Short Seaford	NJ.200. NJ.201	Developed Sunderland aircraft.
Short Seaford	MZ.269	Developed Sunderland aircraft.
Short Shetland	DX.166	Performance trials.
Short Sunderland V	SZ.599. TX.293	Last Sunderlands for trials.
Short Sunderland IV	MZ.269. MZ.271. PP.162	General performance trials.
Supermarine Sea Otter	—	Air Sea Rescue duties.

1947-1955

Saro Shrimp	TK.580	Flying scale model flying boat.
Saro SRA/1	TG.267	Jet fighter flying boat trials.
Short Seaford	NJ.200. NJ.201 MZ.269. G-ALIJ	Performance trials.

206

Short Sealand	G-AKLN	Evaluated for A.S.R. duties.
Short Solent 3	G-AKNS/ WM.759.	"City of Liverpool" performance trials.
	NJ.205. NJ.201	Overload trials. Rough water performance.
Short Sunderland V	SZ.599. PP.162 RN.297	General experimental work.
Supermarine Sea Gull	PA.143	Experimental A.S.R. flying boat.
Supermarine Sea Otter	JM.909	Air Sea Rescue duties.

1956-1961

Westland Whirlwind	XJ.435. XJ.763	No. 22 Squadron Air Sea Rescue Helicopters.

The Titan crane still overlooks the area in this picture from the Dooley Beach in the 1960s, but dredgers and pile-drivers gathering to begin work on the new quays herald a big change in the scene. A small coastal tanker is discharging at the newly erected oil jetty.

Appendix III

Formations Associated with Felixstowe Air Station

Royal Naval Air Service

Experimental Seaplane Testing Unit	Various aircraft.
War Flight.	H.12, F.2, F.2A, F2C, F3.
Felixstowe Seaplane Development Flight.	Various aircraft.

Royal Air Force

No. 4 (Operations) Group.	H.12, F.2, F2A, F2C, F.3.
No. 22 Squadron, "B" Flight.	Westland Whirlwind.
No. 26 (ASR) Squadron.	Air Sea Rescue Launches.
No. 33 Wing.	R.A.F. Regiment.
	(Nos. 2, 16 and 48 Squadrons.)
No. 63 Squadron.	R.A.F. Regiment.
No. 85 Maintenance Unit.	Various marine aircraft.
No. 194 Squadron.	R.A.F. Regiment.
No. 205 Squadron.	Supermarine Southampton III.
No. 209 Squadron.	Short Singapore III.
No.210 Squadron.	Supermarine Southampton III
No. 230 Squadron.	Felixstowe F.5.
No. 231 Squadron.	Felixstowe F.3, F.5.
No. 232 Squadron.	Felixstowe F.2A, F.3.
No. 247 Squadron	Felixstowe F2A, F.3.
No. 259 Squadron.	Felixstowe F2A, F.3. Curtiss H.12.
No. 261 Squadron.	Felixstowe F.3.
No. 320 (Netherlands) Squadron.	Fokker T.VIII.W.
No. 356 Squadron. Air Training Corps.	Training Unit.
No. 928 (Balloon) Squadron.	Barrage Balloon Unit.
No. 1103 (Marine Craft) Squadron.	Air Sea Rescue Unit.
High Speed Flight. 1927, 1929 and 1931.	Schneider Trophy Aircraft.
Link Trainer School Unit.	Instrument training unit.
Marine Training School.	Marine Craft Instruction Unit.
Seaplane Development Flight.	Various aircraft.

Royal Navy

1st Flotilla	60' British Power Boat M.T.Bs.
4th Flotilla.	Vosper M.T.Bs.
6th M.G.B. Flotilla.	British Power Boat M.G.Bs.
10th Flotilla.	Thorneycroft M.T.Bs.

Army

East Anglian Regiment.
No. 409 (Suffolk) R.A. Battery.
National Defence Corps.

Appendix IV

Notable Dates

5th August, 1913.	Station commissioned.
1st July, 1914.	Royal Naval Air Service formed.
17th May, 1916.	First airborne separation performed.
13th April, 1917.	First "Spider's Web" Patrol flown.
1st April, 1918.	Royal Air Force formed.
Autumn, 1919.	First long range flight to Norway.
October, 1920.	Air Ministry Civil Aircraft Competition.
1st April, 1924	Marine Aircraft Experimental Establishment formed.
12th August, 1924.	King's Cup Air Race starts at Felixstowe.
1st October, 1926.	High Speed Flight formed for 1927 event.
Summer, 1926.	Long distance flight to Egypt.
17th May, 1927.	No. 205 Squadron Far East Flight formed.
12th August, 1927.	Northern European Capitals Flying Boat Cruise.
27th September, 1927.	Long distance flight to Karachi.
17th October, 1927.	Far East Flight to Australia and Singapore.
February, 1928.	First large civil flying boat C. of A. (Calcutta)
1st February, 1929.	High Speed Flight reformed. (For 1929 event)
Spring, 1931.	First long range squadron delivery flight. (Rangoons to Basra)
August, 1931.	6,500 mile flight by prototypes to Aden.
Summer, 1935.	First floatplane autogyro tested.
15th September, 1936.	First Short Empire civil flying boat evaluated.
9th May, 1938.	First full-load separation by Mayo Composite aircraft.
3rd September, 1939.	M.A.E.E. evacuated to Helensburgh, Scotland.
June, 1940.	First operational M.T.B. Base in U.K.
May, 1945.	M.A.E.E. returned to Felixstowe.
July, 1945.	Marine Training School formed.
July, 1945.	Link Trainer Instrument Blind Flying School formed.
1st June, 1946.	Felixstowe takes over administration of Martlesham Heath.
April, 1948.	Marine Training School moves to Pembroke Dock.
November, 1949.	First W.A.A.Fs stationed at Felixstowe.
31st January, 1953.	Tragic tidal surge and flood.
April, 1954.	Station moved from No. 11 (F.C.) Group to No. 26 Group.
June, 1958	Station moved from No. 26 Group to No. 22 Group.
26th September, 1958.	Freedom of Entry granted to Air Station.
20th May, 1959.	No. 1103 Marine Craft Units moves to Bridlington.
27th April, 1961.	Last Inspection by Air Officer.
29th May, 1961.	No. 22 Squadron, "B" Flight, moved to Tangmere.
March, 1962.	No. 33 Wing, R.A.F. Regiment leaves.
21st June, 1962.	Final Closure.
1962.	Occupation by Army.

Appendix V

Test and War Flight Pilots

M.A.E.E.

Flight Lieutenant Abrams
Flight Lieutenant Alston
Flying Officer Atcherley
Flight Lieutenant Bainbridge
Flight Lieutenant Barrett
Flight Lieutenant Boothman
Flying Officer Brown
Flight Lieutenant Butler
Flight Lieutenant Cahill
Flight Lieutenant Carnegie
Flying Officer Chadwick
Flight Lieutenant Clift
Flight Lieutenant Cross
Flight Lieutenant D'Arcy Greig
Flight Lieutenant Davies
Flight Lieutenant Davis
Flying Officer Dipple
Flying Officer Flood
Squadron Leader French
Flying Officer Grant-Jones
Flight Lieutenant Hall
Flying Officer Harris
Flying Officer King
Flying Officer Leech
Wing Commander Livock
Flight Lieutenant Long
Flight Lieutenant Lovering
Squadron Leader Major
Wing Commander Martin
Squadron Leader Martin
Flight Lieutenant Martin
Flying Officer Martin
Squadron Leader Maycock
Flight Lieutenant McClymont
Flying Officer Mills
Squadron Leader Orlebar
Flight Lieutenant Parker
Flying Officer Payne
Squadron Leader Pickles
Flight Lieutenant Sawyer
Flying Officer Scholefield
Squadron Leader Scott
Squadron Leader Slatter
Flying Officer Snaith
Flight Lieutenant Smythies
Squadron Leader Squire

Flight Lieutenant Stainforth
Flying Officer Waghorn
Flying Officer Walsh
Flying Officer Wardle
Flight Lieutenant Weblin
Flight Lieutenant Webster
Squadron Leader White
Flying Officer Whittle
Squadron Leader Williamson-Jones
Flying Officer Worsley

War Flight

Aplin	Purdy
Bailey	Rees
Barker	Rhys-Davis
Bath	Samson
Clayton	Tees
Cuckney	Trumble
Culley	Webster
Day	Wilson
Dickey	Young
Duff-Fyffe	
Fauz	Ensign Eaton U.S.N.
Galpin	Ensign Fallen U.S.N.
Galvayne	Ensign Hawkins U.S.N.
Gooch	Ensign Keep U.S.N.
Gordon	Ensign Scheffelin U.S.N.
Hallam	Ensign Sturtevant U.S.N.
Hallinan	Ensign Verys U.S.N.
Hobbs	
Hodgson	
Holmes	
Hope	
Keesey	
MacLauren	
Mackenzie	
Magor	
Martin	
Morrish	
Newton	
Partridge	
Pattison	
Paull	
Perham	
Porte	
Potter	

Appendix VI

TYPICAL FLYING LOG-BOOK ENTRIES

Date and Hour	Aeroplane Type and No.	Pilot	Passenger/s	Time Hr. Min.	Height	Course	Remarks
4.7.28	Calcutta G-EBVG	Flight Lieutenant Cahill	Self and Crew	4·00	0·2000	Local	Consumption Trials
12.7.28	Calcutta G-EBVG	Flight Lieutenant Cahill	Self and Crew	1·00	0·1000	Local	(Oil Tank Burst)
18.7.28	Calcutta G-EBVG	Flight Lieutenant Cahill	Self and Crew	1·15	0·1000	Local	Engine Tests
28.7.28	Calcutta G-EBVG	Flight Lieutenant Cahill	Self and Crew	2·10	0·2000	Felixstowe-Southampton	Take-offs
29.7.28	Calcutta G-EBVG	Flight Lieutenants Cahill, Martin and Clift	Hoare, Self and Crew	0·40	0·2000	Southampton-Channel Isles	
29.7.28	Calcutta G-EBVG	Flight Lieutenants Cahill, Martin and Clift	Hoare, Self and Crew	3·15	0·2000	Channel Isles-Scilly Isles	
30.7.28	Calcutta G-EBVG	Flight Lieutenants Cahill, Martin and Clift	Hoare, Self and Crew	2·10	0·2000	Scilly Isles-Mount Batten	
30.7.28	Calcutta G-EBVG	Flight Lieutenants Cahill, Martin and Clift	Hoare, Self and Crew	6·15	0·2000	Mount Batten-Felixstowe	
17.8.28	Sturgeon N.199	Flight Lieutenant Martin	Self	0·30	0·1000	Local	
18.8.28	Sturgeon N.199	Leading Aircraftsman Grant-Jones	Flight Lieutenant Clift, Squadron Leader Woodhouse	0·25	0·2000	Local	Passing out for Short Service Commission
3.10.28	Southampton N.9896	Flight Lieutenant Martin	Self	1·30	0·3000	Local	Take-offs
15.10.28	Calcutta G-EBVH	Flight Lieutenant Cahill	Self	1·00	0·3000	Local	Fuel Tests
15.10.28	Fairey IIIF	Flight Lieutenant Wardle	Self	0·30	0·1000	Local	
17.10.28	Supermarine Seagull	Flight Lieutenant Clift	Self	0·12	0·1000	Local	Engine Test
21.10.28	Fairey IIIF	Flight Lieutenant Wardle	Self	1·05	0·6000	Local	Partial Climbs
29.10.28	Southampton	Flying Officer King	Self	4·12	0·2000	Local	Fish Patrol
7.11.30	Short Kawanishi	Flight Lieutenant Cahill	Self	1·15	0·2000	Local	Short Climbs
14.11.30	Saunders A/7 N.240	Flight Lieutenant Waghorn	Self	2·00	0·17000	Local	Full Climb. Speeds
17.12.30	Cutty Sark S.1575	Flight Lieutenant Weblin	Self	1·05	0·600	Local	Take-offs and landings
19.1.31	Sydney N.241	Flight Lieutenant Cahill	Self	1·35	0·3000	Local	Tail Observations
24.2.31	Fairey IIIF (Greek Government)	Captain MacMillen	Self, Commander Averoff	1·00	0·14000	Local	Full Climbs

Appendix VII

Cargo handled through the Port of Felixstowe

	Imports Tonnes	Exports Tonnes	Total Tonnes
1957	50,652	32,238	82,890
1967	880,575	381,986	1,262,561
1977	2,816,199	1,841,902	4,658,101
1979	2,821,383	2,070,460	4,891,843
1980	3,235,968	2,261,569	5,497,537
1981	3,220,592	2,274,552	5,495,144
1982	3,922,228	2,799,252	6,721,480
1983			8,530,032

Containers handled through the Port of Felixstowe

1967	18,522 containers	1977	162,202 containers
1982	427,780 containers	1983	456,666 containers

1982	Landguard Terminal	167,965 containers	2,105,207 tonnes
	Dooley Terminal	86,582 containers	1,101,412 tonnes
	Walton Terminal	119,197 containers	1,024,502 tonnes
1983	Landguard Terminal	180,529 containers	2,302,786 tonnes
	Dooley Terminal	97,397 containers	1,200,451 tonnes
	Walton Terminal	125,347 containers	1,282,272 tonnes

Other Cargo

Roll-on, Roll-off	1982	2,547,833 tonnes
	1983	2,972,569 tonnes
General	1982	420,689 tonnes
	1983	439,900 tonnes

Vessels arriving at the Port of Felixstowe to discharge and/or load cargo

1967	2,345 vessels of 1,533,979 net registered tonnage.
1977	4,509 vessels of 9,120,197 net registered tonnage.
1983	4,463 vessels of 32,155,669 net registered tonnage.

Glossary

A.A.A.	Amateur Athletics Association
Aerodynamic	The study of air in motion.
Aileron	Moving surface on mainplane trailing edge used for lateral control.
Air Ministry	Government Department responsible for aviation.
Air Sea Rescue	Life saving at sea carried out by combined air and marine craft operating together.
Airship	Lighter than air aircraft. Powered as opposed to balloons.
Aldis Lamp	Powerful lamp used for signalling Morse Code etc.
Amphibian	In the case of aircraft capable of operating from land or water.
A.M.W.D.	Air Ministry Works Directorate.
A.T.C.	Air Training Corps. Aviation-orientated youth organisation.
Autogiro	Usually wingless aircraft obtaining lift from airflow driven horizontal rotor.
Auxiliary Aerofoil Aileron Balance	Aerodynamic device designed to lighten flying loads on controls.
Auxiliary Power Unit	Small power unit used to supply power when main engines are not running.
Aviator's Certificate	Early Flying Licence, sometimes known as "Ticket".
Beaching Trolley	Carriage used to launch or retrieve marine aircraft.
Biplane	Aircraft with two mainplanes.
Bomb Sight	Instrument used for aiming bombs from aircraft.
Bomber Stream	Formations of bombers flying on target course.
Boom Defence Vessel	Small craft used to maintain harbour defence booms.
Boundary Layer Control	Regulation of moving air or water flow over flying surfaces or hull.
Box-Kite	Slang name for early biplane aircraft. (Bristol Box-Kite)
Brasshat	Service slang name for high ranking officers.
Brock	Explosive type of machine gun ammunition named after makers.
Browning Gun	American designed machine gun adopted by British Services and firing belt ammunition.
Cantilever	Self supporting. Not braced with struts.
Carrier Pigeon	Homing pigeon used for carrying messages from aircraft whilst they were on patrol.
Caterpillar	General name for large track-laying tractor.
Centre of Gravity	Theoretical point on an aircraft structure at which it balances on all axes.
Code Books	Documents containing wireless and signal codes which were changed frequently.
Convoy	Formation used by shipping and designed to combat submarine interference.
Cover Muff	Thick padded protective covers used on engines.
C.O.W.	Coventry Ordnance Works.
Crankshaft	Main rotating component of an internal combustion engine.
Crystal Set	Early wireless receiver.

Cupola	Streamlined enclosure usually for the protection of free mounted machine guns.
De-Icing	Prevention of ice forming on leading edges of flying surfaces and airscrews.
Dihedralled	Upward and outward inclination of aircraft's mainplanes or horizontal tail surfaces.
Direction Finding Station	Powerful wireless station capable of transmitting and receiving signals for navigation purposes.
Ditched	To put an aircraft down on a water surface usually in an emergency.
Dope	Chemical additive incorporated in special fuel use in high powered racing engines.
Doped	To treat aircraft fabric covered surfaces with acetate preparation in order to tauten and preserve them.
Duralumin	Light strong aluminium alloy.
Elevator	Moving surface on tailplane trailing edge used for longitudinal control.
Empire Air Days	Open days and air displays held at many R.A.F. establishments instead of the former R.A.F. Pageant at Hendon.
Ensign	Junior Officer Rank in the United States Navy.
E.R.A.	Engine Room Artificer
Fire Curtain	Pattern of anti-aircraft fire aimed in front of enemy aircraft.
Floatplane	Marine aircraft fitted with floats for water buoyancy.
Float Step	Change of float bottom surface angle to assist in breaking water suction effect.
Flight	Sub Unit of the R.A.F. usually comprising three aircraft.
Fluted Planing Bottom	Ribbed under surface of hull or float designed to assist in reducing water suction.
Flying Boat	Marine aircraft with boat type hull or hulls.
Flying Speed	Forward speed necessary to maintain sustained flight.
Gas Turbine	Commonly known as jet engine in aircraft terms.
G.C.I.	Ground Control Instruction.
Gotha	Large German bombing aircraft.
Gull Winged	Inner section of mainplanes sharply inclined upwards or downwards.
Gun Layer	Naval term for Gunner.
Hack	Used as a general runabout.
Hangar	Large shed used for housing aircraft.
Hendon Air Pageant	Annual Air Display staged at R.A.F. Hendon, London.
High Speed Flight	Unit formed by R.A.F. for participation in Schneider Trophy events.
H.M.M.G.B.	His/Her Majesty's Motor Gun Boat.
Hollow Bottomed Hull	Hull designed with ventilated under surfaces to assist in reduction of water suction.
Hull Ventilation	Induced air flow to hull under surfaces to form barrier between aircraft and water surface to break suction.
Hydro Aeroplane	Original term for seaplane.
Hydrodynamic	The study of fluids in motion.
Hydrogen Gas	Highly inflammable lighter than air gas used in airships.
Hydrophone	Listening instrument used by marine craft for detecting movement or underwater craft.

Interplane Strut	Bracing member between the mainplanes of a biplane or triplane.
Interrupter Gear	Gas or oil operated mechanism allowing machine gun bullets fired from fixed forward firing guns to pass between revolving airscrew blades.
Jankers	Confined to camp for a misdemeanour.
King's Cup Air Race	Annual civil aircraft race for Cup presented by King George V.
Knot	Measure of nautical speed equivalent to 6,080 feet per hour.
Landing Wire	Bracing wire designed to absorb landing loads.
Leigh Light	Powerful airborne searchlight fitted to R.A.F. overwater patrol aircraft.
Lewis Gun	Machine gun designed to fire bullets from drum or pan.
Liberty Boat	Small boat used to ferry naval personnel between ship and shore.
Light Vessel. L.V.	Light ship.
Lighter	A non-propelled large barge-like vessel.
Link Trainer	Instructional device for training air crew in blind flying techniques.
Local Defence Volunteers	Later known as the Home Guard.
Longitudinal Stability	Stable or unstable condition in the fore and aft axis. Pitching.
Luftwaffe	German Air Force.
Main Hatch	Opening in front upper hull roof on Felixstowe type flying boats.
Maintenance Unit. M.U.	Establishment dealing with the repair and maintenance of R.A.F. equipment.
Manual Starter	Means of starting aero engine by hand, i.e. starting handle as opposed to gas or electric starter.
Marine Section	Unit responsible for Marine Craft.
Maxim Gun	Early machine gun designed by Sir Hiram Maxim.
Meteorological Section.	Unit responsible for weather forecasting.
Modifications	Revising and upgrading equipment designs.
Mole	Breakwater protecting a harbour.
Monitor	Naval vessel with large guns used for bombarding shore targets.
Monocoque	Construction without internal bracing where the outer skin carries all loads.
Monoplane	Aircraft with one mainplane.
Morse	Signal code utilizing long and short rounds or flashes.
N.A.A.F.I.	Navy, Army, Air Force Institute.
Nacelle	Streamlined fairing usually behind aero engine.
Naval Air Station	Land base for Royal Naval Air Service.
Oerlikon Gun	Swiss designed gun built under licence in the U.K.
Off-Station	Not on plotted or specified position.
Packet	Fast vessel used for ferry services.
Parachute Mine	Anti-shipping weapon dropped by parachute.
Planing Form	Shape of the bottom of a marine aircraft's hull or float.
Planing Step	Same as Float Step.
Pomeroy	Explosive type of machine gun bullet designed for use against Zeppelins.
Pom-Pom	Quick firing shell gun mainly used by the Royal Navy.

Prototype	First constructed machine from new design.
Pusher	Aircraft fitted with airscrew or propeller behind the main-planes.
Radial Engine	Aero engine with cylinders forming a circle.
Radio Location	Early name for radar.
R.A.F. Regiment	Formed to defend R.A.F. establishments.
R.A.F.V.R.	Royal Air Force Volunteer Reserve.
Ramp	Inclined slipway used to launch or retrieve marine aircraft.
Rankin darts	Small finned and percussion nosed darts which exploded on hitting the fabric of a Zeppelin. They were dropped by hand.
Rating	Seaman rank in the Royal Navy.
R.M.L.I.	Royal Marine Light Infantry.
R.N.L.I.	Royal National Life-boat Institution.
Rotary Engine	Aero engine in which the cylinders rotate around the crank-shaft.
Royal Aero Club. R.A.C.	Governing body for civil aviation.
Royal Air Force. R.A.F.	Formed 1st April, 1918 from R.F.C. and R.N.A.S.
Royal Naval Air Service (R.N.A.S.)	Aviation Section of the Royal Navy.
Rudder/s	Vertical moving surface on fin/s trailing edge giving directional control.
Scale Effect	Relative comparison between model and full scale test measurements.
Scarff Mounting	Type of flexible machine gun mounting invented by Warrant Officer Scarff.
Seaplane	General term for marine aircraft.
Seaplane Carrier	Vessel for conveying, launching and retrieving seaplanes.
Servo Power	Mechanical assistance to lighten control functions performed by aircraft's crew.
Sick Bay	Service term for hospital.
Side-Slip	Descent quickly in a sideways direction.
Spark Set	Early wireless transmitter.
Special Duties Squadron	R.A.F. Unit employed in sustaining patriot forces usually in Occupied Countries.
Sponson	Stub wing on lower hull of flying boat used for water stability instead of wingtip floats.
Sprint Engine	Highly tuned racing aero engine capable of high power over a short period.
Squadron	R.A.F. Unit usually comprising nine aircraft.
Stall	Loss of control due to lack of forward speed.
Standing Patrol	Patrol system devised to place air or marine craft in an area of anticipated activity.
Stressed Skin	Form of construction in which the outer skin or plating carries all loads.
Tarmac	Hard flat surface usually in front of hangars.
Third Reich	Nazi Government of Germany.
T.N.T.	Trinitrotoluene.
Titan Crane	Maker's name for large cantilever crane.
Tracer	Glowing type bullet used for aiming machine gun or cannon fire.

Tractor Aircraft	Aircraft fitted with engine and airscrew in front of its mainplanes.
Trailing Aerial	Long wireless aerial towed behind and below aircraft.
Triplane	Aircraft fitted with three mainplanes.
Turnbuckle	Device used for tensioning control or bracing wires.
Turret	Protected gun position.
U-Boat	German submarine.
U.S.A.F.	United States Air Force (After Second World War).
U.S.A.A.F.	United States Army Air Force. (During Second World War)
Vee-Bottomed	Pointed along the keel line as opposed to flat bottomed.
Very Light	Star cartridge fired by pistol and used for signalling purposes.
V.1	Vergeltungswaffe. 1 — Reprisal Weapon. German pilotless aircraft launched against Great Britain.
V.2	Vergeltungswaffe 2 — Second Reprisal Weapon. Long range altitude rocket launched from the Continent against the British Isles. Sometimes known as the A.4.
Vickers Gun	British designed machine gun firing belt ammunition.
W.R.A.F.	Women's Royal Air Force. Previously known as W.A.A.F. — Women's Auxiliary Air Force.
W/Ts	Wireless Telegraphy.
Zeppelin	German design of airship usually associated with First World War bombing raids on Great Britain.
Zero Thrust Integrating Pitot Tube	Specialised airspeed measuring instrument as opposed to standard air speed indicator.

A rubber-tyred mobile gantry crane handles a container at the Dooley Terminal as one of the port's Tugmaster and trailer units waits to receive it. In the background are two of the rail-mounted cranes on the quayside, each capable of a forty-tonne lift.

The Felixstowe Dock and Railway Company

Bibliography

Aeronauts and Aviators.	Christopher Elliott.	Terence Dalton.	1971
Aircraft of World War One.	Kenneth Munson.	Ian Allan.	1967
Air Defence of Great Britain.	John R. Bushby.	Ian Allan.	1975
Airspeed Aircraft since 1931.	H. A. Taylor.	Putnam.	—
Armament of British Aircraft 1909-1939.	H. F. King.	Putnam.	1971
Aviation — Flight over the Eastern Counties.	Gordon Kinsey.	Terence Dalton.	1977
Avro Aircraft since 1908.	A. J. Jackson.	Putnam.	1965
Battle of the Narrow Seas.	Sir Peter Scott.	White Lion.	—
Blackburn Aircraft since 1909.	A. J. Jackson.	Putnam.	—
Bomber Squadrons of the R.A.F.	Philip Moyes.	Macdonald.	1964
British Aeroplanes 1914-1918.	J. M. Bruce.	Putnam.	—
British Aircraft 1909-1914.	Peter Lewis.	Putnam.	—
British Aircraft.	Kenneth Munson.	Ian Allan.	—
British Aviation. The Pioneer Years.	Harald Penrose.	Putnam.	—
British Aviation. The Great War.	Harald Penrose.	Putnam.	—
British Aviation. The Adventuring Years.	Harald Penrose.	Putnam.	—
British Civil Aircraft 1915-1959. Vols. I, II and III.	A. J. Jackson.	Putnam.	1974
British Floatplanes.	G. R. Duval.	Bradford Barton.	1976
British Flying Boats and Amphibians 1909-1952.	G. R. Duval.	Putnam.	1966
British Aircraft Serials. 1912-1966.	Bruce Robertson.	Ian Allan.	1964
British Naval Aircraft since 1912.	Owen Thetford.	Putnam.	1958
British Racing and Record Breaking Aircraft.	Peter Lewis.	Putnam.	1970
British Test Pilots.	Geoffrey Dorman.	Forbes Robertson.	1950
East Anglian Daily Times.	Various.	—	—
East Anglian Magazine.	Various.	—	—
Eastern Daily Press.	Various.	—	—
Felixstowe Dock and Railway Co.	Handbook.	—	—
Felixstowe Foghorn.	Various Issues.	—	1930's
Flight International.	Various Issues.	—	—
Gloster Aircraft since 1917.	D. J. James.	Putnam.	—
Hawker Aircraft since 1920.	Francis K. Mason.	Putnam.	1961

Know Aviation.	Francis K. Mason and M. and M. C. Windrow	George Philip.	1973
Martlesham Heath.	Gordon Kinsey.	Terence Dalton.	1975
Science at War.	J. G. Crowther and R. Whiddington.	H.M.S.O.	1947
Shorts Aircraft since 1900.	C. H. Barnes.	Putnam.	1967
Squadron Histories since 1912.	Peter Lewis.	Putnam.	1959
The Aeroplane.	Various.	—	—
The Blackburn Story 1909-1959.	Blackburn Aircraft Co.	Private.	1960
The Defence of the United Kingdom.	Basil Collier.	H.M.S.O.	1957
The British Fighter since 1912.	Peter Lewis.	Putnams.	1965
The Mighty Eighth.	Roger Freeman	Macdonald.	—
The Royal Air Force in the World War. Vols. I, II and III.	Captain Norman Macmillan	Harrap.	1950
The Spider Web.	P.I.X.	William Blackwood.	1919
The Story of a North Sea Air Station.	C. F. Snowden Gamble.	Neville Spearman.	1967
Vickers Aircraft since 1908.	C. F. Andrews.	Putnam.	—
Winged Words.	Various.	William Heinemann.	1941

A veteran of the Falklands war, the Townsend Thoresen roll-on, roll-off ship *Nordic Ferry* is employed on the Felixstowe-Rotterdam service. This vessel and its sister *Baltic Ferry* offer twenty-two sailings a week to Europort, carrying 140 trailers and driver-accompanied lorries and containers on each trip.   *The Felixstowe Dock and Railway Company.*

General Index

For Aeroplanes, Airships, Aero Engines and Marine Craft see separate index.
Note: Service Ranks quoted are those of the period unless otherwise stated.

Index of Aircraft, Airships, Aero Engines and Marine Craft

Note: Items in Appendixes II, III and VI are not included.

Aero Engine Index

Marine Craft Index

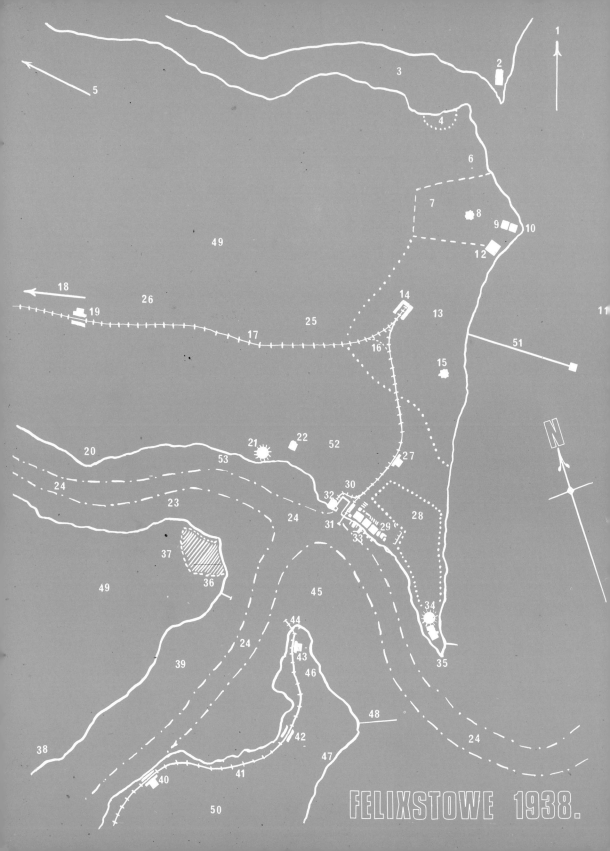

FELIXSTOWE 1938.